CHRISTOPRAXIS

CHRISTOPRAXIS
A Theology of Action

EDMUND ARENS

Translated by John F. Hoffmeyer

Fortress Press   Minneapolis

CHRISTOPRAXIS:
A Theology of Action

First Fortress Press edition 1995. English translation copyright © 1995 Augsburg Fortress. All rights reserved. This book is a translation of *Christopraxis: Grundzüge theologischer Handlungstheorie* (Freiburg im Breisgau: Herder Verlag, 1992). Except for brief quotations in critical articles or reviews, no part of this book may be reproduced in any manner without prior written permission from the publisher. Write to: Permissions, Augsburg Fortress, 426 S. Fifth St., Box 1209, Minneapolis, MN 55440.

Unless otherwise noted, scripture quotations are from the New Revised Standard Version Bible, copyright © 1989 by the Division of Christian Education of the National Council of the Churches of Christ in the United States of America. Used with permission.

Quotations in the text from some published English-language translations have been slightly altered to make their language more inclusive.

Cover graphic: Sketch by Judy Swanson of Louise Nevelson's "Cross of the Resurrection," St. Peter's Lutheran Church, New York.
Cover design: Judy Swanson
Author photo: Scheler Porträt-Foto

Library of Congress Cataloging-in-Publication Data

Arens, Edmund, 1953-
  [Christopraxis. English]
  Christopraxis : a theology of action / Edmund Arens ; translated
by John F. Hoffmeyer. — 1st Fortress Press ed.
    p. cm.
  Includes bibliographical references.   ISBN 0-8006-2746-6 (alk. paper)
  1. Theology, Practical. 2. Communication—Religious aspects—
Christianity. I. Title.
BV3.A6913 1995
230—dc20   95-2302
                                                            CIP

The paper used in this publication meets the minimum requirements of American National Standard for Information Sciences—Permanence of Paper for Printed Library Materials, ANSI Z329.48-1984.   (∞)™

Manufactured in the U.S.A.   AF 1-2746

99   98   97   96   95   1   2   3   4   5   6   7   8   9   10

CONTENTS

PREFACE

The present work focuses on the interdisciplinary project of a theological theory of action. This theory is directed toward the basic structures of Christian and ecclesial praxis, which this theory defines as christopraxis. This volume sketches the steps necessary for carrying out such a project. It contains an outline of a theological theory of action that ties together the biblical, systematic, and practical labor of theology. At the same time the consequences for the understanding of gospel, faith, church, and theology become clear.

Numerous discussions with friends, colleagues, and students have entered into the formation of this book. I owe a great deal to their suggestions and criticisms. The work on this volume was made possible by a Heisenberg Grant of the Deutsche Forschungsgemeinschaft, for which I am very much indebted.

I dedicate this book to a dear friend and a persuasive witness to the truth, who with his person and praxis stands up for the equally dangerous and liberating truth of the gospel: Dr. Smangaliso Mkhatshwa. This book is also dedicated to the Institute for Contextual Theology in Johannesburg, of which Mkhatshwa is General Secretary and which practices a theology that, as contextual, is both prophetic and practical, as explosive as it is relevant.

I appreciate that my work *Christopraxis* is now appearing in English. I hope that my considerations in view of a theological theory of action will thus enter the English-speaking world and will contribute to the intercontinental dialogue and research that both theology and church are much in need of.

My thanks go to Fortress Press for being interested in the book, especially to J. Michael West, who strongly supported its American publication. I would like to express my special gratitude to John Hoffmeyer for his excellent, precise, and flowing translation.

Edmund Arens
Frankfurt

INTRODUCTION:
CONTOURS OF A THEOLOGICAL THEORY OF ACTION

Truth is to be *done* and can be done—that is implied in the statement made to Nicodemus by the Johannine Christ: "But those who do what is true come to the light, so that it may be clearly seen that their deeds have been done in God" (John 3:21). This sentence, which ties together truth, praxis, and their relation to Christ or God, can serve as stating the foundation of a theological theory of action. Such a theory reflects upon the structures, the dimensions, and the theological quality of Christian praxis. Varying the theme of the Johannine metaphor, one could say that such a theory presents an exposition of how and by what means truth comes to light in this praxis, who is thereby elucidated, and what occurs in the execution of this praxis. In short, such a theory presents an exposition of christopraxis.

A social-scientifically and philosophically oriented theory of action such as that developed by Jürgen Habermas in his theory of communicative action will express reservations concerning talk about "doing truth." A theory like his will point out that the claim of validity in the *truth of a statement* must be distinguished from the claim of validity in the *rightness of an action*. Such a theory of action will evaluate the Johannine expression as evidence for the fact that at the time of the New Testament a strict differentiation of validity claims had not yet occurred. Such a theory will pride itself in the reconstruction and explication of these validity claims in terms of a theory of action. A theological theory of action that takes shape and develops in conversation and in critical engagement with the social-scientific and philosophical theory of action fully recognizes that the differentiation of validity claims—as well as the analysis of and reflection upon the constituent parts, structures, and dimensions of human action—delivers both important insights into the foundations of human communication and interaction, and a theologically fruitful set of instruments.

In this context the theological theory of action relates particularly to Habermas's communicative theory of action. It does so in a threefold manner. First, it takes up Habermas's theory, in which it recognizes a most far-reaching analysis of and reflection upon the basic structures and orientations of human praxis. The theological theory of action appropriates the instruments of Habermas's theory in order to apply it to the theological theory's own domain and tradition. Of course this does not occur in the form of a blind adoption. The second aspect of the theological theory of action's relation to Habermas's theory is, namely, that a critique of the communicative theory of action in its current form goes hand in hand with the appropriation of the instruments of the theory of action. A theological theory of action points out the constrictions, deficiencies, and aporias of the communicative theory of action in its current form. As counterpoint to the communicative theory of action, it brings its own tradition into the conversation. On this basis it critically questions the communicative theory of action concerning the latter's scope and boundaries. If thus the current theory of action is criticized in the second step in light of the theologically relevant tradition, in the third step the theological tradition is explained in a new way with the tools of the theory of action. In this way a theological theory of action reflects upon and unfolds its christological, theological, ecclesiological, and ethico-practical implications and consequences.

Inasmuch as the theological theory of action takes up, criticizes, and explains the theory of communicative action, it sees the concept of action as a fundamental theological concept. The theological theory of action attains an understanding of theology as reflection upon a determinate communicative praxis, which it unfolds with regard to the biblical foundations, the systematic status, and the practical theological contents of that communicative praxis. Theological theory of action understood in this manner can at the same time be conceived as the transformation of a theology of the Word of God carried out in terms of the theory of communicative action. This transformation explains the contents of that theology in terms of linguistic pragmatics, whether those contents be formulated within the framework of an existential, a dialectical, or a transcendental theological conception. In this way the theological theory of action at the same time exerts itself to bridge the prevailing division of labor among the theological disciplines in the actual organization of the theological enterprise, and to tie together the plurality of disciplines in theology from the perspective that overarches them all: that of the interconnection between God-talk and human praxis. In this manner the theological theory of action aims at a comprehensive theological conception and brings to expression the unity of theology in the plurality of its disciplines. It sees these disciplines as specific reflections on communicative praxis. In particular the theological theory of action relates biblical, systematic, and practical theology to each other and sees thematized in them the three constitutive dimensions of Christian communicative praxis. The theological theory of action brings out the connection between these three dimensions.

The theological theory of action has a double interdisciplinary orientation: on the one hand, in relation to the social sciences and to philosophy; on the other hand, with regard to the intratheological domain. This double orientation is reflected in the structure of this book. Its first chapter introduces the approach of a communicative theory of action, taking as its starting point the central concept of communicative action, the characteristic features of which come to light in the differentiation and demarcation of other types of action. I will then elucidate the complementary concept to that of communicative action, the concept of communicative rationality. In this process an essential aim is to show both that and how the concept of communicative rationality marks out the parameters for a comprehensive concept of rationality that does not reduce reason to its cognitive-instrumental dimension, but elucidates it from the perspective of its constitutively communicative dimension. Further, I will thematize the relation between ethics and discourse. This includes discussing the basic features of Habermas's and Karl-Otto Apel's moral-theoretical approach to discourse ethics. If the treatment of discourse ethics is concerned with the question of the grounding of norms and with the procedure required by that grounding—a procedure that takes the form of practical discourse—what is finally subject to debate is the question concerning the truth of statements and the possibility of their being tested, as well as the question of whether their truth can be secured by means of discursive argumentation.

In the process of considering these questions I will explain Habermas's proposal for a consensus theory of truth. The fact that the communicative theory of action is not an arbitrary, interchangeable, extratheological theory to which theology can relate follows from three viewpoints. First, Helmut Peukert has shown, by means of an exposition that cannot be presented here in detail, that the communicative theory of action is the consequence of the twentieth-century discussion in the theory of science.[1] In doing so he has made clear and has systematically expounded both the fact that and the extent to which science requires for its grounding the return to communicative praxis. Second, the communicative theory of action is dedicated to precisely those problems of rationality, subjectivity and intersubjectivity, society and history, modernity and postmodernity, on which contemporary theology is also laboring. Third, the communicative theory of action can be made theologically fruitful, and in my opinion demonstrates in its theological reception, critique, and explication that it is capable of approaching central theological questions in an interdisciplinary way and of productively advancing them. The function of chapters 2 and 3 of the present book is to show precisely this in a paradigmatic manner by means of biblical and systematic themes.

Chapter 2 treats the biblical foundations of a theological theory of action. In doing so it concentrates on the New Testament. It first brings out the communicative structure of the gospel, elucidates the essential elements of this structure, and, on the basis of the interdependence of those elements, specifies in terms of a theory of communication and action the characteristic features of the gospel. The person and praxis of Jesus then assume center stage. His communicative actions provide access to his person, and the type and manner of his praxis make clear the theological content of his action. Jesus' communicative praxis is fundamentally concerned with God's rule. What constitutes God's rule? In what way or ways does God's rule come? How does God's rule come to speak in Jesus' parables? These questions are thematized in the ensuing discussion.

Jesus' claim to make the reality of God and of God's rule present and to create space for them in human action leads him into conflicts and confrontations, and eventually brings him to the cross. Under the headings of God's rule and judgment and of Jesus' symbolic actions and execution, I will investigate the way in which Jesus' conflicts become more and more acute, and what this means for the content and the orientation of his communicative praxis. With his shameful death on the cross, Jesus' claim and praxis are called into question on a fundamental level. On the basis of the actions of witnessing and of confessing, I thematize the way in which Jesus' adherents and followers, as well as the developing communities of Jesus Christ, relate to his person and praxis after his death, what they say about him, how they do this, and in what forms they continue and advance his praxis.

Chapter 3 introduces systematic and practical perspectives of a theological theory of action. In a first step the relation between truth and praxis is discussed. The analysis picks up both the discussion of the theory of truth elucidated in chapter 1 and the biblical understanding of truth. In doing so it sketches dimensions of a theological theory of truth that on the one hand are related to the theory of action, and on the other hand christologically burst the boundaries of this theory with the help of the Johannine conception. The next section develops actions of faith and of the church in a systematic and practical way. Having recourse to the biblical discussions, this section shows that witnessing and confessing are two complementary and mutually related actions, which at the same time represent basic actions of faith. Witnessing is an innovatively oriented action of various subjects, while confessing is a basic ecclesial action oriented by memory. Confession is that action in which the community of believers performs, makes present, and makes its own a process of achieving unity. I view the community of the church from the perspective of the action of faith. In doing so it is important to elaborate what follows from characterizing the church as a community of communication, and what the relation is between, on the one hand, those characteristics that are taken from the theory of communication and action, and, on the other hand, the theological qualification of the church as communion or *communio*. The next section sketches a christopractical understanding of *communio*. This understanding in turn represents an element of an ecclesiology conceived in terms of the theory of action.

The conclusion of the volume centers on christopraxis within the horizon of universal solidarity. The theme of solidarity is initially articulated as a watchword of the labor movement. The next step is to question the social teaching of the church concerning its understanding of solidarity. Finally I relate the praxis of solidarity as it has been addressed in ecclesial terms to discourse ethics, and I interpret ecclesial and universal solidarity as christopraxis.

1. THE APPROACH OF A COMMUNICATIVE THEORY OF ACTION

In his two-volume *Theory of Communicative Action*, Jürgen Habermas has presented his approach in its most detailed form to date. In this work he systematically develops studies of the theory of language and action that he has been conducting since the beginning of the 1970s. Habermas takes these studies and integrates them into a comprehensive theory of communicative action. His theory stands in the tradition of the Critical Theory of the Frankfurt School and is situated in a broad research program with an interdisciplinary design. Habermas picks up the interdisciplinary program of early Critical Theory. He advances it on the basis of a shift from one paradigm (that of the philosophy of consciousness) to another (that of the communicatively constituted theory of *action*, as well as that of a communicatively understood *rationality*). Habermas's approach in terms of a theory of action is tied into a broad network of interwoven theories. In this theoretical network, and taking his orientation from the reconstructive sciences, he seeks to work out from one angle after another a comprehensive theory of communicative action. In my opinion the systematic core of this theory is formed by universal or formal pragmatics as the reconstruction of the universal conditions of the possibility of reaching understanding. Habermas develops this pragmatics in conversation with, on the one hand, analytic philosophy of language, in particular the theory of speech acts, and on the other hand, Karl-Otto Apel's transcendental prag-

matics, as well as in critical debate with the major social theories of
the nineteenth and twentieth centuries.

Universal pragmatics in turn is to be located within the broad
scope of Habermas's theoretical endeavors, which include at least
the following theoretical parts:

(1) *a theory of the subject.* This theory, which gives an exposi-
     tion of the intersubjective constitution of the subject, con-
     tains a theory of the unfolding of the subject's cognitive,
     linguistic, and interactive competence;

(2) *a theory of intersubjectivity.* This theory is connected with
     that of the subject, without being reducible to that theory;

(3) *a theory of society.* This theory has a two-level approach,
     conceiving society simultaneously as system and as lifeworld,
     and grasping society on the basis of the interdependence of
     the two;

(4) *a theory of history.* This theory understands itself as a
     theory of social evolution, in the sense of a reconstruction of
     historical materialism in terms of a theory of action; and

(5) *a theory of modernity.* This theory is conceived in decided
     contradiction to the thinkers of postmodernity. In addition,
     this theory casts light upon the function and achievement of
     philosophy in the period of postmetaphysical thinking.

Having at least named the context of Habermas's universal pragmatics, I will not investigate that context more deeply in what follows. Instead I will be concerned with four components of universal
pragmatics:

(1) the concept of communicative action and its demarcation
     from other types of action;

(2) the concept of a rationality based in its constitutively com-
     municative dimension, a rationality that is comprehensive in
     contrast to the instrumental reductions of rationality;

(3) Habermas's reflection on the program of grounding a dis-
     course ethics;

(4)   his reflections on the theory of truth, which have led him to
      sketch a consensus theory of truth.

COMMUNICATIVE ACTION

The fundamental concept of formal pragmatics is that of communicative action. Formal pragmatics seeks to show that this concept is
fundamental to human interaction and life together. Universal or
formal pragmatics understands itself as a reconstructive science. It
reconstructs and reflects upon the universal and necessary conditions of human action, the basic orientations of human action, the
validity claims raised in human action, and the way in which these
validity claims are redeemed.

Habermas's reconstruction picks up on the theory of speech acts
as well as on other approaches to the pragmatics of speech and language. His reconstruction also stands in relation to sociological concepts of action. He proceeds from the differentiation of three types
of action. According to their situation and orientation, he characterizes them as instrumental, strategic, and communicative action. Instrumental action appears in a nonsocial situation of action. Its
reference is to objects that are at its disposal. It is directed toward
intended effects coming to pass and thus toward action being successful. The last point holds equally for strategic action. Strategic
action is admittedly distinguished from instrumental action by the
fact that the former presents a social form of action whose reference is
other human beings. In relation to them, though, it follows the rules of
rational choice in order to exercise an influence upon their decisions.
This is the reason for its being equally oriented toward success. According to Habermas, communicative action distinguishes itself from both
types of action oriented toward success. It has in common with strategic action the fact that it takes place in social situations. The
agents in these situations, however, coordinate their interactions
not by means of calculations aimed at success, but by means of acts
of reaching an understanding. They orient their interactions to each
other in view of the understanding that they are seeking to achieve.

Habermas wants not merely to distinguish the orientation toward
success and the orientation toward reaching an understanding as

two analytic viewpoints of linguistically mediated interaction. He wants to arrive at a normative understanding of linguistic action. In order to do so, it is important to him to demonstrate that linguistic use oriented toward reaching an understanding is primary, while use oriented toward success is correspondingly parasitic, dependent on the former. According to Habermas, linguistic processes of reaching an understanding aim at an agreement. Agreement achieved by means of communication possesses a rational foundation insofar as it is based on acceptance of the offers made in speech acts—an acceptance that results in shared conviction. "Reaching an understanding is the inherent telos of human speech."[1] Thus linguistic use oriented toward reaching an understanding is the original mode.

In Habermas's view this can be demonstrated on the basis of John L. Austin's distinction between illocutions and perlocutions. Austin drew this distinction within the framework of his project of a theory of speech acts.[2] By saying something, a speaker carries out an illocutionary act, with which the speaker pursues a goal that proceeds from the meaning of what is said and that can be made explicit in the speech act itself. By contrast, the perlocutionary goal at which a speech act is aimed can at most be figured out from the context. According to Habermas, the perlocutionary goal is attained by the speaker deceiving her partner about her true intention. Of course, speech acts can serve perlocutionary goals of influencing the hearer or hearers only when those acts also are appropriate for attaining illocutionary goals.

> If the hearer failed to understand what the speaker was saying, a strategically acting speaker would not be able to bring the hearer, by means of communicative acts, to behave in the desired way. To this extent, what we initially designated as "the use of language with an orientation to consequences" is not an original use of language but the subsumption of speech acts that serve illocutionary aims under conditions of action oriented to success.[3]

In Habermas's view, a theory of meaning that uses the approach of formal pragmatics must clarify what understanding a speech act means. A speech act is understood when the hearer knows the conditions of its acceptability. With "yes" or "no" he takes a position with regard to these conditions. Insofar as he accepts the offer made in the speech act, the hearer makes certain commitments concerning his subsequent action. Habermas sets forth the conditions that constitute the meaning of regulative, expressive, and constative speech acts. He also sets forth the validity claims raised by these acts. On that basis he reconstructs the three validity claims that a speaker raises in communicative action in order to reach an understanding with a hearer about something: the validity claims of the truth of a statement, the rightness of the interpersonal relation intended by a speech act, and the truthfulness of what is uttered. A fourth validity claim is that of comprehensibility. This claim, however, is not raised in the action itself, but is presupposed in order for the action to occur at all. In communicative action a speaker must choose a comprehensible expression "in order to come to an understanding with a hearer about something and thereby to make herself understandable."[4]

If the point of communicative action is to attain agreement on all three levels, a speech act must be accepted on these same three levels. According to Habermas, such agreement is rationally motivated insofar as it is open to criticism and, when this happens, must and can be restored by providing grounds. "With his 'yes' the hearer grounds an agreement that relates, on the one hand, to the content of the utterance, and on the other hand, to the speech-act-immanent provision of warrants and to the obligations whose consequences are relevant for interaction."[5] With a speech act the speaker vouches for the fact that, if necessary, she will redeem the validity claims that have been made. She will redeem them by bringing forth reasons for her claims to truth and to rightness and by demonstrating through her own consistent behavior that her claims to truthfulness are justified. All this implies at the same time that each of the three validity claims can be contested. The continuation of action oriented toward reaching an understanding then rests on the restoration of the disrupted agreement. This restoration happens by means of the redemption of validity claims. In the very fact that each of the three validity claims can be contested and redeemed, we can see that the agreement presupposed in communicative action is rationally motivated: it can be examined, grounded, and renewed as need be.

In Habermas's view, analysis of the three validity claims at the same time delivers

> the key for the identification of the basic functions of the linguistic process of reaching an understanding. Language serves: (a) the establishment and renewal of interpersonal relations, by which the speaker makes reference to something in the world of legitimate structures of order; (b) the presentation or the presupposition of conditions and events, by which the speaker makes reference to something in the world of existing states of affairs; and (c) the manifestation of experiences—that is, self-representation—by which the subject makes reference to something in the subjective world to which she has privileged access.[6]

Habermas sees three basic attitudes that agents can assume and that correspond to the three basic functions of linguistic understanding and to the three types of reference to a world—reference to the social world, the objective world, and the subjective world—by means of which persons engaged in communicative action raise the three validity claims. These three basic attitudes are an objectifying attitude, an expressive attitude, and an attitude in conformity with norms. These basic attitudes manifest themselves for their part in three basic modes of linguistic usage: in the constative, the expressive, and the regulative use of language. At the same time they form the pure types of linguistic use oriented toward reaching an understanding. As classes of speech acts the constatives, the regulatives, and the expressives are to be correlated with them. In each of them one of the validity claims is highlighted and explicitly brought to expression: in the constatives, the claim of truth; in the regulatives, the claim of rightness; in the expressives, the claim of truthfulness.

That completes the naming of the fundamental formal-pragmatic distinctions that Habermas seeks to reconstruct as elements of action oriented toward reaching an understanding. His formal-pragmatic analyses aim at "hypothetical reconstructions of that pretheoretical knowledge that competent speakers bring to bear when they employ sentences in actions oriented to reaching an understanding."[7] At the same time they seek to explain the universal conditions and rules of interaction oriented toward reaching an understanding. They have the further goal of demonstrating that the orientation toward reaching an understanding and agreement is the characteristic feature of communicative action, with this action in turn underlying the other forms of social interaction. This reconstruction and reflection form the normative core of the theory of communicative action. They also deliver the normative foundation for a critical theory of society that judges and measures societies according to the degree to which they have developed or limited the potential for communicatively reaching an understanding and for communicative rationality.

Habermas works out his categories of formal pragmatics by picking up on insights of linguistic pragmatics and especially of the theory of speech acts. But he also explains them with regard to sociological concepts of action, which he differentiates with respect to their types of world-relation and with respect to their aspects of rationality. By doing so he distinguishes concepts of teleological, norm-regulated, dramaturgical, and communicative action. According to Habermas the concept of teleological action—action that chooses between alternative actions with regard to the realization of a purpose—has stood in the center of the philosophical theory of action since Aristotle. The strategic model of action is understood as an extension of the teleological model. Both models are oriented to the aspect of purposive rationality. They presuppose only one world: the objective world. By contrast, the concept of norm-regulated action has as its reference the members of a social group who order their action in accordance with mutual expectations of behavior that are recognized as valid. This type of action presupposes, in addition to the objective world of existing states of affairs, the social world of normatively regulated interactions. According to Habermas the concept of dramaturgical action likewise presupposes two worlds: the inner world and the outer world. The primary focus of dramatic action is the relation of the agent to her own subjective world and to its authentic expression. This expression can take on latently strategic features. In the concept of communicative action the three types of an agent's world-relation come into play together.

At the same time they are reflected as such in the medium of language. In the validity claims related to the individual worlds, they also bring the problem of rationality as a problem of the coordination of action by means of reaching an understanding "into the perspective of the agent herself."[8]

COMMUNICATIVE RATIONALITY

The concept of communicative action is closely connected with that of communicative rationality. The concept of communicative action seeks to secure a comprehensive concept of action against an understanding of action that, in its orientation toward the purposive rationality of instrumental action, is overly narrow. The concept of communicative rationality stakes out the parameters for a comprehensive concept of rationality that does not reduce reason to its cognitive-instrumental dimension. If, from the perspectives of the theories of language and action, rationality has to do with how subjects make use of knowledge, two kinds of rationality can be distinguished in an initial step according to the way in which they make use of knowledge. On the one hand is a rationality directed toward the effectiveness of actions and thus toward instrumental control. On the other hand is a rationality that aims at reaching an understanding by communication. The goal of this rationality is the truth of what is known. Both rationalities involve claims that can be criticized and defended, and thus can be grounded. If the rationality of an utterance or of an action is to be traced back to its capacity to be criticized and to be grounded, then assertions on the one hand, and goal-directed actions on the other hand, "are the more rational, the better the grounding is that can be given to the claim (to propositional truth or efficacy) that is connected with those assertions or actions."[9]

Reconstruction of the universal conditions of action oriented toward reaching an understanding has already made clear that validity claims are connected not only with assertions and teleological actions. They are also raised in those actions that concern the relation of the agent to his surrounding social world and to his own subjective world. Norm-regulated actions and expressive self-presentations are connected with the claims of rightness and of truth-fulness. As validity claims they can likewise be criticized and are capable of being grounded. To that extent they likewise embody a form of rationality that Habermas pulls together under the comprehensive concept of communicative rationality.

For the development of the concept of communicative rationality, it is then important to analyze the procedures by means of which contested validity claims can be grounded. In general terms, this grounding occurs through argumentation. Habermas understands argumentation as a continuation of communicative action by other—reflexive—means. He characterizes argumentation as a type of speech "in which participants thematize contested validity claims and attempt to redeem or criticize them through arguments."[10] He distinguishes between discourse and critique as two types of argumentation. Discourses must approximate the conditions of an ideal speech situation. In Habermas's view we can speak of discourses only "when the meaning of the problematic validity claim conceptually forces participants to suppose that a rationally motivated agreement could in principle be achieved . . . if only the argumentation could be conducted openly enough and continued long enough."[11] With the type of argumentation known as critique this supposition is not required. Nor must the conditions of a speech situation free from both external and internal constraints be regarded as fulfilled in critique.

Habermas characterizes as theoretical discourse the form of argumentation in which contested truth claims are thematized and grounded. By contrast, practical discourse has to do with the contested status of norms of action. Practical discourses are conducted with the goal of consensually resolving the dispute about the normative rightness of action, and thus of justifying by argument the corresponding norms of action. The truthfulness of expressive utterances is likewise accessible to examination by means of argument, although not to examination by means of discourse. The examination of expressive utterances follows the model of therapeutic critique, which focuses on clearing up systematic self-deceptions. In the domain of evaluative utterances, aesthetic critique is the means of carrying out argumentation and examination—likewise nondiscursively. Finally, the validity claim of the comprehensibility of an utterance, the claim that the utterance is well formed, is also accessible to rational examination, which occurs in explicative discourse with the goal of getting rid of disturbances to communication.

Communicative rationality as Habermas conceives it includes cognitive-instrumental rationality, while not reducing reason to the latter. Communicative rationality likewise encompasses the moral-practical, evaluative, and expressive dimensions of human action and knowledge. With this concept of communicative rationality, Habermas has at his disposal a critical standard against which he measures rationality by means of the applied procedures for grounding and justification.

Habermas goes on to demonstrate that a concept of communicative rationality is also necessary for the formation of sociological theory. By picking up on and critically engaging Max Weber, Habermas shows both the achievements and the deficiencies of Weber's concept of rationality and of rationalization. Weber's theory of rationalization provides Habermas with the framework in which the dimensions of social rationalization emerge. But due to its narrow concept of rationality and action, Weber's conception leads to contradictions that keep it from drawing out its full explanatory potential.

Habermas discerns a central contradiction in Weber's theory of rationalization. Habermas argues that in Weber's investigations of cultural tradition a comprehensive concept of practical rationality emerges that Weber does not, however, apply on the level of institutions. Instead Weber articulates their rationalization exclusively in terms of purposive rationality. Weber tries with his thesis of the loss of freedom and of meaning to grasp the pathologies that emerge in the modern period. In doing so he employs the concept of rationalization in an ambiguous way. According to Habermas, in order to give an adequate analysis of those pathologies, we need a comprehensive concept of rationality as well as a two-level theory of society. One can indeed find in Weber's work indications of how to develop such a concept and such a theory, but they do not acquire a systematic role. This is due to his understanding rationality and rationalization in terms of purposive and instrumental rationality, and to his theory of action, which is tailored to the model of action in terms of purposive rationality. On the one hand, Weber equates the historical form of rationalization effective in capitalist modernization with social rationalization in general. On the other hand, according to Habermas, Weber's reflections on the condition of his time implicitly contain "standards by which he can assess and criticize a rationality that has shrunken to a totalized purposive rationality."[12]

In Habermas's view the basis for a differentiated and comprehensive concept of rationality is present in the systematic content of Weber's theory. This concept of rationality contains the cognitive-instrumental rationality institutionalized in the scientific enterprise, the aesthetic-practical rationality institutionalized in the artistic enterprise, and the moral-practical rationality of the ethics of brotherhood of a religion of salvation. But for this moral-practical rationality Weber does not take into consideration a secularized form: that is, "a communicative ethic detached from its foundation in salvation religion."[13] Weber characterizes social rationalization as paradoxical, instead of more correctly as partial. Yet Habermas sees him as pointing in the direction of a selective model of rationality. This model comes into view from the perspective of a comprehensive concept of communicative rationality. On this basis it becomes possible at the same time for Habermas to judge processes of rationalization, which he conceives as learning processes, with regard to possible instances of one-sidedness and distortion. Communicative rationality serves for him as a normative criterion for the judgment and critique of the unfolding and restriction of this rationality's potential as it inhabits all dimensions of social relations. Communicative rationality also serves as a normative criterion for the critique of social pathologies and of those social situations in which the potential for rationality that has been attained has not been fully exploited or has been realized only in a one-sided manner.

ETHICS AND DISCOURSE

As has been presented above, Habermas distinguishes three forms of discursive argumentation: theoretical, practical, and explicative. All three are procedures by means of which contested validity claims can be criticized and grounded with arguments. The goal of discursive argumentation is to reach a rationally motivated understanding concerning the intersubjectively binding recognition of validity claims. By focusing on this goal it is possible to point out, on the basis of the structures of discursive argumentation, foundations of ethical action. The fundamental ethical principles that are presupposed and drawn upon in every discourse are explained by Habermas on the basis of that discourse which explicitly thematizes normative questions: practical discourse. Practical discourse centers on the justification of the claim to rightness of norms. For Habermas practical discourse is the point of departure for the project of a discourse ethics—a project that he is pursuing along a path that in part is parallel to that of Karl-Otto Apel, and in part diverges in certain characteristic ways from Apel's transcendental pragmatics.[14] Discourse ethics reflects upon the presuppositions and the procedure of rational argumentation. In this way discourse ethics elaborates the foundations of the process of reaching an understanding by means of argumentation.

According to Habermas, discourse ethics stands as moral theory in the Kantian tradition and is to that extent characterized by four features proper to every Kantian ethics. It has a deontological, a cognitive, a formal, and a universalistic character.[15] First, discourse ethics is deontological, insofar as it is concerned with the validity of the "oughtness" of norms that determine right or just action, and whose validity is in turn "to be justified in light of principles worthy of being recognized."[16] Second, discourse ethics is cognitive, insofar as it conceives of normative rightness as a validity claim analogous to truth: that is, as something that can be rationally grounded. Third, discourse ethics is formal, insofar as it does not distinguish specific normative contents. Instead, similar to Immanuel Kant's categorical imperative, it constitutes a formal criterion as a principle of justification for norms of action. In discourse ethics the procedure of moral argumentation assumes the place of the categorical imperative. Finally, discourse ethics is universalistic, insofar as it claims that its moral principle of universalization is related not only to a specific culture or epoch, is meaningful and valid not only for a specific culture or epoch, but has universal validity. According to that principle of universalization, "only those norms may claim validity which could find approval by all those affected by them, were all affected parties to be participants in a practical discourse."[17]

The exposition of these four characteristics should at the same time make clear that discourse ethics is not an ethics for the conduct of discourses. Rather discourse ethics ascertains from the structure of discursive argumentation principles of the communicative process of reaching an understanding—principles that norms of action must satisfy. In working out these principles, the focal point is occupied by the question of how to secure a consensus to be attained by means of argument. According to Habermas, the attainment in practical discourse of a consensus concerning a contested norm is guaranteed and intersubjectively secured by the formal conditions of discourse, which must satisfy "to a sufficient degree of approximation"[18] those of an ideal speech situation. This means that there is no limitation with regard to participants and theme, that communication does not stand under the burden of action and is free of constraint, that the participants in the discourse can switch from one form of discourse to another, and that they all potentially "have an equal chance to put forward interpretations, assertions, recommendations, explanations and justifications, as well as to render them problematic, ground them or refute them. The result is that no prior opinion remains immune over time to being thematized and criticized."[19]

Picking up on Habermas's theory of discourse, Robert Alexy has set up rules of practical discourse, which Habermas in turn appropriates for his reflections concerning the program of grounding a discourse ethics.[20] Along with the fundamental rules that concern the logico-semantic level, the procedural rules are of particular importance for discourse ethics. In Habermas's formulation they are:

(3.1) Every subject with the competence to speak and act is allowed to take part in a discourse.

(3.2) a) Everyone is allowed to question any assertion whatever.

      b) Everyone is allowed to introduce any assertion whatever into the discourse.

c) Everyone is allowed to express his attitudes, desires, and
needs.
(3.3) No speaker may be prevented, by internal or external coer-
cion, from exercising his rights as laid down in (3.1) and (3.2).[21]

Of decisive importance for practical discourse is a principle that is
supposed to secure the process of using arguments to reach an understanding concerning contested norms of action, and thus to
ground these norms in an intersubjectively binding manner. The
principle is that of universalization. It is implied in Kant's categorical imperative. According to the categorical imperative, only those
norms are accepted as valid which are suited to be a universal law.
In Habermas's view the categorical imperative can be "understood
as a principle that requires the universalizability of modes of action
and maxims, or of the interests furthered by them (that is, those em-
bodied in the norms of action)."[22] If this is so, then discourse ethics,
in contrast to Kant, does not tie universalization to the reflection
and the conceptual power of the isolated individual subject who in
each particular case attempts hypothetically to assume for himself
the universal perspective. Instead discourse ethics ties universalization to the real argumentation and the actual discourse of potentially
all those concerned. The principle of universalization takes as its
point of departure the position that valid norms must merit recognition on the part of all concerned. From this starting point, the
principle of universalization has the function of ensuring that the interests of all are taken into account, and thus of ensuring the formulation of an interest common to all that at the same time can count
on universal agreement and intersubjective recognition. In Habermas's words,

> the principle of universalization has the function of compelling the
> universal exchange of roles that G. H. Mead called "ideal role
> taking" or "universal discourse." Thus every valid norm has to ful-
> fill the following condition:
>   (U) All participants can accept the consequences and the
>   side effects its general observance can be anticipated to
>   have for the satisfaction of everyone's interests (and these

> consequences are preferred to those of known alternative possibilities for regulation).[23]

According to Habermas, this principle of universalization ("U") is not to be confused with a moral principle that already expressed the basic conception of discourse ethics. The principle of universalization designates solely a procedure by which a consensus concerning norms can arise and can be intersubjectively secured. If each person who engages in argumentation must make presuppositions that correspond to the rules of discourse presented above (3.1–3.3), and if norms are only justified when they regulate the common interest of those concerned,

> then everyone who seriously tries to discursively redeem normative claims to validity intuitively accepts procedural conditions that amount to implicitly acknowledging (U). . . . But once it has been shown that (U) can be grounded upon the presuppositions of argumentation through a transcendental-pragmatic derivation, discourse ethics itself can be formulated in terms of the principle of discourse ethics (D), which stipulates,
>> Only those norms can claim to be valid that meet (or could meet) with the approval of all affected in their capacity as participants in a practical discourse.[24]

Contrary to Apel, Habermas refuses to derive basic ethical norms in an immediate way from the presuppositions of argumentation. He therefore characterizes universalization as a formal-procedural principle and not as an ethical principle. According to Apel, by contrast, the principle of universalization shows itself "a priori to be a principle of generalized reciprocity and to be aimed at consensual-communicative implementation. To that extent it cannot be applied in contentless or arbitrary ways. Instead it points to the possible result of a universal process of reaching an understanding."[25] The principle of universalization contains the "basic norm that all communication partners enjoy equal rights as a matter of principle."[26] It also contains the "obligation to share in the responsibility for finding a solution by means of arguments (and in this sense a solution that as a matter of principle can be the object of a consensus on the part of all possible partners in argumentation) to the morally relevant problems that emerge in the lifeworld."[27]

In his earlier works Habermas made strong claims that in discourse a counterfactual anticipation of an ideal speech situation and of an ideal form of life occurs. In his more recent works Habermas is considerably more restrained. He now brings out only the formal and procedural character of discourse ethics. Discourse ethics makes no statements of content. By contrast, Apel understands his transcendental-pragmatic discourse ethics as a reflection upon the norms of an ideal community of argumentation and as an ultimate grounding of these norms. This ideal community of argumentation is counterfactually anticipated in the real community of argumentation. The ideal community of argumentation serves as a challenge to take the norms that are founded in a transcendental-pragmatic way in discourses of grounding and to make them fruitful in discourses of application in the lifeworld, with the goal being an intersubjectively valid ethics of responsibility in solidarity. In Apel's view the real community of communication is directed toward the realization of an ideal community of communication. At the same time discourse ethics must be clear that as a regulative idea this ideal community will never exist in reality, although the ideal community is always to be presupposed and anticipated.[28]

TRUTH AND CONSENSUS

The goal of practical discourse is to attain justification of a claim of the rightness of norms after that claim has been rendered problematic. The focus of theoretical discourse is the grounding of the truth claim of statements. Habermas defines truth as a validity claim that is explicitly raised in the constative use of language with regard to facts that are claimed to exist in the objective world. In Habermas's view the speaker at the same time offers to provide grounds for raising this claim, and thus to demonstrate that the claim is rational. If the "speech-act-immanent obligation to provide grounds"[29] proffered in the constative use of language cannot be immediately redeemed in the context of interaction on the level of communicative action—for example, by recourse to experiences—because this offer is not accepted or continues to be rendered problematic, the prescribed remedy is engagement in theoretical discourse. Theoretical discourse aims at grounding and securing in an intersubjectively binding manner the truth claim that has been rendered problematic. The common goal of both theoretical and practical discourse is consensus attained by means of arguments. The central questions of Habermas's discourse or consensus theory of truth are these: By what means is the attainment of that goal guaranteed? What demonstrates that the consensus is intersubjectively secured?

Habermas undertakes elaboration of his theory of truth in two essays published at the beginning of the 1970s.[30] His reflections on the theory of truth have been the object of various criticisms, to which we also need to turn our attention briefly. So far Habermas has not further pursued his theory of truth in a systematic way, aside from cursory self-criticism. One can find reflections in Apel's work, however, that in my opinion are fruitful for the further development of a discourse or consensus theory of truth. Inasmuch as Habermas defines truth as a validity claim that can be discursively redeemed, he distances himself from every ontological theory of truth. He conceives of truth as essentially related to language systems and to statements, and also bound to the potential agreement of all to those statements. In his view, the criterion of truth cannot be either the representation or the reproduction of reality. Nor can it be the evidence of experiences. The criterion of truth can only be the rational consensus of all. If a statement is true when the predicate attributed to the named object belongs to that object, then I may "attribute a predicate to an object if and only if everyone else who could enter into a conversation with me would attribute the same predicate to the same object."[31] According to Habermas such a consensus can be attained and is intersubjectively secured by means of the formal conditions of discourse, which are those of the ideal speech situation. The ideal speech situation comes into play with the question of (1) whether the conditions under which a consensus, which is always a consensus of only a few factual participants in a discourse, can count as true, and (2) how this consensus is to be distinguished from a false consensus. Habermas has claimed that in order to acquire an adequate criterion for distinguishing between true and false consensus, we "are compelled in every discourse to assume an ideal speech situation. We are compelled to anticipate counterfactually an ideal speech situation, just as we are compelled to anticipate the accountability of the subjects who act in contexts of interaction."[32]

The concept of the ideal speech situation is an abstraction, in accord with the model of pure communication, from the conditions and dependencies of real processes of communication. It is thus an idealization in the sense of the subtraction of all the external conditions and internal inadequacies that disrupt or burden communication. In addition, the concept of the ideal speech situation fulfills the specific function of explaining why we can act communicatively at all, what we presuppose in engaging in such action, what assumptions we make, and what our orientation is in such action. Accordingly, in defining the concept of the ideal speech situation it is necessary to consider, along with the aspect of the idealization of actual communication, the converse aspect of the forming of real communication. It is this latter aspect that provides the standard for evaluating real communication. The ideal speech situation means simultaneously the presuppositions of real communication, the question concerning the conditions of the possibility and validity of real communication. This question concerns the normative foundation of real communication.

Habermas's explanation of the possibility of reaching an understanding through discourse contains the claim "that in every discourse we mutually assume an ideal speech situation."[33] He has understood this assumption as an "anticipation" that both provides the guarantee for regarding an actual consensus as true, and delivers the critical standard for calling into question and examining each actual consensus with regard to whether it indicates that an understanding has really been reached. Habermas has termed a speech situation "ideal" in which communication is impeded neither by external influences nor "by constraints that result from the structure of communication itself."[34] In other words, an ideal speech situation excludes systematic distortions of communication and every form of constraint. As Habermas shows by means of the four classes of speech acts, this implies equality of chances with regard to the choice and employment of communicatives and constatives, and is dependent on the presupposition that equal chances in employing regulatives and representatives are guaranteed for the speaker as agent.

"The counterfactual conditions of the ideal speech situation prove to be conditions of an ideal form of life"[35] because and insofar as they not only represent conditions for the success of discourses, but at the same time circumscribe a model of pure communicative action with reference to interaction—a model that is anticipated in interaction. Habermas has characterized as counterfactual the status of this anticipation of an ideal speech situation and the status of the model of pure communication. Neither of them coincides with the conditions of empirical speech and of actual interaction. It belongs

> to the structure of possible speech that in carrying out speech acts (and actions) we do so counterfactually, as if the ideal speech situation (or the model of pure communicative action) were not merely fictional, but real. . . . The normative foundation of interaction is therefore both: anticipated but also, as an anticipated foundation, real.[36]

Habermas's conception, which he has sketched out in his "Preliminary Remarks on the Theory of Communicative Competence" as well as in "Theories of Truth," has run up against various criticisms. This has in part contributed to a productive further development of Habermas's initial undertaking.

Ansgar Beckermann has called attention to the "realistic presuppositions of J. Habermas's consensus theory," which he claims that Habermas fails to observe. Habermas overlooks the fact "that the idea of grounding has meaning only if one clings to the idea of an independent reality."[37] Habermas's theory comes to grief on the impossibility of giving, within the framework of a consensus theory, "a viable distinction between reaching a rational and reaching an irrational understanding."[38]

In his "Critical Reflections on the Consensus Theory of Truth," Otfried Höffe comes to the conclusion that Habermas cannot simply assume as a matter of course that truth is the truth of statements, and thus from the outset tie truth to discursive speech. Höffe argues that inasmuch as Habermas confines himself to the problem of validity and excludes the problem of constitution, his theory of truth is philosophically inadequate. Moreover, Habermas's own logic of discourse cannot get by without an "element of coherence theory" in articulating the redemption of claims to truth. The *adaequatio*-formula is "an ongoing point of reference for his validity theory of claims to truth."[39] In Höffe's view, the moments of coherence and of correspondence remain criteria of truth for Habermas as well.

Bruno Puntel's critique is similarly situated. First, he highlights the unclarified character of Habermas's metatheoretical conceptual apparatus. Second, he elucidates the objective components, neglected by Habermas, for the definiens of truth. Third, he understands Habermas's theory as an "intersubjective version, in terms of linguistic pragmatics, of the coherence theory of truth."[40] "The fact that Habermas grasps consensus not as a contingently de facto consensus, but as a grounded consensus—that is, a potentially universal consensus—means that the consensus he has in mind means nothing other than universal coherence."[41]

Puntel sketches his systematic coherence theory of truth in a critical and systematic exposition of "Theories of Truth in Recent Philosophy." This exposition surveys the correspondence theory, Alfred Tarski's semantic theory of truth, intersubjectivity theories, and the coherence theory of truth. His own view closely follows Nicholas Rescher's coherence theory,[42] while going beyond Rescher's criteriological understanding of coherence. For Rescher, coherence is a necessary (authorizing) but not sufficient (guaranteeing) criterion of truth. According to Puntel, coherence is not merely that, but must be regarded as the single and thus also sufficient criterion of truth. Puntel argues that this criterion thus also shows itself to be the essence of truth.[43]

For both Rescher and Puntel, the idea of system is decisive for the concept of coherence. This idea implies comprehensiveness, consistency, cohesiveness, and unity.[44] According to Puntel, the correspondence theory and the consensus theory must and can be integrated in the coherence theory. "To establish an equivalence means that . . . ; a predicate holding good of an object signifies that . . . ; the discursive redeemability, that . . . the corresponding statement can be incorporated into a (into the) framework of coherence."[45] If in Puntel's view the concept of truth is to be specified as the relation between the two poles of "validity claim" and "the subject matter," then the two poles "and the structural elements that form the connection between them receive their own proper—that is, their ultimate—determinacy by being integrated into a (into the) framework of coherence or, alternatively, by showing themselves to be integrated into it."[46]

Hans Kraml raises concerns about Puntel's giving preference to the coherence theory. These concerns are then systematically reflected in Apel's work. If the coherence version, as Puntel says, is the abstract formulation of the meaning of truth, then when difficulties arise around abstract problems, "sooner or later the recourse to pragmatic reflections and examinations is unavoidable."[47] For this reason Kraml argues for giving preference to the consensus theory.

In the meantime Habermas himself has taken a critical position toward his early reflections on the consensus theory of truth. He admits that he neglected the referential dimension of the concept of truth. He continues to regard the coherence theory of truth as too weak to explain the concept of propositional truth, but he sees that the coherence theory has its rightful place on the metatheoretical level.[48] Above all, though, he makes a decisive restriction, in relation to his earlier conception, with regard to his understanding of the ideal speech situation. He no longer recognizes in the ideal speech situation a necessary presupposition of discursive argumentation and an already established goal to be anticipated in such argumentation. He relativizes the ideal speech situation inasmuch as he now assumes that its conditions are fulfilled in discourse only "to a sufficient degree of approximation."[49] As Apel and A. Wellmer rightly highlight and criticize, with this relativization Habermas gives up the attempt to distinguish a criterion of truth. Instead he now speaks of criteria of truth that change with the standards of rationality.[50]

Karl-Otto Apel has sketched a transcendental-pragmatic concept of truth that retains consensus as the basis for finding truth, and at the same time seeks to take into account the dimensions of reference (correspondence), coherence, and evidence. In a critical analysis of Tarski and picking up on Charles Peirce, he develops an explication of the meaning of truth. In this explication he argues against Puntel, seeing the transcendental-pragmatic alternative to the coherence theory in the systematic connection of the various criteria of truth as moments of an integrative concept of truth.[51] He highlights the moment, neglected by Habermas, of the adequate interpretation of the facts—a moment that must also receive its due in a consensus theory of truth. Apel calls this the moment of the evidence of correspondence in a coherent framework of interpretation. On this basis Apel defines truth as consensus concerning the coherence of the evidence of correspondence. He thus advocates a concept of truth that integrates the correspondence theory, the evidence theory, and the coherence theory in a consensus theory of truth. I will return to these four dimensions of a comprehensive theory of truth when I investigate (1) whether and to what extent they must also be observed for a theological understanding of truth, and (2) in what way a theological theory of truth and of action distances itself from those dimensions, inasmuch as it insists that truth is to be done, that truth can be done, and that truth receives its due in christopraxis.

THEOLOGICAL RELEVANCE, RECEPTION, AND CRITIQUE OF THE COMMUNICATIVE THEORY OF ACTION

In my opinion the theological relevance of the communicative theory of action presented by Habermas shows itself in a threefold way. First, its categories and concepts furnish a fruitful set of instruments for doing theological work. The categories of the theory of action, the concept of communicative rationality, the conception of discourse ethics, and the consensus theory of truth are open to a theological use and are suited to being taken into the formation of theological theory. Second, the possibility presents itself for theology, in working through the communicative theory of action and in demonstrating the structure of its aporias, to engage in self-reflection with regard to the theory of science[52] and of action, and thus to lay the foundation for a theological theory of action. Third, there is the prospect, particularly on the just-mentioned basis in fundamental theology, of theologically taking up individual elements of Habermas's conception, criticizing them, and constructively developing them with regard to the requirements and interests of each of the theological disciplines.

The communicative theory of action is theologically relevant first of all insofar as it is engaged in a reconstruction of, and a reflection upon, the basic structures of human praxis. Compared with a merely synthetic philosophical reflection upon praxis, the analytic reconstructive approach of the communicative theory of action has the advantage that on the one hand it develops a set of instruments that picks up on empirical research in linguistics and the social sciences, while on the other hand it does not positivistically deny philosophical reflection. In my opinion, when theological reflection critically appropriates Habermas's theory of communicative action, it arrives at deepened insights into the structure of individual and collective, social and historical, praxis. These insights contribute to a greater precision in theology's own categories and concepts.

The communicative theory of action is of particular relevance for reflection at the level of fundamental theology. The communicative theory of action is constituted in an interdisciplinary manner and oriented in an interdisciplinary direction. It thus fits nicely with a fundamental theology that: (1) among the theological disciplines, represents the place of institutionalized interdisciplinary work; and (2) has the task of engaging in the investigation of theological foundations in conversation and critical debate with other sciences and with philosophy. The communicative theory of action takes a multiplicity of the most divergent disciplines and positions of theory formation in the social sciences and humanities, relates them to each other, and processes them into an integrative approach. For precisely this reason the communicative theory of action is interesting and relevant for a fundamental theology that lays claim to its place in interdisciplinary exchange, seeks to make itself comprehensible in that exchange, and advances its own claim to truth within that exchange, explicating and defending its own claim to truth in conversation and critical debate with the consensus theory of truth.

The central concepts of communicative action and of communicative rationality are relevant for theology insofar as they sharpen theology's perception concerning several key questions. Does Christian faith represent a communicative praxis that should be the object of theological analysis and reflection? If so, to what extent? Do the rationality claimed by the Judeo-Christian tradition and the rationality of theology correspond to the criteria of communicative rationality? If so, to what extent? Are there places where they contradict these criteria? If so, where?

Helmut Peukert has undertaken the most comprehensive effort to work through the theory of communicative action and to demonstrate the structure of its aporias so as to show the possibility of a responsible way of talking about God, and so as to lay the foundation of theology, in terms of the theory of science, as a practical theory of action at the level of fundamental theology. In his "Analyses concerning the Approach to, and the Status of, the Formation of Theological Theories,"[53] he reconstructs this century's discussion of the theory of science, as that discussion begins by contesting the very possibility of theology. He elaborates the way in which this discussion increasingly encounters communicative action as the basis of scientific rationality, so that the questions asked by the theories of science and of action converge in a theory of communicative action. With regard to Habermas's development of such a theory, he argues that the normative implications of such a theory both for the identity of subjects and for the structure of a society end in aporias "where the attempt is made to conceive of the historical constitution of humanity united in solidarity."[54] He demonstrates that a theory of communicative action that defines the normative foundation of interaction as unconditional equality, reciprocity, and solidarity runs into three kinds of limitations that it cannot overcome in the form in which it has so far been developed.

The first limitation is the impossibility for the theory of communicative action in its present form to thematize at all the question of "an absolute freedom as the presupposition of finite historical freedom."[55] A second limitation is presented by the temporal structure of communicative action, which Habermas does not take into account. Concerning this structure, Peukert writes with reference to Martin Heidegger's analysis of the temporal structure of existence: "A theory of temporal, communicative action in which one's own death and the death of another are both incorporated as the farthest horizon of consciousness is yet to be developed."[56]

Third, the basic way in which the theory of communicative action as it has so far been developed ends in aporias is seen in its breakdown when it attempts to claim that the universality and solidarity that it demonstrates to be the normative foundation of interaction are really unlimited. The question is radically and paradigmatically posed when we ask how solidarity can be lived precisely with those dead who were destroyed on account of their engagement on behalf of the realization of solidarity.

> Can we simply exclude the question of a reality to which communicative action in solidarity is directed? Precisely at this point, does not the theory of communicative action pose the question of the reality that is the subject matter of theology, the question of a reality witnessed for the other in the face of his death by acting in solidarity with him?[57]

From the confrontation with these aporias, Peukert develops the foundations of fundamental theology by unfolding two theses. First is the claim "that the Judeo-Christian tradition is concerned with the reality experienced in the foundational and limit experiences of communicative action and with the modes of communicative action still possible in response to these experiences." Second he claims "that a fundamental theology can and must be developed as a theory of this communicative action of approaching death in anamnestic solidarity and of the reality experienced and disclosed in it."[58]

Peukert has further developed his approach to a theological theory of action in various essays. He has applied his approach to the pragmatics of ethical speech. On the basis of his approach he has undertaken a critique of the functionalist understanding of religion as the overcoming of contingency. He has explained the resulting concept of both fundamental and practical theology. And he has interpreted theology as a critical project of "enlightenment" that resists those systems engaged in amassing power.[59] He emphasizes that theology and the communicative theory of action have a common interest, since they are both uncompleted projects that stand over against the mechanisms for amassing power. At the same time he pointedly formulates his theological questions to the theory of communicative action with regard to the conditions for breaking through these mechanisms, and introduces reflections on an ethics of intersubjective creativity. Such an ethics is the central concern of his critical reception, analysis, and further development of the communicative theory of action. This ethics is the hinge on which turn his works of the last several years on pedagogy and the theory of action. Yet although they explicitly focus on conceiving a pedagogical theory of action, they also have theological questions in mind, and to that extent can at the same time be read as an underground development of a theological theory of action.[60]

From the theological side the concept of communicative rationality has been criticized in particular for excluding religion, or at least for paying it no attention. To be sure, today Habermas is no longer certain whether religion dissolves into a communicative ethics, and in his most recent works he is prepared to allow for communicative reason temperately coexisting with religion "as long as no better words for what religion can say are found in the medium of rational discourse."[61] Yet this offer of provisional coexistence is not acceptable to theology. In the sense of Habermas's own understanding of communicative rationality, the way in which he places communicative reason and religion over against each other is untenable, for communicative reason cannot *eo ipso* exclude religion from itself and distance religion as something that does not belong to itself. Within the framework of a procedural, communicative rationality, it is only from participation in the procedures of argumentation and from the conversation of those who participate in that argumentation that the contribution religion has to make to that process can be seen. Rather than standing over against communicative reason, religion is thus to be regarded as an element and dimension of an essentially open communicative rationality.

For that reason it is my opinion that the goal cannot be to claim for religion a separate sphere of validity beyond communicative reason. Religion must rather be conceived as related to communicative rationality, as having an indispensable dimension to introduce into communicative rationality: namely, the dimension of revealing and creatively changing reality on the basis of the memory stored in religion, the experience attested in religion, and the hope nourished by religion. Understood as communicative praxis, religion creates community and establishes identity. In a theological critique of Habermas, religion itself is to be conceived as a communicative praxis, which "as praxis, and thus as communicative action, claims God for others and seeks to verify this God in action."[62]

The theory of communicative action has been theologically discussed, criticized, and received in a variety of ways. I have presented this elsewhere, and there is no need to repeat the whole discussion here.[63] Therefore I will limit myself to examining two authors who have recently concerned themselves with Habermas theologically, and in particular have examined his discourse ethics and his theory of truth.

The discourse ethics conceived within the framework of the communicative theory of action has been variously criticized by Hans-Joachim Höhn from the perspective of a theological ethics, the foundations of which he seeks to elaborate by starting from the limit questions of discourse ethics.[64] For him discursive reason alone is inadequate. Therefore the capacity of reason to be in relation with its "outside" needs to be restored. Reason needs to draw into relation the "other" of discursive rationality, including the prediscursive conditions of the possibility of discursive rationality. This is precisely what Höhn wishes to attain with his extension of discursive reason to a "comprehensive rationality." Over against the formal and procedural rationality of discourse, Höhn intends this comprehensive rationality to secure and preserve in a rational way those creative and creaturely pre- and transrational impulses that are articulated, for example, in aesthetic and religious language games. In Höhn's view, a comprehensive ethics that would be developed from such elements begins its trajectory "by uncovering and exploding the limits of discourse morality."[65]

Höhn highlights two fundamental limitations of discourse ethics, which in his opinion can only be overcome theologically: the problem of recognizing those who are without reason as persons, and the problem of the mortality of human beings. In Höhn's view, discourse ethics makes the recognition of persons dependent on their capacity to argue, and thus on their rationality. By contrast, he demands that the ultimate proof of the morality of those who are rational be their relation to those who are without reason. He recognizes a second dilemma of discourse ethics in its inability to remove the contradiction between morality and the mortality of rational subjects, and in the inattention in its grounding of ethics to the finitude of personal and social existence.[66]

In Höhn's words, Christian faith contains precisely that "more" and "other" of reason which is able comprehensively to extend discursive ethics, and thus in connection with discursive ethics to introduce those moments which "can be justified as keystones of human life together."[67]

Höhn's proposal theologically to subsume discourse ethics under a comprehensive ethics appears problematic to me for several reasons. First, by assuming that communicative rationality is valid only for those with reason, he passes over communicative rationality's self-understanding and amputates discourse ethics. Second, in taking a position on the temporality of communicative action and on the death of those who act communicatively, he does not, unlike Peukert, use the practical theory of action. Instead he uses the theory of meaning to superelevate this fundamental aporia of discourse ethics, dissolving it in the religious certainty of an ultimate "ground of the being and meaning"[68] of the world. Third, inasmuch as he focuses on a supposedly religious component of human action, highlights faith's ground of meaning, and then only on that basis elucidates practical consequences of faith, he remains within the framework of an idealistic theological theory of meaning and precisely thereby misses the mark of a theological theory of action.[69]

Wolfgang Pauly has investigated the consensus theory of truth with regard to its theological relevance.[70] He recognizes in the consensus theory a concept of truth that is founded in the lifeworld and procedurally determined, and that in his opinion fulfills not only the necessary conditions but also the sufficient conditions of a theory of truth. Pauly makes clear that, as a process, truth "itself [represents] something that is communicative and changeable," and that is thus "not predetermined, but given to be determined."[71] In particular his analysis yields the insight that the view of reality given with the consensus theory avoids every form of ontologizing and grasps human action as the point of reference for the theory of truth. Pauly throws into relief the theological implications of the epistemo-logical framework of the consensus theory. In his opinion these implications also hold valid for discourse ethics. He understands truthfulness as a "truth-conditioning decision"[72] in the sense of an existential engagement directed toward the dialogical discovery of truth. He sees in truthfulness "a validity claim that on the purely formal level is set up in such a way as to shatter the discursive sys-tem."[73] In his view, the validity claim of truthfulness coincides with genuinely theological and central biblical statements. According to Pauly, it has theological implications, just as Habermas's idea of true, successfully lived life implies an experience of meaning and of hap-piness and thus evinces "connotations that can be interpreted in a theological way."[74]

Pauly concludes that the theory of communicative action offers opportunities for theological discourse. He first considers them with regard to Habermas's diagnosis of our times and his specifica-tion of the subjects of experience. Second, Pauly argues that, on the basis of Habermas's recognition that in communicative action expe-rience is "always founded in interactive processes carried out within the framework of a social lifeworld,"[75] we can conceive of theologi-cal sentences themselves as the result of communicative experi-ence, confess and predicate "God" as an experience, and conceive of theology as a science of experience. Finally, the consensus model provides a point of connection for reflections that understand the church as a conciliar, universal community of communication.

Pauly's concern is not a theological critique of the consensus theory of truth, but rather the exposition of affinities with theology and the search for theological connotations, implications, and points of connection. He rightly points to theological and biblical connections that result from Habermas's conception. As chapter 3 will attempt to show, though, these are not limited to the validity claim of truthfulness. On the one hand, they include all dimensions of the concept of truth. On the other hand, they must also be given a new explication over against Habermas. In attempting to pick up

theologically on the communicative theory of action, Pauly makes
Habermas more an implicit or anonymous theologian[76] than a theologically relevant conversation partner whom theology must critically engage for the sake of its own claim to truth, whose set of
instruments in the field of the theory of action theology can use, and
whose conception theology can make fruitful by examining it,
showing its aporias, and by working through them in the sense of a
theological theory of action.

2. BIBLICAL FOUNDATIONS OF A THEOLOGICAL THEORY OF ACTION

THE COMMUNICATIVE STRUCTURE OF THE GOSPEL

The Concept of "Gospel"

To constitute its approach, to clarify its set of methodological instruments, and to acquire its categories, a theological theory of action must have recourse to conversation and critical debate with extratheological theories of action. It acquires its genuinely theological contours, though, by assuring itself of its biblical foundations. The following discussion will articulate exemplary instances of these foundations.

I will concentrate on the New Testament, for which the Markan programmatic formula "the gospel of Jesus Christ" (Mark 1:1) could serve as the heading. But what is the (or a) gospel? Otto-Hermann Pesch rightly notes an "expansive linguistic usage"[1] of the concept of gospel that understands it on the one hand as a qualifier and legitimator of Christian theological statements, and on the other hand as an apologetic and critical category, as well as ultimately a basic theological concept. The concept of gospel itself has a multiplicity of meanings and dimensions, insofar as it encompasses various aspects that can in different specific cases be designated by this concept. On the one hand, it applies to a specific linguistic form, literary genre, or type of text that can be treated and investigated as having its own semantic function and identity. How this might logically play itself out is seen in the work of Erhardt Güttgemanns.[2] This approach highlights primarily, if not indeed exclusively, the text as text. On the other hand, other approaches define gospel as the form of the life of Jesus, as a "little unit" preformed for both the New Testament authors and for Jesus himself by early Judaism. In this "little unit" Jesus himself, as well as later both the communities of the early church and the evangelists, have given his life a form that also shapes its content.[3] Detlev Dormeyer places the text in relation to its content and to its intention by his undertaking to define gospel as a theological genre of kerygmatic-historiographic biography. Subjected to analyses of textual pragmatics, this genre enables us to see the communicative dimension of the gospel.[4] A communicative concept of gospel comes to expression most clearly in the work of Reinhold Reck. He grasps the gospel, itself communicative, as the initiating power of early Christian communication. He analyzes the messengers and addressees, content, intention, and effect of this communicative gospel on the basis of the processes of communication of Pauline communities.[5]

In my opinion, the communicative structure of the gospel and thus the multidimensional concept of gospel are most readily clarified within the framework of a theory of action. In what follows, this clarification will make use of the basic insights of both the communicative theory of action presented above and the pragmatic theory that has been appropriated and systematized in the communicative theory of action.[6]

Basic Insights of Pragmatic Reflection

Among the basic insights of pragmatic reflection is the idea that reality does not appear independently of language. Pragmatic reflection shares this insight with all theories and philosophies that have made the "linguistic turn" from ontology and philosophy of consciousness to philosophy of language. On the most basic level this means that human beings are *animales linguales* who approach reality by means of language and communication. The reality of this "linguistic animal" is not only socially constituted, but also linguistic. Our reality does not exist as such independently of communication, so there is no access to this reality independently of language. Instead this reality is always already linguistically constituted, made available, and interpreted, so that it is experienced, known, and changed by means of language.

In the course of the formation of pragmatic theory, five decisive characteristics of language and of linguistic communication have been elaborated. First, a constitutively intersubjective character is proper to language. Language is something that is given a priori to the individual, something that the individual always already shares with others. As the individual acquires language in the form of a particular language, she is at the same time integrated into a community of communication, in which fundamental assumptions about and ways of access to the external, the social, and the internal "world" are shared. These assumptions are to be taken on by the individual in such a way that the individual learns at the same time to identify with all others, to demarcate herself from them, and to conceive of herself as a subject, thus learning to say "I."

A second fundamental insight concerns the propositional and performative character of language. On the one hand, language is about something; on the other, action[7] is performed by means of language.[8] This character of language comes to expression in the basic units of human communication, the use of sentences in utterances. An utterance is characterized by a double structure. On the one hand, it contains a propositional component—that is, what is being talked about—which is carried out in a propositional act of reference and predication. On the other hand, it combines the propositional component with an illocutionary component. The latter indicates what is done when someone says something. The illocutionary component with which the illocutionary act is carried out thus specifies the sense in which the propositional component is to be understood. By contrast, the perlocutionary act, if it arises, concerns what is actually accomplished in and with the hearer by what is said. The perlocutionary act concerns the effect of the speech act. Accordingly, language can be adequately analyzed only with the inclusion of pragmatics. Specifically, language is an intersubjective process of carrying out rule-governed speech acts that are realized according to conventions, and that consist of acts of utterance, propositional acts, illocutionary acts, and intentionally perlocutionary acts.

All sorts of things are done with speech acts. Social relations are established, maintained, and changed. With actions of questioning, petitioning, promising, and so forth we intervene in reality. With speech acts the internal, the social, and the external "world" as such are constituted, made available, called into question, contested, changed, and so forth.

Third, a constitutively textual character is proper to language. Communication is carried out in situations by means of texts. In communication the textuality of language manifests itself. Texts are media of communication, which is carried out by means of them either in oral or in written form. An understanding of this sort does not limit texts to written texts, but recognizes in texts an element of every instance of communication. In communicative processes, actions are performed by means of texts. In communicative processes, texts are produced, used, and received. Embedded in interaction, interwoven with nonverbal actions and thus situated in concrete situations of action and communication, texts have specific intentions and fulfill specific functions with regard to the process by which the partners to the communication or interaction come to an understanding concerning that which is thematized.

Fourth, textually mediated communicative action always happens in concrete situations. It is localized and situated in its specific context, and thus situationally defined. The fifth and final feature of linguistic communication to be highlighted, along with its intersubjective, its propositional and performative, its textual, and its situational character, is its orientation toward reaching an understanding. This orientation is the characteristic that universal- or transcendental-pragmatic reflection upon the conditions of the possibility of linguistic communication and upon the foundations of linguistic understanding shows to be determinative for the original mode of communicative action.

Linguistic action oriented toward reaching an understanding—one could equally say communicative action—thus possesses a basic structure that is oriented toward solidarity, equality, and reciprocity. This basic structure is always already counterfactually presupposed in the actual communication within a real community of communication in order for an understanding to come about at all.

This understanding in turn aims at the realization of this basic structure in an ideal community of communication.

A Communicative Concept of the Gospel

Subjects of the Gospel.   To what extent can we say that the
gospel is intersubjective, propositional and performative, textual,
situational, and oriented toward reaching an understanding? In
order to answer this question I will look at the subjects who in the
New Testament are brought into connection with the gospel. In addition I will treat the contents enunciated by the gospel. Third, I will
examine the texts that speak about the gospel. Fourth, I will clarify
the situations into which the gospel is spoken, in order to obtain a
view of its structure of action, its intentions, and its goals.

If we start with New Testament word usage we see that the concept "gospel" appears 76 times in the New Testament. It is found 12
times in Mark and 4 times in Matthew. The concept is absent from
Luke and the Gospel of John. It has two occurrences in the Lukan
Acts of the Apostles. It is employed 60 times in Paul and in the Deuteropauline letters alone. First Peter and the Apocalypse of John contain the remaining two passages where it is found. While Luke
avoids the substantive, he uses the verbal form 25 times: 10 times in
his Gospel and 15 times in the Acts of the Apostles. The verb is to-
tally absent from Mark and John. It is employed only a single time by
Matthew. It appears 21 times in the Pauline and Deuteropauline
writings. In addition, it appears twice in Hebrews, 3 times in 1 Peter,
and finally twice in the Apocalypse.

On the concept "gospel" among the Greeks, Gerhard Friedrich
writes: "*euangelion* is an adjectivally based substantive. Like *euan-
gelizesthai*, it derives from *euangelos*. It means that which is proper
to a *euangelos*. This gives *euangelion* a twofold sense. For those to
whom a *euangelos* comes, what is proper to him is good news; but
for the *euangelos* himself, what is proper is his reward."[9] The intersubjective dimension of the concept of gospel comes to expression
already here. A gospel is a piece of good news, in profane Greek usually news of a victory, which a messenger delivers to his addressees,
whom the message affects and concerns, and for the delivery of
which the messenger receives due payment. In the New Testament

understanding, in accord with later Greek usage, the meaning of
"payment for a message" falls away and "gospel" means the message itself. Still, the intersubjective dimension remains relevant.

"Gospel" is a noun of action. On the one hand, it designates an
activity that a messenger performs with regard to his addressees. On
the other hand, it designates the content of this action. *Euangeliz-
esthai* is an intersubjective process: it takes place between subjects.
Participants in this process are, on the one side, the messenger as
the bringer of the gospel, and on the other side, those who receive
the gospel, its addressees and recipients. The messenger delivers to
them a piece of news to which he has access on the basis of his own
knowledge: for example, by having seen or heard firsthand. Mediated by the messenger, the piece of news likewise becomes accessible and available to his addressees. That which is communicated to
the addressees, the gospel, is evidently as important as it is welcome
to them. It concerns them, and is perhaps even of life-changing importance. Precisely in order for them to share [*teilen*] in it, it must
be communicated [*mitteilen*] to them by the messenger. Such a
gospel is always about something. The messenger makes a statement about that something. Of course the messenger's activity is
not limited to providing information about his object. Instead the
goal of the messenger is to see to it that what he delivers as something for which he vouches becomes effective so that it really becomes good news for the addressees.

With regard to the question of which subjects in the New Testament are brought into connection with the gospel, Jesus is to be
named first of all. It is he of whom the gospel says that he proclaims
the gospel. In particular, the gospel is mentioned in this way in summary statements, without the concrete addressees of specific cases
being named. The Gospel of Mark designates itself already in its
heading as the gospel of Jesus Christ (Mark 1:1). The construction
leaves open whether the genitive "of Jesus Christ" is to be understood as an objective genitive or as a subjective genitive. Possibly it
is holding itself open for both understandings.[10] The historical Jesus
is explicitly the subject of the gospel in Mark. The text says that he
proclaimed the gospel of God. Otherwise in Mark the concept appears only in direct address by Jesus. Jesus summons his addressees,

who are not more precisely specified, to repent and believe in the gospel (Mark 1:15). At Caesarea Philippi Jesus calls the crowd and his disciples to himself and makes clear to them that being a disciple and following him represent a risky, if not indeed a mortally dangerous, business: "those who lose their life for my sake, and for the sake of the gospel, will save it" (Mark 8:35). In his apocalyptic address on Jerusalem's Mount of Olives, Jesus communicates to his disciples that before the end the gospel must be proclaimed to all peoples (Mark 13:10). Sharing table fellowship in the house of Simon the leper in Bethany, Jesus, after having been anointed by a woman, says to those present that people will remember her and tell of her deed "wherever the gospel is proclaimed in the whole world" (Mark 14:9). In the inauthentic conclusion to Mark, the risen Christ commissions the Eleven to go out into all the world and proclaim the gospel to all creatures (Mark 16:15). Mark identifies Jesus as the messenger of the gospel that he proclaims to his addressees, his disciples and adherents, those with whom he participates in table fellowship, and the people in general. If Mark identifies Jesus in this way, then at least the disciples are indirectly seen as those subjects who are to proclaim his gospel to all peoples.

In Matthew Jesus is likewise the primary subject of the gospel. Matthew characterizes the gospel three times with the pithy phrase *euangelion tēs basileias* (Matt 4:23; 9:35; 24:14). In a summary way, Matthew brings the gospel together with Jesus' teaching in the synagogues and his healings. In accord with Mark 13:10, Jesus in Matthew explains to his disciples on the Mount of Olives that the gospel of God's reign will be proclaimed in the entire world in order that all peoples might hear it (Matt 24:14). In Matthew and Luke Jesus, in response to John the Baptist's question, has recourse to formulations from Second Isaiah and explicitly names the poor as addressees of the gospel. Picking up on Isa 61:1, Matt 11:5 (par. Luke 7:22) reports that "the poor have the gospel proclaimed to them." It is an object of dispute whether the historical Jesus "understood himself as the messianic evangelist to the poor in accordance with Isa. 61:1,"[11] or whether he was first identified with Second Isaiah's messenger of good news in the early church.[12]

In Luke in any case Jesus is the one who is sent to proclaim good news to the poor (Luke 4:18). It is his role to proclaim the gospel of the rule of God (Luke 4:43). He gives his followers, and in particular the Twelve, a part in this proclamation. He sends them out to go into the villages, where they proclaim the gospel and heal the sick (Luke 9:6). What Jesus initiates and does in many places, among them the Temple, where he teaches the people and proclaims the gospel (Luke 20:1), his disciples and witnesses continue after his death and resurrection. In Luke the subjects of the action of evangelizing— which appears ten times in Luke's Gospel and once in the Acts of the Apostles—are, besides the angel Gabriel and John the Baptist, above all Jesus and his apostles, disciples, and witnesses. While the gospel that Jesus proclaims has the *basileia* as its content, his apostles, disciples, and witnesses proclaim him, Jesus Christ, as the Word of God (Acts 4:31; 8:4; 13:5, 46; 16:32; 17:13). In Acts the following are named as doing this vis-à-vis their addressees: the apostles, who teach in the Temple and the houses and who proclaim "the gospel of Jesus, the Christ" (Acts 5:42); Peter and John, who do this in many villages of the Samaritans (Acts 8:25); Philip, who proclaims in Samaria the gospel of God's reign (Acts 8:12), proclaims the gospel of Jesus to the Ethiopian (Acts 8:35), and proclaims the gospel to all the towns through which he goes (Acts 8:40). Most frequently Paul and Barnabas appear in Acts as subjects of the gospel. Either they themselves talk about how they are commissioned to proclaim the gospel to their addressees (Acts 13:32; 14:15; 16:10), or others say of them that they did this in Lycaonia, Lystra, and Derbe (Acts 14:7), or that in Athens Paul proclaimed "the gospel of Jesus and of the resurrection" (17:18). In his parting speech at Miletus Paul gives a pithy summary of the ministry handed over to him by Jesus: "to testify to the gospel of God's grace" (Acts 20:24).

In the Lukan Acts of the Apostles the proclamation of the gospel is the task and the activity of various persons: the apostles, including Paul, and their co-workers. Paul in his letters highlights the proclamation of the gospel as an activity that is quintessentially his. He understands himself as having been called to be an apostle, "set apart for the gospel of God" (Rom 1:1). As he writes to the church in Rome, he is concerned to proclaim the gospel in Rome as well (Rom

1:15). He conceives of himself in the service of the gospel of God's Son (Rom 1:9). By God's grace he understands himself as a servant of Christ Jesus, working for the Gentiles and handling the gospel of God like a priest (Rom 15:16). He can even speak pointedly of "my gospel" (Rom 2:16; 16:25), by which he underscores the dignity of his own ministry. With this assertion he is not, however, claiming to deliver a gospel of his own. In particular the Letter to the Galatians makes this clear. In this letter Paul emphasizes to his Galatian addressees that there is no other gospel than the one gospel of Christ that Paul proclaimed (Gal 1:6ff.). This gospel does not originate from human beings, but from Jesus Christ himself, who revealed it to Paul, and which in addition Paul presented to the Jerusalem church and especially to "those who were supposed to be acknowledged leaders" (Gal 2:6). These authorities recognized, though, that Paul "had been entrusted with the gospel for the uncircumcised" (Gal 2:7) and they acknowledge him as the apostle to the Gentiles. Paul "sees the initial proclamation as his specific task."[13] Therefore he is careful "to proclaim the gospel, not where Christ has already been named . . ." (Rom 15:20). Instead of building on the foundation of another, he initiates the proclamation of the gospel there where it has not yet occurred. Moreover, he leaves to the churches themselves and to his co-workers the further communication of the gospel. To that extent he can likewise characterize Titus, Timothy, Silvanus, and others as fellow workers for the gospel of Christ (1 Thess 1:5; 1 Cor 9:14; 2 Cor 8:18).

In the New Testament "gospel" always signifies an oral message. It is the announcement that the messenger Jesus or his apostles and disciples deliver to their addressees. To be sure, even if such a meaning lies outside New Testament usage, the written text is also a gospel, by means of which its redactor or author communicates with his community. The gospel writers tailored their gospels to their particular addressees, to the specific recipients whom they had in mind. Thus at this level of the written gospel, the gospel again appears as a communicative undertaking, which as an element of communication between evangelist and community itself has an intersubjective dimension.[14]

The Double Structure of the Gospel. Together with the inter-subjective dimension of language, I named as a second dimension the propositional and performative one. This latter dimension shows itself in the double structure of linguistic communication, in which the propositional and the illocutionary are bound together. The linguistic material itself likewise suggests speaking of a double structure of the gospel. One side of this double structure consists of the fact that the gospel is about something: this, its content, represents its propositional substance. The other element of the double structure concerns what happens with the propositional substance in the course of the act of evangelizing: that for which the propositional substance is employed in the illocutionary act.

From a pragmatic point of view the proclamation of the gospel demonstrates itself to be a communicative action in which something is done with words and sentences. Inasmuch as the messenger proclaims something, something happens. Inasmuch as the messenger delivers a gospel, the messenger evangelizes and does various things that are connected with one another. Those things that one does in speaking have been investigated in detail by both speech act theory and the theory of communicative action, which picks up on speech act theory. The propositional and performative double structure of the gospel is already seen indirectly when Gerhard Friedrich writes, "That a specific content is to be declared with *euangelion* is clear from the fact that it is combined with different verbs of speaking and hearing."[15]

Employing the instruments of a communicative theory of action, Reinhold Reck conceives of the proclamation of the gospel as a communicative process and analyzes "the communicative action: preaching of the gospel."[16] He divides the components of this action of communication into two sides. On the side of the communicator he differentiates the contents and its power of persuasion, the methods and their appropriateness, and the communicator and her credibility. On the other side he places the recipients and their predisposition. The verbal action of evangelizing can be further explained with the help of the instruments of speech act theory. Later on we will take up what is done, with what means, and with what goal in the act of evangelizing: that is, what is done in an illocutionary mode and in an intentionally perlocutionary mode. At this point we shall first address the propositional element.

In asking about the propositional substance, the content of the gospel, we need to differentiate, in accordance with the distinction made above between various subjects, between the gospel of the historical Jesus (independently of whether he himself designated his message by this term), the gospel of early Christian preachers, and the gospel writings that were put forward by early Christian authors under the later designation of "gospel."

The central content of the gospel of Jesus is the rule of God. We find this central content echoed in the Gospels, embedded in the linguistic form of gospel. The rule of God appears in Mark, Matthew, and Luke as the basic substance of Jesus' communicative praxis. Both in his verbal action and in his nonverbal behavior, he brings this substance to expression as that which defines his person and his praxis. In so doing he places himself and his deeds in a particular relation to God and God's rule. He claims at least indirectly that God's rule is coming in his person and praxis. God, God's will and rule, and the consequences that result for human life together are the object of Jesus' gospel. This gospel thus becomes, in accord with its content, a "gospel of God" (Mark 1:14) and a "gospel of the rule (of God)" (Matt 4:23; 9:35; 24:14). At the same time Jesus implicitly objectifies himself in his particular participation in the coming and the praxis of God's rule.

The early Christian preachers, by contrast, make Jesus the explicit content of the gospel. The first instances in which this can be grasped are the early Christian confessional formulas. These bring to expression what happened with Jesus in his death, and both how and wherein God acted on him. The content of the gospel is now that Jesus is the Christ. Paul can thus also talk explicitly about the gospel of Christ. Helmut Merklein summarizes in the following way the Pauline concept of gospel in its commonalities and its differences in relation to pre-Pauline, Palestinian Jewish-Christian, and Hellenistic Jewish-Christian concepts:

> The "gospel" thus has Jesus Christ as its content. It is the good news of his salvific work in his death and resurrection. In that

regard Paul agrees with the tradition. The specifically Pauline idea lies in the fact that Paul brings this christological content of the "gospel" to a head in God's action in the Crucified One. On this basis Paul can interpret the "gospel" as a message and at the same time as the effective event of the new creation.[17]

The Synoptic Gospels make Jesus Christ the content of a theologically accentuated narrative of his history, his life and action, his suffering, death, and resurrection. According to Peter Dschulnigg, in Mark "the essential content of the gospel is both the proximity of God's rule (1:14-15) and the destiny in life and suffering of the proclaimer of the *basileia*, Jesus himself." Dschulnigg notes at the same time that for Mark's addressees the word "gospel" "certainly also [carries] an undertone of political criticism" as part of its meaning: "Not Caesar and his empire,[18] but Jesus and the rule of God are the true gospel."[19] As has already been presented, Matthew brings Jesus' "gospel of the *basileia*" (Matt 4:23; 9:35) into connection both with his teachings in the synagogues and with his healings. For Matthew the gospel of God's rule, the gospel that occurs in Jesus' communicative action, is the content of the gospel:

> Matthew designates Jesus' proclamation in word (chap. 5-7) and deed (chap. 8-9) as *euangelion tēs basileias*. The unity of verbal and nonverbal action, of proclaiming and doing the gospel, is thus secured from the outset (cf. 11:2, 4, 5, 19). And a second point: The earthly Jesus both proclaims and realizes the *euangelion tēs basileias*. According to Matthew, Jesus' disciples also have nothing other to do than that done by Jesus (cf. Matt. 10:7-8, among others).[20]

In Luke's Gospel the rule of God that has begun in Jesus' communicative praxis is the content of the gospel. In the Acts of the Apostles, Luke designates Jesus Christ or the Word of God as the object of the gospel. In his view of salvation history, Luke emphasizes the continuity between Jesus' communicative praxis and that of the early Christian preachers. Luke is concerned with making clear "that Jesus as *euangelizomenos* (Luke 4:18) initiates and grounds a dynamic process of proclamation and salvation that is to be continued after Easter in the initial witnesses and the church's preachers."[21] In this context one can explain directly on the basis of the Lukan terminology of witness how, to what purpose, and with what means the content of the gospel of Jesus Christ is propositionally transmitted, has an illocutionary mediation, and can have a perlocutionary effect.

Gospel Texts.   Along with its intersubjective and its propositional and performative character, I named as the third distinctive feature of linguistic communication its textuality. The textual character of language comes to expression in the fact that communication is carried out by means of texts. Texts are media of communication; textuality represents the "universal social mode of manifestation, binding in everyday language, for the execution of communication."[22] The gospel is also textually mediated. Whether the form be oral or written, it is in texts that the gospel is transmitted by its subjects. It is in texts that they hear it, read it, and appropriate it.

In asking about the types of texts in which a gospel is articulated, we need to distinguish between Jesus' texts—those types of texts that he himself used—and those that are about him, that tell a story or report about his person and praxis. If the central content of his gospel presents the rule of God, then a privileged place is to be accorded to those texts which talk about that rule. This is particularly the case in Jesus' parables and within the framework of those parables. For this reason the parables can count as the "gospel in parable."[23] The parables of Jesus represent the fundamental form of his preaching. In them Jesus makes clear to his addressees both his message and himself. Parables are narrative texts. In them Jesus, by telling stories about processes of nature and about the course of human actions, communicates to his hearers what the rule of God is like, in what type of human relationships God rules, and what God's rule means for the transformation of human structures of action. Along with the narrative texts of Jesus in which he unfolds his gospel are other, primarily narrative texts that tell stories about his action and his person: for example, call stories, stories of healings and exorcisms, further miracle stories, stories of encounters with sympathizers and opponents, stories of table fellowship and of conflicts, stories of discipleship, and so forth. I assume that at least a part of these texts was already in circulation during Jesus' lifetime, before they were gathered, passed on, and later integrated into the larger text of a gospel.[24]

The early Christian preachers not only continue to narrate Jesus' texts and texts that are about him, adding to them and applying them to their specific situations. One also encounters new types of texts in which the early preachers condense and pass on the gospel: confessional formulas and catechetical, parenetic, and kerygmatic formulations in which they record and communicate the gospel of Jesus Christ. The letters of Paul[25] are a type of text in which the gospel, always understood in the New Testament as an oral message, nevertheless finds an early written expression. They represent a type of text that takes up the gospel and supports it, protects it against misinterpretations and misuse, and strengthens and preserves it.

Finally, the textual dimension of the gospel comes to expression in the New Testament in the Jesus narratives of the Gospels. The authors and redactors of the Gospels arrange the texts that they have before them and integrate these into a new type of text called a gospel. In each specific Gospel this arrangement and integration takes place in a particular way with regard to the addressees of that author and in order to transmit the contents and intentions that are relevant to them. Even if "gospel" in the New Testament always means an oral message, "through the process of giving fixed literary form to the most important elements of the basic early Christian kerygma" and of the Jesus narratives, "the *euangelion* becomes quotable."[26] The seeds for the identification of the gospel with the book "Gospel" are sown in Matthew, and then explicitly carried out in the *Didache*. On the basis of the programmatic heading in Mark 1:1, "gospel" becomes a designation of that literary genre of primarily narrative texts that connects texts by and about Jesus texts in an original way to form a new literary and theological genre of Jesus narrative. That the parables as characteristic texts of Jesus became paradigmatic for this new genre is no more to be excluded than that the miracle stories could have played a role in the process. This does not mean, of course, that the gospel genre could be traced back in a unilinear manner to one of these two types of texts.[27]

Situations. Fourth, along with the intersubjective, the propositional and performative, and the textual dimension of the gospel, is its situational character. Texts are localized in specific situations; they are employed by subjects in situations; they are produced for and received in these situations. In the concrete situations in which they develop and are employed, texts pursue specific goals. They are embedded in situations of action and applied to them in order to constitute or to criticize them, to legitimate them or to call them into question, to stabilize them or to break them open and change them. Form criticism already had the situational character of the New Testament texts in view insofar as it correlated them with a "setting in life" and understood them from that perspective. By "setting in life" are meant the typical, recurring situations of origin and of use of early Christian texts: those social locations in which the texts arose and were used in the life of communities. The gospel is thus situational insofar as its subjects express its contents and bring them to bear by means of specific texts in their contexts and situations of action.

In general we can in turn distinguish between situations of action of Jesus, of the early Christian preachers, and of the Gospel writers. On each of these levels we need to presuppose a multiplicity of situations of action to which the gospel of Jesus, the gospel of Jesus Christ, and the Gospels relate. Among Jesus' typical situations of speech and action, in which he formulates, defends, explains, and addresses his gospel of God's rule in view of his specific addressees, are: public situations of proclamation in synagogues and other gathering places, in which Jesus addresses a multiform public; familiar situations of conversation in encounters with sympathizers and adherents when Jesus has been invited into houses and to table fellowship; situations of conversation in the closer circle of his disciples; situations of call and conversion; situations of encounter with persons who are needy and marginalized, who expect from him a change in their unbearable situation; situations of conflict with opponents and rival groups; and so forth. On the level of the early Christian communities we can likewise distinguish typical situations to which the gospel of Jesus Christ in each particular case relates and in which this gospel is brought to bear: for example, situations of initial proclamation, catechesis, teaching, baptism, regular worship, persecution, struggles against heresy, and so forth. And of course, the written texts of the Gospels also have their situations, from which they proceed, which they want to influence, and in which they find their employment.

Intentions. Finally, the gospel's situational dimension is connected with its intentional dimension. What the intention and the goal of a messenger are depend on the situation in which she finds her addressees. Whether the messenger with her gospel attains her goal has essentially to do with whether she is able properly to illuminate, to interpret, to stabilize, or to change the situation. On all the levels treated, the gospel has an illocutionary and perlocutionary structure. In being made known, its message aims not only at being understood in its illocutionary dimension, but also at being accepted and thus having a perlocutionary effect. The messenger wishes to come to an understanding with her addressees concerning what she communicates to them in order that they might share in it.

On the level of the gospel of Jesus we should note that his texts "are not intended simply to give information or to prescribe something but to open the eyes of the listeners; their purpose is to lead the listeners to see something and to assent to it."[28] Jesus' gospel of God's rule has primarily the intention of mediating the experience of the *basileia* to human beings and of inviting them into the praxis of God's rule. Jesus' gospel aims at an understanding with its addressees concerning God's reality and rule. It wishes to open up this reality to them and to win them for this reality. It thus definitely occurs with the intention (with the intended perlocutionary effect) of persuading. Its goals are insight and the arrival at an understanding, which are to express themselves in a shared conviction that manifests itself in the praxis of the *basileia*. Jesus' message of the gospel is at the same time an innovative action that changes the situation insofar as that message not only declares, announces, and makes known God's reality, but opens up this reality itself, transmitting it and enabling it to take effect in its salvific power (*dynamis*). Precisely in this way Jesus' gospel overcomes separations, removes excommunication, creates solidarity and community, invites people to take part in carrying them out, and summons people to do so.

The early Christian missionaries' gospel of Jesus Christ continues to aim at reaching an understanding and retains the gospel's inviting character, now with a kerygmatic-missionary edge. This is increasingly combined, though, with the identity- and community-forming aspect, the expression of a shared conviction that both asserts itself and delineates its particular contours in critical engagement with others. The gospel of Jesus Christ soon articulates itself in confessional formulas and formulations, whose primary foci are the confessors' attainment of a self-understanding among themselves and their community with each other.

Finally, these intentions also make their mark in the Gospels committed to writing. In them as well the Gospel writers pursue the goal of opening up the reality of God's rule and of Jesus' person and praxis, and of issuing the invitation to follow Jesus. At the same time they have the intention of coming to an understanding with their communities concerning the story and history that is determinative for those communities, and of strengthening and consolidating those communities in their shared conviction and identity. The goals set here are a combination of the missionary, the parenetic, the pastoral, and the antiheretical.[29] Of course these goals are embedded in the overarching intention of the Gospel writers to transmit the messenger Jesus' salvation message of the rule of God into the situation of their addressees, in order to tell the history of Jesus and of God with him as an offer and as an invitation to the addressees to discover themselves together in that history.

Now that we have presented the intersubjective, the propositional and performative, the textual, the situational, and the intentional dimensions of the gospel, we have sketched its communicative structure. What follows will examine some of these elements more closely. To this end I will first concern myself with Jesus' communicative actions. Under the rubric of God's rule and parables I will then turn to the content of his gospel and to the texts that fit this rubric. Third, I will elucidate Jesus' confrontation with the powerful and his resulting death on the cross. Finally, I will consider the action of his disciples and witnesses.

JESUS' COMMUNICATIVE ACTIONS

The Context of Jesus' Action

The preceding discussion has shown that in the Gospels Jesus is the
primary subject of the gospel, that the gospel occurs in his communicative action, and that the gospel's content is the rule of God. This
needs now to be elucidated. In accordance with the pragmatic
model I will again look at the subjects, contents, texts, situations,
and intentions of Jesus' communicative praxis. But before I start
talking about individual addressees and concrete situations of
action, I must first sketch the larger context within which Jesus'
action occurs.[30] In general, Jesus' situation of action is determined
by the sociocultural, political, and religious relations in the Palestine
of his time. At that time and place there is no longer an autonomous
Jewish state. Political power lies with the occupying Romans, who
beginning in 6 c.e. rule in Samaria, Judea, and Idumea through
Roman governors, while Galilee, Perea, and northern Transjordan
are under the rule of Jewish princes dependent on Rome. At the
time of Jesus Palestine is economically and fiscally tied into the
Roman Empire. In the domain of religious and cultic life it has preserved a certain autonomy.

The Sadducees were lay nobility who were allies of the powerful
priestly nobility. They were conservatively oriented toward the old
ways of Judaism and represented a national eschatology of election.
They had come to terms with the Romans so that they could maintain their own economic and religious privileges. After the death of
Herod the Great (4 b.c.e.) they attained decisive political weight in
the Sanhedrin, the highest non-Roman authority, responsible for
Jewish judicial and administrative functions and for religious matters. The Sadducees thereby became the most politically influential
group and appointed the High Priest.

Their opponents both ideologically and politically were the Pharisees, a lay movement shaped by members of the lower middle class.
At the time of the Hasmoneans this movement had developed into
an opposition party and on occasion exercised great political influence. Since Herod, however, the political party had turned into a
missionary religious movement. It was democratically organized in

associations. In these associations the schools of Hillel and Shammai opposed each other over the correct interpretation of the Torah. The conception of a sanctification of daily life through voluntary acceptance of Levitical purity, and thus the conception of a "perpetual ritualization of daily life,"[31] was common to all Pharisees and determinative of them. This sanctification was to occur with the help of an oral tradition given equal value alongside the written Torah. This oral tradition contained additional stipulations, specifications, and applications to concrete cases. In this way the Pharisees were pursuing the goal of an order of life that would be disengaged from the worship of the Temple and determined by the Torah, and that would include broader strata of society.

At the time of Jesus the Pharisees' primary interest was in the religious community and the life of the synagogue. They exhibited widespread abstinence from, and indifference to, politics as long as the former concerns were respected by the political power. The Zealot party, a split-off from the Pharisees,[32] assumed an opposing standpoint in this question. The Zealots combined strongly apocalyptically inspired nationalistic and particularistic expectations of a restoration of the Davidic kingdom with military struggle against the Roman forces of occupation. After the collapse of the Roman forces Israel would again rise up.

The Sadducees, Pharisees, and Zealots pursued their religious-political goals within society. The Essenes, by contrast, withdrew from society. They organized themselves into monastic communities with a strictly hierarchical structure. These communities were sealed off from the outside world; as communities of the pure and elect, they awaited in the near future the fall of this evil age in the eschatological war of vengeance. After the annihilation of evil they were sure of a new creation.[33]

Jesus' appearance on the scene is to be located in the midst of the religious-political situation marked by these party divisions. He himself was marked by yet another movement, that of the prophetic preacher of judgment and repentance, John the Baptist. He was baptized by John, and it is possible that he was numbered for a short time among John's adherents before he began at the end of the 20s C.E. to deliver his gospel of God's rule. It is common both to the Baptist and to Jesus that their message is urgent, since for both of them what they are prophetically announcing has come near. Yet their way of appearing on the scene and their action also exhibit decisive differences. John preaches threatening judgment and carries out his baptism of repentance as an ascetic in the wilderness (Mark 1:3; Matt 11:7 par.) near the Jordan, away from Temple and synagogue. Jesus goes into the villages and towns, to the locations of human beings, in order to declare to them the rule of God that has come near. Showing no trace of asceticism and fasting, he accepts invitations into people's homes, and can even be criticized, in explicit contrast with John, as "a glutton and a drunkard" (Matt 11:19).

Addressees of Jesus' Communicative Praxis

Jesus' public action in Galilee brings him into contact with various groups of addressees toward whom his communicative praxis is directed. In my opinion we can differentiate four more or less precisely definable groups of persons whom he encounters in situations typical for each of them, and with regard to whom he acts. As the four groups of addressees of Jesus' communicative action I differentiate first, concretely needy and marginalized persons; second, competitors and opponents; third, supporters and adherents; finally, the people in general in the sense of the mass of the population in the area of his activity.

Concretely needy and marginalized persons are those who are excluded from normal social intercourse and religious life, and those who for diverse reasons have excommunication imposed upon them. Numbered among these are, on the one hand, the sick, the leprous, and the possessed and, on the other hand, those who suffer social discrimination, such as lawbreakers, sinners, and prostitutes. A series of New Testament texts talk about Jesus' relations with persons belonging to this group. There are reports of Jesus performing healings and exorcisms. Even if the authenticity of these texts is hotly contested in individual cases, the fact that Jesus healed sick persons and drove out demons nevertheless counts as historically certain.[34] Even his opponents do not call that into question, indeed they presuppose it (Mark 3:22; Matt 9:34; 12:24; Luke 11:15, 18). Jesus' opponents do not dispute that he performs deeds of power.

The only points of contention are in whose name and with what authority he does this, and what he demonstrates by doing this.

I understand his healings and exorcisms as communicative actions of Jesus, insofar as in his deeds of power he directs his action toward persons who are concretely needy and frees them from their suffering. This suffering was both personal and socioreligiously imposed. In the understanding of the time this suffering was a sign of one's own sinfulness or of that of one's parents. In Jesus' deeds of power his everyday relations with those who are possessed, leprous, or suffering from other diseases are intensified. By establishing contact with them, he brings them out of their isolation, removes their excommunication—at least temporarily and symbolically—and enters into solidarity with them and their suffering.

In my opinion the primary reason for understanding Jesus' healings as communicative actions is the following. They are precisely not spectacular deeds in which a wonder-worker stages a strategically oriented, grandiose, self-centered performance aimed at overwhelming the astounded public. Instead they are directed toward the concrete other, the needy, toward his or her healing and salvation, in order that the excluded other be included again in the community. Jesus' miracles are communicative actions that provide concrete help and healing. They represent the exact opposite of instrumental and strategic theatrics in which one's own power is put on stage.[35] This understanding of Jesus' miracles sees them as striking intensifications of Jesus' communicative praxis, intensifications in which the healing and liberating power of God's rule is concretized and materialized. In them it is not only those who were previously possessed who learn that God's rule is present if Jesus drives out demons with the finger of God (Luke 11:20).

If the marginalized sick are excommunicated from social intercourse and religious life, so are other persons against whom society discriminates. It is especially true of them that the guilt for having become what they are is their own. Sadducees, Pharisees, and Essenes all agree on that, albeit for different reasons. The Pharisees argue for mercy in punishing lawbreakers, but they refuse to associate with them. Jesus of course associates with them. He even acts communicatively in relation to them by participating in table fellowship with sinners. The terms "sinners" includes all those who did not know the Torah, did not keep it, or could not keep it, as well as lawbreakers such as those who belonged to a dishonorable profession. Many Pharisees counted the entire rural population (*'am ha'aretz*) among this number. Mostly illiterate in any case, they did not study the Torah and did not keep the regulations for purity and tithing. It was not only according to the understanding of the Pharisees that tax collectors practiced a dishonorable profession. The educated despised them across the board. The merchants, whom they often cheated, attacked them.[36] The Zealots fought them as collaborators with the occupying power.

By contrast, Jesus consorts with sinners, lays claim to their hospitality, and participates in table fellowship with them. In the context of the ancient Near East, invoking the claims of hospitality, shared eating, and table fellowship are communicative actions of great symbolic substance. To eat with another signifies an intense experience of and attestation to community. It can indeed be understood as the dawning of the rule of God, in whose reign people will come from east and west, from north and south, and sit at table (Luke 13:29). This kind of communicative action on the part of Jesus in relation to persons against whom society discriminates signifies at the same time that Jesus enters into solidarity with them. Jesus' solidarity includes both practical and active assistance and healing, and the opening of the possibility of changing. Jesus' solidarity removes socially imposed excommunication and creates community. Such behavior gives rise to the burning question concerning the partiality of solidarity. Solidarity evidently includes entering into solidarity with groups of notorious exploiters and at the same time with their victims. This type of communicative action leads to conflict with those for whom the removal of social and religious excommunication goes against the grain of their construction of reality.

The question concerning Jesus' opponents as addressees of his communicative action is a difficult issue. We must first work out who they are and what it means that they are opponents of Jesus. The Synoptic Gospels name primarily "Pharisees," "scribes of the Pharisees," and "Pharisees and scribes" as opponents of Jesus. Reference is seldom made to the Sadducees. The Zealots and the Essenes are not mentioned at all by name. It would, however, be precipitous to draw from the Synoptic material the historical conclusion that, for the predominant time of Jesus' activity, his actual opponents were the Pharisees. That conclusion would transfer to Jesus' situation relations that were decisive for the Gospel writers at the time of the composition of their Gospels.

In any case the Essenes, characterized by their rigoristic obedience to the Torah, their ideology of election, and their dualistic separation between community and outside world, form a clear counterpole to Jesus. But, due to the monastic seclusion of the Essene communities, whose members were forbidden to have contact with nonmembers, one would not speak of an actual opposition. For this reason Jesus would not have publicly engaged the Essenes.[37]

Jesus likewise "never openly refers to the Zealots."[38] The Zealot underground movement operated as a secret society. Jesus would no more have encountered it in public than he would have encountered the Essenes. As a Galilean in Galilee, a center of resistance to foreign rule,[39] however, he could not avoid taking a position on this movement of uprising. Jesus' rejection of Zealot zeal is known to us at least indirectly from the command to love one's enemies (Matt 5:21ff., 38ff. par.), his answer to the question about paying taxes (Mark 12:17 par.), the third beatitude (Matt 5:5), and his behavior in the temptation story (Matt 4:8-11 par.). Jesus' communicative action in relation to tax collectors, prostitutes, and sinners contradicts Zealot action as radically as his invitation into God's rule runs counter to the Zealot program of God's exclusive rule in a theocracy to be brought about through military struggle. The Zealots must be regarded as opponents of Jesus, yet we can say little about Jesus' action with regard to them, since on the basis of their strategy and their form of organization there would hardly have been direct contact with them.

Since the Sadducees' theater of action was Jerusalem, it was only after Jesus' arrival there that he came into direct contact with them. The personal confrontation with the Sadducees, which soon led to his execution, can only date from this time forward. This does not exclude the possibility, though, that already in Galilee Jesus had critically engaged the ruling circles of Jerusalem. If the Sadducean party "had a decisive part in Jesus' condemnation and death, there must have been considerably broader conflicts between Jesus and the Sadducees than the single mention of the Sadducees in the Synoptic dispute about the resurrection of the dead leads one to suppose."[40] Jesus' denunciation of the violence of rulers (Mark 10:42 par.), his rejection of the *ius talionis* (Matt 5:38 par.), his rejection of cultic purity (Mark 7:1-15 par.), and his critique of the Temple, culminating in the Temple prophecy (Mark 14:58 par.) and the cleansing of the Temple (Mark 11:15-19 par.), indicate a thoroughgoing opposition to the Sadducees. Yet for the time of his activity in Galilee they remain the distant opponent with whom he did not have immediate dealings.

Thus it is probably the Pharisees, whose scribes were active in the synagogues of the villages and towns, who were the primary actual opponents of Jesus. The Pharisees' religious renewal movement, with its missionary tendency, became the natural competitor of the Jesus movement. Jesus engaged them critically in Galilee. He disputed with them concerning the interpretation of the Torah, concerning his and their understanding of reality, and concerning the orientation of their and his action. "Jesus' opponents in disputes during his public activity in Galilee were to a large extent Pharisees, who would have had substantially more influence than any other groups on religious life in the synagogues."[41] They are addressees of his communicative action, conversation partners with whom Jesus debates basic questions of life together, and thus basic questions concerning the interpretation of the Torah. The Pharisees stand in opposition to his action concerning the excommunicated, while he critically engages their ideal of piety and behavior.

Jesus also presents his interpretation of scripture in the synagogues of Galilee. In doing so he enters into the Pharisaic dispute between competing teachings. From this perspective one can certainly take him at first to be one of them, especially since he goes into the houses of Pharisees and participates in table fellowship with them (Luke 7:36; 11:37; 14:1). His communicative action thus explicitly includes them. It seeks community with them, too. When Jesus accepts invitations from Pharisees to eat with them, he attests to his interest in them, to his readiness to enter into dialogue with these people whose common life was defined by table fellowship.[42] At the same time basic conflicts arise between Jesus and the Pharisees. They are reflected in stylized form in the disputes in the Gospels. At issue in these conflicts are theological questions with practical relevance.

It is a consistent feature of the New Testament texts that Jesus measures the Pharisees' teaching by what they actually do, denounces them on occasion, but always seeks dialogue with them. Communication between Jesus and the Pharisees does not break off. It seems to have been carried by mutual interest and by the act of wrestling with each other over the correct interpretation of God's will and God's reality. In particular I will attempt to show on the basis of Jesus' parables, which were at least in part told to Pharisees, that he accepts his dialogue partners, argues with them, seeks to win them over, and attempts to persuade them.

Just as Jesus' communicative action in relation to his opponents is significant, so is his praxis with regard to his supporters. Jesus gathers adherents around himself. Like the rabbis, he lives with a group of pupils. There are of course characteristic differences. In the case of the rabbis the pupils choose their teacher on their own initiative and take instruction from him in scripture and tradition in order, after the apprenticeship is fulfilled, to become rabbis themselves.[43] Jesus, by contrast, issues an authoritative call for people to come with him. He calls them into an ongoing "common life and fellowship"[44] with himself, which assumes the place of their old family ties. Like Jesus, the wandering charismatic, those who follow him, leaving home, family, profession, and possessions,[45] become collaborators in his movement of gathering. As a consequence he gives them a part in his communicative action. He sends them out so that they, too, might proclaim the message of the inbreaking rule of God, and in the praxis of the *basileia* might heal the sick and drive out demons (Mark 6:7-13).

In particular the constituting of the circle of Twelve, which he sends out to the "lost sheep of the house of Israel" (Matt 10:6), points to the fact that in his communicative action in relation to his adherents Jesus also acts in a prophetic and symbolic way in and on them. He establishes the Twelve as a sign "that God turns to God's people with a grace that bursts boundaries and is itself boundless, and that 'all Israel' is being brought into the eschatological *basileia*."[46] The circle of the Twelve thus makes symbolically clear that Jesus' communicative praxis applies to Israel as a whole, which he is gathering and symbolically reconstituting in the praxis of the *basileia* in anticipation of the eschatological rule of God.

Besides the Twelve and the other disciples who follow Jesus and who share his wandering existence, Jesus' adherents include "settled groups of sympathizers."[47] The wandering charismatics are taken into the homes of these sympathizers. They receive hospitality and material support from them. Women belonged not only to these adherents of Jesus who had a set residence—women were also presumably among the wandering charismatics. In the patriarchal society of the ancient Near East, Jesus' public action in relation to women was something new, breaking social norms. Jesus' community of life with women who "had followed Jesus from Galilee" (Matt 27:55), and who thus were traveling with him as disciples, documents the fact that his movement of gathering had the intention and praxis of not excluding anyone, including on the basis of gender. This movement represents a "discipleship of equals"[48] that undermines structures of domination[49] and oppression, including patriarchal ones, and which in the praxis of God's rule enables and realizes new forms of human relationships. This is reflected in the composition of the circle of disciples, which encompasses men and women, the marginalized and the religiously observant, tax collectors and sinners. In the structure of this community the contours of a movement become visible in which social barriers to communication are broken down and communicative community is realized. Merely the composition of the circle of disciples entails a structure of action that, in the sense of the intention of the movement, attempts to break open the antagonistic structures of domination, and which, in real life together, makes it possible to experience in the praxis of the *basileia* the proclaimed message of the inbreaking rule of God.

Jesus' action with regard to the people in general, whom he encounters concretely in great numbers of the needy and marginalized discussed above, is his answer to the situation of the majority of the population of his home, Galilee. Along with the merchants and craftspersons living in the villages and towns, a large part was constituted by the uneducated rural population (*'am ha'aretz*). These are the poor, tenant farmers dependent on landowners, small farmers, shepherds, fishers, day laborers, and beggars. The economic situation of Palestine was bad in any case.[50] Within this situation, these persons were particularly economically disadvantaged. They did not know the Torah or could not keep it. These were the people who played a particular and privileged role with Jesus. A series of parables are about such persons. The beatitude that Jesus pronounces on the poor says that the rule of God is theirs (Luke 6:20; Matt 5:3).[51] Jesus' eschatological prophecies against the rich (Mark 10:25 par.; Luke 6:24) likewise make clear that he is on the side of the poor. As a wandering charismatic without possessions, he is in fact one of them. He shares their existence and enters into solidarity with those who are really needy, insofar as they cannot satisfy the basic needs of life. They are addressees of his liberating message and praxis, insofar as Jesus changes them from objects of human oppression to subjects of God's rule, suffers with them, and promises them God's solidarity.

He identifies himself with those who have neither political, social, nor economic power, who seem to be forced to remain in a dependency that gives them no future. He gives them hope for a change in their situation. It is a short step from this to their regarding him as a sociorevolutionary liberator.[52] Jesus, however, did not expect a fundamental change from military victory over the Romans. Nor did he have in mind the violent overthrow of existing economic relations. In Jesus' view, something new would arise from the liberation of human beings as they overcame the difficulties of their situation through solidarity. Borne by commonality among each other and with Jesus' liberating God, they would act differently and relate to each other differently. They would be able and ready to overcome structures of domination and oppression by introducing new structures of action. Where God rules, human beings can no longer rule over human beings. With Jesus, God's rule is already here, because in Jesus' communicative action "communication free from domination"[53] blazes a trail for itself. At the same time, God's rule is still to come, because while it is present in Jesus' action, it is still infinitely far removed from being realized in a way that will "rule" all human action. This realization is possible for God alone. Through God it becomes an eschatological reality.

Jesus' communicative action in relation to those persons and groups whom he encountered and with whom he lived during his activity in Galilee—needy seeking help, Pharisees opposing him and engaging in disputes with him, disciples and supporters, members of the rural population—is characterized by a common basic feature. His communicative praxis demonstrates a communicative orientation toward others.[54] It also brings to expression the communicative intention of the Jesus movement. This movement aims at the healing of social antagonisms and malignant structures, at solidarity, equality, and health-giving wholeness, which manifest themselves in the "domination-free relationships in the community of disciples."[55]

The Reality and the Will of God

Jesus' communicative action in relation to his various addressees is guided by his experience of the reality and the rule of God, and by his interpretation of God's will. For him as for every Jew, it goes without saying that the will of God is laid out in the Torah. Thus he does not in any way advocate getting rid of the Torah. Rather he returns to its original intention, which he sees formulated in the double commandment to love God and one's neighbor (Mark 12:28 par.). All other instructions must take their orientation from this double commandment. To the extent that they run counter to its sense, Jesus rejects them.

Jesus opposes both a rigorous interpretation of the commandment to observe the Sabbath (Mark 2:23ff. par.) and the prescriptions for cultic purity with their ties to "externalities" (Mark 7:1-23 par). He knows the danger that lurks in them for pious people: namely, that in their concern for the success of their communication with God in sacred cultic life, they neglect communicative action in relation to their fellow human beings, or even that in the name of the former they refuse to do the latter. The Pharisees' striving to sanctify everyday life by taking on Levitical purity thus implies nothing less than an excommunication of that which is impure. From the effort aimed at permanent worship and service of God[56] follows the refusal to serve human beings. Jesus does not reject service of God carried out in cultic and ritual forms. Rather, he participates in such service as a matter of course and at the same time "makes [it] a matter of indifference."[57] In contrast to such service, Jesus emphasizes the practical worship and service of God that is carried out in interaction between human beings. This is the presupposition of the first type of worship and service of God (Matt 5:23; Mark 11:25) as well as its genuine form of realization. For Jesus, worship and service of God mean doing the will of the Father, which is not satisfied by means of ritual correctness, but which aims at intersubjective action that breaks through cultic forms.

In Jesus' communicative action the instructions of the Torah are sublated into the "rule of God as a principle of action."[58] He claims to follow the trajectory of the Torah and to radicalize and concentrate it in such a way as to bring his experience of God's reality near to human beings; to confront them with God's will; to make his own behavior, in its deviation from the norms of social intercourse, conceivable and convincing to people in terms of its relation to God; and thus to depict God's reality to them in such a way that they can experience it. What fascinates or provokes his addressees in all this is the fact that Jesus identifies his experience of God's reality with God, who in Jesus is at the point of making God's rule reality.

In the midst of the diverse expectations of salvation in his day, Jesus proclaims the rule of God neither in the Saducean sense of an enduring order of creation nor in the manner of the Zealots as a purely future event. Nor does he share the Pharisees' view, according to which it is essential to take the yoke of God's rule upon oneself now through penance, observation of the commandments, study of the Torah, and the practice of charity, in order to bring the day of the Messiah closer. On the one hand, Jesus announces the *basileia* as having come near: that is, as imminent (Mark 1:15). On the other hand, he speaks of it in the present tense (Luke 11:20 par.; Luke 17:20-21; Matt 11:12).

In the message of God's rule that undisputedly stands in the center of Jesus' proclamation, there is a tension between God's rule already having dawned and its fulfillment still being outstanding. This tension is marked by the juxtaposition of present-oriented statements and future-oriented ones. Within this tension, the accent is placed on the present experience of the *basileia* in Jesus' praxis: "But if it is by the finger of God that I cast out the demons, then the rule of God has come to you" (Luke 11:20). This says nothing other than that in Jesus' healing praxis, it becomes possible to have real experience of the eschatological *basileia*. In Jesus' healing praxis, the eschatological *basileia* becomes reality. This in no way eliminates the relation to the future. Precisely the symbolic actions of Jesus point beyond themselves to what is still outstanding, which they at the same time announce. Jesus' message of the *basileia* is to be elucidated in the light of his communicative praxis, which Jesus himself understood by means of that message. One example of this communicative praxis is the expulsion of demons. On the one hand, it is made possible by God's action, as is graphically depicted by the vision of Satan's fall.[59] On the other hand, it anticipates God's eschatological action and practices it already in the present in a symbolic way. This becomes clear, for example, in Jesus' mighty acts, in which the rule of God becomes "currently and symbolically visible."[60] It becomes clear in Jesus' table fellowship with tax collectors and other sinners, with Pharisees and with women, in which he acts so as to anticipate symbolically the meal fellowship of those who "will sit at table with Abraham and Isaac and Jacob in the rule of God" (Matt 8:11).

Because for Jesus the experience of God's rule and of the "action made possible"[61] by this rule is located in the present, his communicative actions concentrate on what is happening now, what is made possible now, and what ought to be done now.

The *basileia* that is present in Jesus' experience and communicative praxis thus stands in the center of his understanding of his own action and of his person.

> Inasmuch as Jesus invokes the *basileia* for his appearance on the scene and for the way in which he relates to people, wherever in

Palestine he might encounter them, the domain of human history is
shown to be the location of the *basileia*'s present. This is not to say,
of course, that it is possible to pin it down to one location in history
(cf. [Luke] 17:21).[62]

For Jesus, the presence of the *basileia* is tied to his action and his
person. In Jesus' action, the God who is benevolent, merciful, and
liberating offers God's rule to human beings. God wills to win them
for Godself, so that they will let themselves be "ruled" by God, in
order thus to "enter into"[63] the eschatological *basileia*. This is just
what Jesus does: he lets himself be ruled by God. For this reason
God's rule dawns in him. At the same time it is still outstanding, still
future. It is not yet the case that all human beings in their action
place themselves under God's rule. Social relationships are anything
but free from domination (cf. Mark 9:35 par.; 10:42-44 par.).[64] Both
will really become fully possible only in a new reality brought about
by Godself—the eschatological *basileia*. This can be neither described nor calculated nor effected by human beings. It can, however, be experienced where Jesus acts and where human beings act
and interact in christopraxis.

GOD'S RULE AND PARABLES

Experience and Praxis of the *Basileia*

When Jesus talks about the rule of God, he usually speaks of it in
parables.[65] In a multiplicity of images and picture stories he compares aspects of the experience of the *basileia* with processes in
nature and with the action of human beings in both everyday and
extraordinary situations. The use of parabolic speech in talking
about the rule of God is hardly just happenstance. The material at
issue suggests it, and may even require it. When Jesus says that the
rule of God is like a mustard seed that becomes a tall bush, or like
the owner of a vineyard paying wages, he uses processes that can be
experienced in nature and in human action to make clear what
God's rule means, how it comes, what experiences it mediates,
what possibilities for action it opens up, or in what praxis it manifests itself.

In the parables of nature—for example, the parable of the seed that grows on its own (Mark 4:26-29), the parable of the mustard seed (Mark 4:30-32 par.), the parable of the leaven (Matt 13:33 par.), and the parable of the weeds among the wheat (Matt 13:24-30)—the primary concern is to depict the contrast between the tiny beginning, which has to do with the present experience of God's rule, and the abundance of the fulfillment of that rule. By contrast, the parables in which human actions are discussed sometimes demonstrate the forms of human interaction in which God rules. This is directly thematized in the example stories of the merciful Samaritan (Luke 10:25-37) and of the father and the two sons (Luke 15:11-32). It is also thematized by means of the opposite behavior in the parable of the unmerciful debtor (Matt 18:23-35). More frequently the parables of action address the question of the action that is provoked by God's rule and to which people are invited by God's rule, and the question of how human beings behave in view of the *basileia* and gain or lose it.

Action in view of the rule of God is discussed, under the aspect of the self-evident readiness to risk everything, in the parable of the treasure and the pearl (Matt 13:44-46), in the parable of the talents (Matt 25:14-30 par.), and in extremely drastic form in the parable of the deceitful overseer (Luke 16:1-8). It is articulated under the aspect of prudence in the parable of building a tower and making war (Luke 14:28-32), and under the aspect of importunity in the parable of the unjust judge (Luke 18:1-8). The parable of the servant's reward (Luke 17:7-10) thematizes action as unconditional service; the parable of the ten virgins (Matt 25:1-13) and that of the doorkeeper (Mark 13:33-37 par.), untiring preparedness. The parable of the foolish rich man (Luke 12:16-20) can count as a negative foil in this regard. The question of the action that is provoked by God's rule and to which people are invited by God's rule is addressed under the aspect of generosity in the parables of the workers in the vineyard (Matt 20:1-16) and of the two debtors (Luke 7:41-43). It is addressed with regard to the act of seeking and finding what has been lost in the parables of the lost sheep (Luke 15:4-7 par.) and of the lost drachma (Luke 15:8-10).

It is characteristic of Jesus' parables that they almost never speak of God. It is precisely this feature, though, that shows "Jesus' simple and concrete speech about God."[66] Just as in his action Jesus speaks about God in an indirect and practical manner, so in the parables he leads his addressees in an indirect and practical way to see those contexts of action in which it is right to speak of God.[67] Precisely because God never appears thematically in Jesus' parables, they make it possible to thematize God in a new way. This does not occur in such a way that where human beings act, the action under discussion would actually be God's. Instead the statement runs in the opposite direction: God acts where human beings do God's will. God acts where, on the basis of the experience of God's proximity, human beings in turn draw nearer to others, thus overcoming distance and alienation. God acts where, on the basis of the experience of God's solidarity, human beings in turn enter into solidarity. God acts where, on the basis of the experience of God's goodness, human beings in turn are good. God acts where human beings in this way mediate and make it possible to experience God's proximity, solidarity, and goodness. It is in this way that God's rule becomes present.

Parables as Communicative Actions of Jesus

I understand the New Testament parables primarily as communicative actions of Jesus. In the sense of the basic insights of pragmatic theory discussed above, I see the parables distinguished by five characteristic features. For one thing, they are texts. More specifically, they are fictional-metaphoric texts. Second, they are elements of communication between subjects. Third, with regard to Jesus' situation of action, we need to ask who the addressees are with whom he is communicating in his parables. Fourth, the parables have a specific content. They are about something: namely, the rule of God. Finally, they have specific intentions. They pursue their goals, which we need to work out in relation to their addressees and contents.

First, parables are narrative texts. Since they do not depict any actual reality, but give imaginative expression in themselves to a textual world, they are fictional texts. They can be readily conceived as aesthetic or poetic texts and understood as literary works of art.[68]

As has been elaborated by Paul Ricoeur, fictional texts are characterized in particular by the fact that they deploy their own world, the
world of the text, which is relatively autonomous in relation to everyday reality. According to Ricoeur, though, this world of the text
invites its hearers to understand the text "as the laying out of a
world that I can inhabit in order to lay out within that world one of
my essential possibilities."[69]

Fictional texts lay out their own proper world. This world is a reality with its own plausibilities and structures of action, a reality that
deviates from and breaks through everyday reality. In their projec-
tion of an opposing world, fictional texts at the same time remain
related to the socially constituted reality of experience and action.
This latter reality is broken through, but it also remains present in
the texts. It provides the foil against which the fictional alienation
and redescription of reality unfold. As a socially constructed and
sanctioned world of communicative, strategic, and instrumental
action, everyday reality is both the point of departure and the end
point of fictional texts. Inasmuch as such texts, in Ricoeur's words,
open up new possibilities of being-in-the-world, they want, by
means of their imaginative transformations, to initiate transformations of the everyday experience of reality and transformations of
social action. How the imaginative distancing and transformation of
reality proceed in Jesus' parables is clarified by elucidating a further
feature of parabolic texts: namely, their metaphorical character.[70]

Parables are fictional and metaphoric texts. As pictures/stories
they represent extended metaphors that agitate and unsettle human
imagination, and in so doing issue an invitation to participate in the
reality expressed imaginatively by the metaphors. They are a "raid
on the articulate,"[71] in which the imaginative shock confuses the
conventions of predication in the interest of a new view of the
world. Ricoeur succeeds in bringing together the realism of Jesus'
parables with their potential for metaphoric innovation. Starting
from his understanding of metaphor as a semantic innovation that
resolves semantic dissonances, Ricoeur argues that one can "tenta-
tively define a parable as a figure of speech that applies a metaphoric
process to a narrative form."[72] In a parable, metaphoric process,
narrative form, and hyperbole all come together. To be sure, the par-

able functions on the level of everyday life, telling what is at first glance an everyday story. As a fictive scene, though, it at the same time stands in tension with everyday reality. This is expressed in particular in the hyperbolic and paradoxical features of the parable, which collide with and break through everyday reality.

In Ricoeur's conception the moment of fictional-metaphoric texts that comes most clearly to expression is the breaking open and the creating of reality. On the basis of Ricoeur's conception one can also show the extent to which the parables, as metaphoric-fictional texts, represent innovatively oriented communicative actions of Jesus. In the tension between the fictive world of the text and the world of everyday life, they not only break through everyday reality, but at the same time they introduce semantic innovations. They point toward a new reality with plausibilities and structures of action that deviate from everyday reality. They invite their hearers to enter into this reality with their imagination. By means of the imaginative alienation of their reality, the hearers are to receive an impetus to real change and then to respond to the text in the innovative praxis of life. On this level the innovation offered and required by the text of the parable is that of the imagination: namely, the possibility of experiencing reality otherwise, in order to act innovatively on the basis of this experience.

Second, the parables are elements of communication between subjects. The people whom Jesus encountered in Galilee are the probable addressees. On the level of Jesus' situation of action, there are primarily two groups of addressees to whom Jesus' parabolic speech could have been addressed: his adherents and his Pharisaic opponents—the only opponents with whom he publicly came together in Galilee. To the needy whom he encountered, he would have communicated himself less by means of words than through practical, healing solidarity. The masses of the population would likewise have probably been more interested in the presence of solidarity than in "theological" conversations. Admittedly, the texts of the parables often talk about people from the masses of the population, about farmers, servants, fishers, shepherds, day laborers, debtors, and beggars. Whoever compares the rule of God with what such people do and with how things go for them is hardly address-

ing such people themselves in those texts. Moreover, Jesus' parables—unlike, for example, his beatitudes—do not address promises
to the listeners, but rather tell stories. The parables thematize natural processes and human actions in such a way that in view of the
basileia, orientations of action become transparent with regard to
their theological consequences.

To this extent the parables of nature are also concerned with the
orientation of human action, because real, seemingly insignificant
experience is contrasted with the visible fulfillment in abundance
that is still outstanding. In the orientation toward certain fulfillment,
patient action is possible without resignation. This seems to point
toward Jesus' adherents at least as addressees of the parables of
nature. In these parables Jesus comforts and strengthens them, placing their action and their experiences in the horizon of God. Of
course, because of their brevity and their metaphoric richness, and
because they lack clear relations to specific situations, the parables
of nature fit various situations of action. Jesus certainly could have
told them in conversation with his disciples. They could originally
have been told in view of the lack of success of the disciples' mission, in view of Jesus' adherents' doubts concerning the social reality of the rule of God, in view of their experience of the rejection of
their own message, in view of the flagging commitment of his sympathizers in the face of the marginality that they experienced as
hopeless, or in view of disappointment among Jesus' adherents at
the fact that the great liberation had not yet come.

In my opinion, the relations with addressees are clearer in the
parables that thematize the forms of human interaction in which
God rules. Persons appear in these texts who point to the identity of
the addressees. With the priest and the Levite in the parable of the
merciful Samaritan (Luke 10:25-37), with the older son in the parable of the father and the two sons (Luke 15:11-32), and with the
first debtor in the parable of the unmerciful debtor (Matt 18:23-35),
the issue is the behavior of persons who, based on their understanding of reality and on their orientation of action grounded in that understanding, refuse to interact with others. The priest and the Levite
reject such interaction because contact with a dying person would
make them unclean; the older son, because he asserts the preroga-

tives that lifelong service have brought him in relation to the younger son; the first debtor, because he does not make the forgiveness of debt that he has received the principle of his own action as well.

The dramatization of such persons in my opinion makes clear allusions to Pharisaic addressees. The open ending of the parable of the father and the two sons supports the view that the situation in which it was originally spoken was Jesus' wrestling with Pharisaic opponents whom he was trying to persuade to accept his understanding of reality and his orientation of action. He was challenging them to critically engage his view of God's reality. That critical engagements of this sort came to pass is historically plausible for the following reasons. For Jesus and the Pharisees, Galilee was a shared area of operation. In part they had identical locations of action: the synagogues of the villages and towns. The Jesus movement and the Pharisaic movement were competing as renewal movements. Jesus and the Pharisees both were oriented toward conversation and persuasion, which included shared theological conversations.

Many of Jesus' parables that thematize the action that is provoked by God's rule and to which people are invited by God's rule, or that thematize how human beings behave in view of the *basileia*, likewise contain clear indications of Pharisaic addressees. It is likely that the theme that is presented with variations in the parables of the lost sheep (Luke 15:4-7 par.) and the lost drachma (Luke 15:8-10)— the theme of losing and finding, and of the resultant rejoicing— concerns Jesus' situation of action. In view of Jesus' table fellowship with tax collectors and sinners, "the Pharisees and the scribes were grumbling and saying, 'This fellow welcomes sinners and eats with them' " (Luke 15:1-2). In response Jesus tells them these parables. These parables metaphorically process the situation of those who are, in the eyes of the Pharisees, lost before God. These parables bring to expression the fact that the excommunicated tax collectors and sinners are found by Jesus and are invited to the table fellowship of the *basileia*.

Three further parables fit this situation of action. In the story of the laborers in the vineyard (Matt 20:1-16), those who have worked a full day grumble about the fact that all are treated equally in the payment of wages—something that in their view is unjust. It is likely that their grumbling in response to the generosity of the landowner reflects the real protest of Pharisaic groups against Jesus' equal treatment of tax collectors and sinners. This issue is also addressed in the parable of the two debtors (Luke 7:41-43). Finally, in the parable of the great banquet (Luke 14:16-24), the question of table fellowship itself is given narrative development. Because the first to be invited decline, people are brought from the highways and the hedges—obviously people with whom those who were originally foreseen as guests would not sit at table. The host fills his house with them. It is an obvious step to see in the addressees of the parable of the banquet people who do not respond to the invitation to the table fellowship of God's rule.[73] Precisely the contrast with people who live in the streets, and who accept that invitation, suggests Pharisees. The parable of the playing children (Matt 11:16-19 par.) also points toward Pharisaic addressees. The quotation that Jesus builds into the parable—"Look, a glutton and a drunkard, a friend of tax collectors and sinners!" (Matt 11:19 par.)—likely reflects a pointed Pharisaic evaluation of his person. In Jesus' parables of action the basic issue is the metaphoric-fictional confrontation between Jesus' understanding of reality and of God with the Pharisaic "construction of reality,"[74] and within that construction, their understanding of God's reality.

The Pharisaic reality is constituted and defined by the written and the oral Torah. By freely taking up Levitical purity, the Pharisees want to realize their goal of a sanctification of everyday life. They are striving for a "perpetual ritualization of daily life"[75] in the sense of an ordering of life that can be disengaged from the cultic life of the Temple and that is available to broader strata of society. Pharisaic reality is thus constituted as a sacred order. The Pharisees' orientation of action, derived from their understanding of reality, is defined by the goals of securing the fulfillment of the divine will in everyday life, and of thus making the Torah practicable. In their construction of reality, God is the guarantor of the order of the Torah. This order forms the foundation of their "world" from a religious, ethical, and social perspective. The order of life realized in the Pharisees' associations derives its legitimacy from God. In this order the Pharisees identify themselves as "separate," "pure." They assert their identity by defining themselves over against the alien groups of sinners and tax collectors, as well as of non-Israelites. The sanctification of everyday life in cultic purity applied to the whole of life contains at the same time an excommunication of those who are stigmatized. This excommunication in turn derives its legitimacy from God, who wills to call a holy people God's own. God thus ultimately becomes the guarantor and stabilizer of an order that is defined by, and that takes its identity from, the excommunication of those who are stigmatized.

Jesus' communicative action does not excommunicate anybody. It thus sparks the controversy between him and the Pharisees. "The dispute about a specific mode of communicative action is at the same time a dispute about the reality of God."[76] Jesus intervenes with his parables in the dispute that has broken out between him and the Pharisees concerning the principles of the social construction of reality. In the parables he engages in action directed toward his hearers and undertakes to work through the conflict. The conflict is to be resolved by his seeking to make his understanding of reality and his orientation of action narratively plausible to his opponents. To this end he makes use of fictional-metaphoric texts that take up the real situation of the existing dispute and work it through textually. In doing so Jesus interlaces his narratively mediated understanding of reality with that of his Pharisaic addressees. The latter can see in the parables an offer to them to go beyond the existing differences to an agreement, doing so on the basis of a shared understanding of the situation in question, as that understanding has been created by the parables.[77]

The Thematized Rule of God

Jesus' parables are about the rule of God. They articulate God and God's *basileia* in an indirect and practical manner. This occurs indirectly because "God is spoken about only . . . in the framework and implications of the action, in the actions and interactions of the participants."[78] It occurs in a practical manner because Jesus "invokes 'God' in actual situations (healings, forgiveness of debt/guilt,[79] deviant behaviour, commerce with the socially unacceptable)."[80] God's

rule is articulated in the textual world of the parables. God's rule is
given imaginative textual expression and is communicated in them
as a reality of a particular sort. Jesus' communicative actions thematize the *basileia* by enabling it to become visible in a fictional-metaphoric manner in pictures/stories.[81]

Jesus' parables talk about processes in nature and about human
actions. In the parables of nature the particular, unemphasized initial human action is followed by a new thing that is *automatē*, arising without human contribution. Reality that is experienced in an
everyday manner thus is represented as itself being full of miracles.
The world of nature appears as open for God's miraculous action in
it. The parables of nature acquire their metaphoric character relating processes of nature to the *basileia*. If there is an analogy between the rule of God and the process in which a tiny mustard seed
becomes a large bush, or in which with the help of a small amount
of yeast a huge mass of bread dough is thoroughly leavened, then
the *basileia* is thematized, in the images of nature, as a reality in the
everyday world that is experienced through the parables as standing
in contrast to the *basileia*. Specifically, the *basileia* is thematized as
that reality which, while located in the everyday world, surpasses
the boundaries of human action. The *basileia* is a reality in which
God is creating something new. In this sense the parables can be
termed "narrated creation."[82] In the images of nature it is said concerning the *basileia* that the apparent insignificance of its present
experience contrasts with the imaginatively anticipated abundance
of its completion. The latter automatically follows the tiny beginning. The completion comes from God alone. This says concerning
God that God will realize God's complete rule on God's own. By the
same token, God is metaphorically named as the one who carries
out the initial action, who lets God's *basileia* dawn at all.

The parables of nature thematize God's rule as God's sovereign
action. Nevertheless, they are also concerned with human orientation of action in reaction to the *basileia* that has dawned. By contrast, the parables of action articulate, first, the form of human
interaction in which God rules. Second, they elucidate the action
that is provoked by the *basileia* and to which people are invited by
the *basileia*, and the question of how human beings behave in light

of God's rule. The picture stories of the parables of action thematize the *basileia* as a principle of action. For example, the new reality of God's rule imaginatively expressed in the parable of the merciful Samaritan is one in which neither religious nor ethnic boundaries impede the praxis of neighbor love. God rules in the interaction between father and "lost," returned son—an interaction borne by prevenient generosity and responding acceptance.[83] God's rule comes metaphorically to expression in the action of the debt-forgiving lord in the parable of the unmerciful debtor. Of course, in this parable the debtor does not make the experienced praxis of the *basileia* his principle of action and does not carry it forward in his interaction with his own debtor.

In other parables of action the rule of God is thematized in an indirect and practical manner by virtue of the fact that these picture stories set the stage of human action in light of the *basileia*. In both daily and extraordinary situations, actions are dramatized that demonstrate praxis that corresponds to the experience of God's rule. In the parables of the treasure in the field, the pearl, the talents, and the deceitful household overseer, the aspect of the self-evident readiness to risk everything stands in the foreground. In the parable of building a tower and of making war, the moment of prudence is emphasized; in the parable of the unjust judge, the aspect of importunate insistence on a rightful claim; in the parable of the servant's reward, the aspect of service. The parables of the ten virgins, the doorkeeper, and the rich fool imaginatively depict in various ways an inexhaustible readiness to anticipate in present action God's expected completion of God's rule. According to these parables, this readiness corresponds to the experience of the *basileia*. The action that is provoked by God's rule, and to which people are invited by God's rule, is demonstrated by the parable of the laborers in the vineyard and the parable of the debtors in a way that emphasizes a generosity that surpasses every just distribution according to merit. God's generous action is thus metaphorically elucidated and made plausible and persuasive. This also occurs in the parables of the lost sheep, the lost drachma, and the father and the two sons. In these parables, by means of the constellation of seeking and finding, and of resultant rejoicing, God's joy over everyone who is found after having been lost is articulated fictionally and metaphorically.

As a thematization of the rule of God, Jesus' parables are innovative verbal actions. They depict the *basileia* and elucidate God's reality and the rule of God that has dawned with Jesus. They elucidate that reality and rule as something radically other and new in contrast to human rule. They dramatize human possibilities of action in light of the reality and rule of God, which Jesus actualizes in such a way that his action and his person interpret them. He thus anticipates the miraculous completion of the *basileia* through God's creative act. In his action, Jesus anticipates God's eschatological innovation.

The Goal of Jesus' Communicative Praxis

Finally, the intention and the goal, the intended perlocutionary effect of Jesus' parables, must be articulated. As the basic goal I see that of reaching an understanding both with his disciples and supporters and with his opposing addressees, whom he seeks to win over and whom he attempts to convince of his understanding of reality and of his orientation of action. He pursues this goal by telling persuasive stories about joy in view of what was lost having been found, about generosity that enters into solidarity, and so forth. In telling these stories he pursues this goal by relating to his opponents in a way that corresponds to the attitude mediated in these stories.

Accordingly, Jesus' concern is to communicate with his addressees and opponents in such a way that he reaches an understanding with them. In his texts and in his action he communicates to them an understanding of reality defined by the rule of God. He offers this understanding to them and invites them to a new form of action, of which he wants to persuade them. The substance that is communicated in the telling is not to be separated from the form in which it is communicated. The content of a series of parables is a certain structure of communication and interaction. This structure of communication and interaction is mediated with regard to the rule of God, which is always also included in the thematized substance of the parables. This mediation occurs in a form that precisely realizes the structure: in the communication [*mitteilender Mitteilung*] of this structure of communication [*Kommunikation*] and interaction, with the goal of its being shared by the addressees.

From the perspective of a communicative theory of action, Jesus' speaking in parables manifestly has to do with the problematization of two validity claims: the claim of the truth of his statements, and the claim of the rightness of his actions and of the norms underlying these actions. Jesus and his Pharisaic opponents share no background consensus that would make it possible to continue communicative action in an unproblematic manner. There is profound disagreement between them with regard to the rightness of his communication with tax collectors and sinners, of his table fellowship with them, and of his transgression of ritual and cultic laws that do no less than define and stabilize the Pharisaic construction of reality. The dispute about the legitimacy of Jesus' action is at the same time a dispute about the truth of his theological statements, "a dispute about the reality of God."[84]

I understand Jesus' parables as an attempt to settle this dispute, to move beyond disagreement to a consensus. Insofar as discourses serve the goal of finding a consensus, I regard Jesus' parables as quasi-discursive. In them he justifies on three levels his communicative action and the reality that grounds this action. First, as a substantive argument for his attention to those who exist on the margins, he adduces the claim that these persons are in need of persons to stand in solidarity with them. On the basis of his self-understanding and his understanding of reality, he uses the narratively alienating representation of his Pharisaic opponents' excommunication of tax collectors and sinners—a practice whose legitimation they trace back to God—to demonstrate the self-evident nature of his action. The goal is that, in this narrative representation, Jesus' opponents will both recognize themselves and see themselves confronted with Jesus' generous Abba who enters into solidarity with human beings. From the perspective of Jesus' Abba, then, their way of relating to those who have been stigmatized will show itself as absurd and inhuman.

Jesus justifies his parabolic action toward his opponents in a second way. In discursive communication that anticipates the goals of the discourse, he gives them to understand that the norms of behavior that in their view are legitimated and sanctioned by God as guarantor of those norms, are rendered passé in a communicative action that breaks those norms. This communicative action is innovative and liberating, and at the same time gives joy. It is precisely this which Jesus practices in relation to them as well.

Third, he grounds the truth claim of his statements about God and God's rule by showing, in his communicative action in relation to those who are discriminated against as well as in relation to those who discriminate, that this truth claim is the ground of what he does. He thus also justifies this praxis with reference to its ground. On this basis he reveals his praxis as self-evident—unconditionally understandable and, conversely, making manifest the logic of this basis.

Jesus' parables can be understood as quasi-discursive speech because they serve to justify the claim to rightness made for Jesus' action. With them he pursues not only the goal of an apology for his praxis, but first the goal of a consensual settlement of the conflict existing between him and his opponents. In quasi-discursive speech and in a way that anticipates the arrival at an understanding, he struggles to reach an understanding with his opponents. In this way he attempts to convince them of the rightness of his action and of the norms underlying this action. He struggles with them by showing them, in a metaphoric-distancing way, that their action, bound to particular interests and norms, is absurd in view of the inbreaking universal rule of God—inbreaking in Jesus—into which all are to go.

CONFRONTATION AND DEATH ON A CROSS

God's Rule and Judgment

Obviously, Jesus did not attain his goal that his communication of the reality and the rule of God be shared in the praxis of the *basileia*. At least the majority of his Pharisaic addressees rejected what Jesus communicated to them. Jesus did not reach the Zealots and the Essenes to communicate it to them. The Sadducees understood quite well its dangerousness for the maintenance of the social and religious status quo. The understanding that Jesus sought again and again to reach with the Pharisaic movement did not come about. On the whole, Jesus' company of adherents remained small and insignificant. Regardless of temporary agreement and success, it is hardly to be assumed that he was able to win the masses of the people in a lasting way. According to Joachim Gnilka, Jesus' words of judgment "provide the insight that Jesus' activity, which was an activity exclusively directed toward Israel, was without success. The masses of the people rejected him, did not understand him."[85]

In the view of a number of interpreters, the rejection that Jesus experienced in his homeland of Galilee led him into a second situation of proclamation. The first situation had been an open one of offering and inviting into the rule of God. By contrast, the second situation was characterized by a changed perspective and praxis. According to this interpretation, Jesus had found no lasting resonance with the people. Instead, after a tremendous movement at the beginning, a "Galilean spring," the people had withdrawn from him. He had been rejected not only by the ruling strata, but by entire towns. In view of this fact, a "Galilean crisis"[86] came about, on the basis of which Jesus' message and praxis changed decisively. A withdrawal from the public arena occurred, and with it a stronger concentration on the circle of disciples, which now received a new function as the "seed of the coming salvation community of the Messiah Jesus."[87] Jesus now showed himself as the suffering Messiah, and immediately set out on the path to his Passover death.

Other scholars connect Jesus' experienced rejection with a change in his message, in which the theme of judgment moves increasingly into the foreground.[88] R. Schwager wonders whether it is possible to divide Jesus' proclamation into distinct periods: a time of offer and a time of rejection. Schwager regards a "Galilean crisis" as a possibility for the beginning of the second situation of proclamation, but thinks it is conceivable that Jesus maintained his proclamation of salvation, and in view of the incipient rejection revealed the inner consequences of that proclamation by means of words of judgment. It seems to Schwager that a third possibility most readily corresponds to the Synoptic material: namely, that Jesus soon ran into opposition from the Pharisees, "but that his immediate response was to continue his unconditional proclamation of salvation, and at the same time to start talking about judgment."[89]

Within the framework of Schwager's dramatic doctrine of redemption, he differentiates five acts in which the drama of salvation
is performed. The first act is constituted by Jesus' proclamation of
the rule of God that is dawning in his action; the second act, by the
new situation of proclamation resulting from the rejection of Jesus'
offer of salvation on the part of his addressees—namely, the situation of judgment. The third act is the judgment itself as the judgment of Jesus by human beings, which leads to his execution. The
fourth act is defined by the verdict and action of the heavenly Father
in raising Jesus from the dead. The New Testament drama of salvation is
concluded in the fifth act by the sending of the Spirit and the new gathering that proceeds from the disciples and gives rise to the church.[90]

I see no reason to divide the proclamation of the rule of God and
the proclamation of judgment into two periods of Jesus' activity. In
my opinion the proclamation of judgment constitutes a consistent
trait of the Jesus who was marked in his beginnings by John the Baptist's message of judgment.[91] The proclamation of judgment is an in-
tegral component of Jesus' communicative praxis. This means, of
course, that the proclamation of judgment is integrated into Jesus'
communicative praxis and is to be understood from that perspective. The proclamation of judgment does not replace the proclamation of the *basileia*, but belongs together with it and heightens its
explosiveness. This can be seen in the fact that Jesus articulates the
proclamation of judgment primarily in precisely those texts that also
thematize the rule of God. Aside from various sayings, it is parables
in particular that talk about judgment. Parables of action such as
those parables of the deceitful overseer (Luke 16:1-8), the unmerciful judge (Luke 18:1-8), the talents (Matt 25:14-30 par.), and the unmerciful slave (Matt 18:23-35) elucidate (in a manner that is at times
dramatic) the dramatic situation of action in which the addressees of
the rule of God find themselves. Jesus metaphorically confronts
them with the ultimate consequences of their action in light of the
basileia offered to them. Refusing to take part in the praxis of the
basileia, they definitively separate themselves from it. They thus
judge themselves. The sayings and parables of judgment do not run
counter to Jesus' invitation into the rule of God. Rather, they give
imaginative expression to the urgency of a praxis that corresponds

to this invitation. Precisely with their threatening and warning images, they are a summons to repentance and "to an action that ventures everything . . . for that which is really good enough to be worth the venture: the rule of God."[92]

In various ways the objection has been made that my elaboration of the communicative structure of Jesus' parables neglects the theme of judgment. Rudolf Pesch cautions that my thesis of Jesus' action orientation that excommunicates nobody

> needed to be checked against precisely those parables in which "excommunication" is thematized: for example, Matt. 13:47-50 or Matt. 25:1-13. Along with the aspect of "gathering," that of "separation" and thus of decision is also frequently thematized. Where this second aspect is neglected, Jesus' claim is presented in only partial form.[93]

In the dissertation of Johannes Gysbertus du Plessis, in which he constructively and critically engages my parable theory, he insists that Jesus' parables not only "communicate," "offer," and "invite," but "most certainly deprive, threaten and exclude."[94] Rudolf Siebert claims that I am "hesitant to face the inconsistencies in Jesus's narrative theology. He is particularly hesitant to deal with the negativity of God."[95]

The judgment imaginatively depicted in Jesus' parables does indeed have to do with excommunication. On that basis a correlation is required between the communicative and the excommunicative dimensions of the parables. I would attempt to make the correlation in the following way. In terms of their intention and their goal, Jesus' parables are communicative, directed toward coming to an understanding, persuading, and converting. Where this intended perlocutionary effect does not result, they can have a de facto excommunicative effect. Or better, they can bring to light the de facto (self-) excommunication of the addressees who are unwilling to repent. It is this that becomes manifest *en tē synteleia tou aiōnos* (Matt 13:39) and when the bridegroom comes (Matt 25:1-13).

Although I reject the thesis that in a second phase of Jesus' activity he replaced the theme of the rule of God with the theme of judgment, I do not exclude the possibility that the sharper accentuation of the dialectic of rule of God and judgment indicates an intensification of the conflicts into which he comes precisely with his Pharisaic opponents, among others. Nevertheless, I consider it historically improbable that Jesus was rejected by whole towns and that he pronounced judgment upon them as in the case of the Galilean towns of Chorazin, Bethsaida, and Capernaum, and that he did this "shortly before setting out to his last Passover festival in Jerusalem."[96] In any case he decided to go to Jerusalem with his disciples for Passover, most likely to await the final, decisive phase of the breaking in of the *basileia*. He must have known the danger of such a step, and indeed in Jerusalem the decisive confrontation occurred with the Sadducees and the Roman force of occupation, who straightway prepared a violent end for him. Precisely the events of the final days in Jerusalem show once again that he neither ran into unanimous rejection, nor withdrew from the public arena to the smaller circle of his adherents, nor gave up the message of the *basileia* and replaced it with that of judgment.

Symbolic Action and the Execution of Jesus

According to the way Mark lays out events, a single parable of Jesus has its location in Jerusalem: the parable of the murder in the vineyard (Mark 12:1-9 par.). If Jesus indeed narrated this text to Sadducees in Jerusalem during the last days of his life,[97] we should see in this event a final attempt to reach out in communication to them. This attempt would have occurred in a situation that for him was life-threatening, a situation of direct confrontation with those whom he metaphorically addresses as responsible for the vineyard of Israel. It would have been Jesus' will to deter them from their murderous intention, and at the same time to depict for them the theological and political consequences of their action with a picture story that in the Jewish tradition was as pregnant with associations as it was clear.

But the Sadducees were interested in maintaining the existing socioreligious order, centered on the Temple. In this they were protected by the Romans. The Sadducees were the people whom Jesus was least able to persuade. The initiative to get rid of Jesus as a re-

bellious and blasphemous troublemaker proceeded from the Sadducees. The occasion for taking Jesus into custody was provided by a
symbolic action that Jesus performed in what was both the symbolic
and the real center of Sadducean power. The action in question is
the so-called cleansing of the Temple. In my opinion the cleansing of
the Temple was a "symbolic action of Jesus,"[98] the core of which
really happened. By putting a scare into the merchants, buyers, and
money changers who were gathered in the courtyard (Mark 11:15),
Jesus protested against Sadducean cultic practice. In reality Jesus'
Temple action was presumably hardly anything spectacular. Nevertheless, it was public and thus created "public aggravation." Following up on his Temple action, Jesus probably also formulated his
critique of the existing Temple business in a saying, the original
form of which lies behind Mark 14:58. This saying places Jesus' symbolic action in the horizon of a future destruction that threatens the
Temple as a whole, and at the same time in the horizon of the Temple's "reestablishment at the ultimate coming of God's rule."[99]
Jesus' verbal and tangible prophetic and symbolic critique of the
Temple provoked the Sadducees, specifically the chief priests, to intervene against him.

Before Jesus was taken into custody and put on trial by the
Temple hierarchy, he celebrated with his disciples a farewell meal
that was to become the summation of his communicative action
toward and with his disciples. The meal was held at night in Jerusalem. According to the authors of the Synoptic Gospels, it was a Passover meal (Mark 14:12-16 par.). According to John, by contrast, it
occurred on the eve of Passover (John 13:1; 18:28; 19:14). In this
meal, Jesus summarized his life and action in the form of an "eschatological symbolic action"[100] in the signs of bread and wine. Jesus
had become certain of his violent death. In view of that death, he
confirmed his community with his disciples in the rule of God, confirmed that this community would extend beyond his personal end.
This is what finds expression in the certainly authentic saying of
Mark 14:25. In its combination of a "prophecy of death" and a temporal specification with regard to the coming of God's rule, this
saying represents "a final confirmation of the message of the
basileia."[101] Jesus holds fast to this message even unto death.

Indeed, in the moment of greatest danger to his life he underlines his confidence that he will take part with his disciples in the table fellowship of the coming rule of God. In my opinion Jesus' last meal with his disciples is a communicative symbolic action that presents in compressed form his life and his praxis of the *basileia*. In this symbolic action he communicates himself to his disciples one last time and shares his life with them one more time in symbolic form. Nevertheless, I concur in the view that the questions "must remain open" whether and, if yes, how Jesus "interpreted more precisely" the violent death that stood immediately before him.[102]

Still, during the night of the Last Supper, Jesus was taken into custody, at the command of the High Priest currently in office, by a detachment from the Sanhedrin. His disciples, who were left unmolested, fled. On account of the heightened tensions of the situation at Passover, the members of the Sanhedrin feared insurrection—for example, on the part of the Galilean pilgrims to the festival. For this reason Jesus was put on trial that same night.[103] The trial consisted, first, of an investigation before the Sanhedrin (Mark 14:53-65), in which the charges against Jesus were compiled and formulated. These charges were then to be brought forward in a Roman trial against him. Because the Sanhedrin did not have authority to impose the death sentence, the charge had to formulated in such a way that it would also stand up before a Roman court as a crime punishable by death. The charge was fixed as insurrection against the Temple, which touched not only Sadducean but Roman interests in a sensitive place. After all, the Temple was not only the center of Sadducean religious, economic, and political power—the Temple also stood under the oversight of the Romans. Daily sacrifices for Caesar and the Roman people were presented in the Temple. To that extent the Temple was "the privileged location of the political interplay between the remaining Jewish self-government and the *imperium Romanum*."[104]

The members of the Sanhedrin, who were involved in the Jewish trial, met as usual behind closed doors. They came to the decision to turn Jesus over to the Roman court of the governor Pontius Pilate. The public Roman trial took place the following morning and ended with a formal death sentence. Jesus was condemned to death on account of *perduellio*:[105] that is, for being an enemy of the state. From a Roman point of view, this was noted with precision by the inscription on the cross—such inscriptions corresponding to the practice of the day—"King of the Jews" (Mark 15:26). Concretely, he was condemned for insurrection against the Temple order sanctioned by the occupying Roman power and by the Sadducean Temple hierarchy. In concrete terms, it was probably his symbolic action of cleansing the Temple, and the critical words uttered against the Temple in that context, that led to the final outcome. In broader and fundamental terms, his claim to usher in God's reality and rule in his communicative praxis naturally also helped tip the balance.[106] Jesus was thus condemned on the basis of a political crime that was also a punishable religious offense due to the intertwining of politics and religion on both the Roman and the Jewish-Sadducean sides. He was sentenced to crucifixion, the punishment provided for capital crimes of a political nature committed by non-Roman inhabitants of the provinces—and a punishment that was applied excessively in Palestine.

After being condemned, Jesus was flogged by the soldiers who were to carry out his execution. They then brought him to the place of execution, Golgotha, and crucified him. He died a wretched, horrible death, the death of a slave.[107] Abandoned by his disciples, with the exception of a few women who watched "from a distance" (Mark 15:40), he died a shameful death that from a Jewish perspective exposed him as cursed by God (Deut 21:23). As one who was crucified, Jesus' person and praxis had to be reckoned as publicly disavowed and definitively excommunicated. His message of the *basileia* was thus taken care of, just as he was exposed as a false prophet and a blaspheming troublemaker.

The violent, shameful end of this man, who in his communicative praxis had proclaimed God as the generous and liberating reality who excludes no one from the divine love, must have "forced upon his disciples the question: Did this assertion not hold good for Jesus himself in his death? . . . Can one assert God as a saving reality for him in his death?"[108] Or did Jesus' shameful death on the cross refute his assertion and communication of God's reality and rule, just as that death exposed Jesus' communicative praxis as "deadly"?

When the one who with his existence asserts God for others is himself destroyed, is not this assertion refuted? Is it still possible to talk about God at all in this situation? Moreover, does this not show the absurdity of the attempt at an existence that in being there for others points to something that is unconditioned?[109]

The reaction of the disciples to Jesus' imprisonment shows the kind of basic crisis in which they landed: in the moment of greatest danger, they abandon him and flee. Disillusioned, robbed of their life community and of their perspective on life, they return to their homeland, to Galilee, in order to take up their old existence. The chapter of Jesus seems to have come to an end. The theopolitical realities of the powers of the Temple and the Roman occupation seem to have overtaken and disposed of the supposed rule of God and community of disciples.

COMMUNICATIVE ACTION OF THE DISCIPLES AND COMMUNITIES OF JESUS CHRIST

The Earliest Witnesses and Confessors

A short time after Jesus' crucifixion, the disciples who had fled returned to Jerusalem and made known that Jesus was alive, that God had raised him from the dead. In Jerusalem they gathered anew as a community of disciples, as the original community of Jesus Christ. This community confessed the Risen One and witnessed to him as living. This occurred in the communicative action of Jesus' disciples and witnesses. In this action they brought to expression the fact that Jesus' person and praxis were not annihilated with his execution. Instead Jesus' person and praxis are definitively confirmed, vindicated, and delivered by God. In my opinion, the communicative praxis of Jesus' disciples can be defined as witnessing and confessing. Both are actions that exhibit a communicative structure: that is, they are intersubjective, propositional and performative, textual, situational, and oriented toward reaching an understanding.[110]

A witness witnesses to what she has seen and what has become evident to her. In her (text of) testimony[111] she communicates to others (the recipients of her testimony) that to which she bears witness, so that it might likewise become accessible and evident to them, so that it can be shared by them. Witnessing has its locations and its contexts. It is a political act that takes place in public. It thus can also be publicly called into question and disputed.

Witnessing occurs with the intention, with the intended perlocutionary effect, of persuading. Witnessing is directed toward reaching an understanding. It seeks "to produce an agreement in a shared experience. It does not aim at a conceptual consensus, but at a shared story and history."[112] The witness tells this story as an offer and an invitation to us to jointly find ourselves in it.

Witnessing is the disciples' action in the face of Jesus' life, death, and resurrection. This action is exhibited in many and various ways in the New Testament. In the disciples' communicative praxis, they point to Jesus as the ground of that praxis. In their own action they make him accessible, comprehensible, and visible. They thus bear witness to what they have seen and to what they have experienced through, with, and in him. They thus bear witness to Jesus himself as a witness who in his communicative action made the reality of God present and accessible to experience. They bear witness to Jesus as a witness in whom the rule of God became manifest to them.

Confessing is likewise a textually mediated communicative action. It has reference to a subject, an object, a text, and a situation, and it exhibits a goal. The action of confessing has much in common with that of witnessing. For both, their public character is constitutive. Both are structured communicatively. Both refer to the same subject matter. There exists between them, however, a characteristic difference that in my opinion makes them complementary actions. I am persuaded that confessing does not have agreement as its goal. Rather it expresses agreement [*Einverständnis*] and completes it. To confess is to achieve consensus. Confession can be made only on the basis of an agreement [*Einigung*], which manifests itself textually in the confessional text.

Those persons who had the experience of being Jesus' apostles and disciples are the earliest witnesses to Jesus. It is impossible to circumvent them. They have a special relation to him that enables them to report authentically about him. Their competence to speak as witnesses is derived from their experience as witnesses. Since they became eyewitnesses and "earwitnesses" to Jesus' life, communicative praxis, death, and resurrection, they are in a position to bear witness to him. For their addressees, those who receive the testimony, it is their act of bearing witness that first creates the link to Jesus, whom in their own action they both make accessible and make present. For that reason *christopraxis*[113] is the best characterization of their communicative action as it carries forward Jesus' praxis of the *basileia* and transforms that praxis with regard to the power of the risen Christ in a manner that is both christological and christopractical.

The key to the earliest witnesses being witnesses is their encounter with the risen Christ. In his Easter appearances they can experience and identify Christ as alive and thus can show him to others. In the encounter with the risen Christ, they have an experience as witnesses that radically defines their life from that time onward. They experience themselves as involved in an "original event of testimony"[114] for which their eyes and ears do not suffice. Precisely therein they learn to see and to hear in a new way, and to see and to hear a new thing that "breaks open the previous horizon of knowledge and of action, and gives it a fundamentally new structure."[115]

Within the framework of this new horizon opened up by the reality of the resurrection, the earliest witnesses see and hear Jesus himself first of all. They experience themselves as the first addressees of the Lord exalted into "universal, communicative competence."[116] They recognize in Jesus the Christ who by God's action was delivered from death and exalted to God, and who from his dwelling in glory makes himself effective among them. They recognize in him the Christ who wills to continue to be active and effective through the mediation of their christopraxis. As the first addressees they experience themselves at the same time as the first agents charged with passing on their experiences with Jesus. Their experience as witnesses impels them to speak as witnesses. It makes them competent to do so, and finds articulation in their speaking. In their christopractical witnessing they carry out their charge to be witnesses.

The encounter with the risen Christ and the charge to be witnesses that was issued in that encounter make possible, evoke, and legitimate the earliest witnesses' action of bearing witness. Insofar as this is the case, we must also regard the earliest witnesses as recipients of testimony. They are addressees of Jesus Christ, who in his appearances himself bears witness to them concerning himself,[117] who shows himself to them. In their encounter with him his resurrection reality becomes accessible to them. As addressees of his act of making himself accessible, they become witnesses and are called to communicate in their act of bearing witness the reality that has been made accessible to them.

For the apostles and disciples, their encounter with the risen Christ constituted the possibility of seeing the reality of the risen and exalted Christ as also affecting and changing their own existence in a fundamental way. The apostles and disciples grasped this possibility existentially and practically in a "total and *existentiell* decision in freedom."[118] By doing so and by allowing the risen Christ to take hold of them, they became the "first witnesses of faith."[119] They came to faith in the risen Christ and at the same time experienced themselves as witnesses of the faith. Their competence and calling consisted in bearing witness to Jesus Christ before others and for others, in order that these others might come to faith in him.

According to the Lukan understanding of witness, the earliest witnesses are composed of the apostles and those disciples who had known the earthly Jesus, stood in community with him, experienced his death, recognized the risen Christ when he appeared to them, and were charged by the risen Christ to bear witness to others concerning what they had experienced with, about, and in him. If in Luke "witness" is to be understood not, as is frequently assumed, "as an ecclesial office," but rather "as an evangelical function,"[120] then the category of earliest witnesses can include all those who, because of their specified qualification and competence, exercise as their own essential activity the function of bearing witness to Jesus Christ and to his gospel. A circle of earliest witnesses understood in this manner, even if it is not limited to the Twelve or to the apostles in the Lukan sense, is nevertheless limited in number. Only a specific group of human beings fulfills the condition of having been together with the earthly Jesus: namely, Jesus' disciples. The earliest witnesses of the risen Christ come from their midst. To that extent their number is limited. Yet they could encompass "a relatively large, numerically unspecified contingent of disciples."[121]

Finally, Paul is also to be numbered among these earliest witnesses. To be sure, he was not an eyewitness of Jesus' life and action. But the risen and exalted Christ appeared "last of all" to him (1 Cor 15:8). The risen Christ thereby mediated to Paul the experience of Christ's Easter reality, called him to be an apostle, and charged him with bearing witness concerning Christ and for Christ. From that time onward Paul did just that, throwing his whole existence into the endeavor—an existence that changed from the ground up once Paul encountered Christ. Paul became nothing less than the paradigm of the kerygmatic-missionary witness, who in his communicative action authentically communicates to his addressees the experience of the risen Christ that has been imparted to him and the gospel of Jesus Christ that he has received.

The goals of the kerygmatic-missionary witness with respect to his or her addressees are the following: that the witnesses' addressees allow themselves to be "instructed" concerning Jesus' person and action, as well as concerning God's action in Jesus; that Jesus become manifest to them as the Christ; that they convert to him, and that, through the person of the witness of Christ, they enter into a relationship with Christ. On the basis of this relationship they can then for their part become witnesses of Jesus Christ. In their own christopraxis they can pass on Jesus' action and carry it forward, pointing to Jesus in their own action. Gerhard Ebeling casts a revealing light on this state of affairs when he writes that "every believer is summoned, as believer, to be a witness to the Risen One. For faith establishes a relation to Jesus himself. Christian faith is not faith in the apostles, and through them indirectly also faith in Jesus; but it is faith, by means of the witness of the apostles, in Jesus himself."[122]

The act of witnessing has its foundation with the earliest witnesses of Jesus Christ. Likewise, the act of confessing has its origin with those who were the first to confess [bekennen] Jesus Christ and the first to declare themselves for [sich bekennen zu] Jesus Christ. The subject of the earliest Christian acts of confession is first of all the community. Gathered for worship, the community acclaims Jesus as *Kyrios* and declares itself for him as its Lord (Rom

10:9-10; 1 Cor 8:6; 12:3).[123] In this common confession the community constitutes itself as a confessional community. Even where the acclamation occurs spontaneously in ecstatic speech on the part of individual members of the community, this acclamation is tied to and carried out with reference to the common confession. Confession in worship is that collective act of the early Christian community in which the community recognizes, acknowledges, and praises Jesus as its Lord, confesses him, and thus places itself under his rule.

The claim that the community is the primary subject of confession also holds good with respect to the baptismal confession that can be documented for the late New Testament period. Hebrews 10:23 and Ephesians 4:5 presuppose or make reference to such a confession. Inasmuch as the individual being baptized speaks this confession, or those being baptized make the confession in common before the community, they take over and appropriate the community's confession. They make the faith of the community their own and join their voices in the community's confession, in order to declare themselves for Jesus from then on in common with the community.[124]

The relation between confession and the community is likewise manifest in the context of the struggle against heresy. In the Johannine letters (cf. 1 John 2:22-23; 4:2-3; 4:15; 2 John 7) it is the Christian community that confesses Jesus, the Son of the heavenly Father, over against anti-Christian teachers of false doctrine. With the confession of Jesus the Christ who has come in the flesh, the community records and carries out the separation between heretics and the orthodox community that exists in community with God and with each other.[125]

There is also a relation between the community and confession in the context of persecution, to which Luke 12:8-9 par. refers. To be sure, the community is not named as the subject in this context. But the saying about declaring oneself for Jesus or denying him—a saying that is concerned with the public confession of early Christian itinerant prophets "before others"—makes clear that what is at issue in the shared situation of persecution is both a collective confession of Jesus that touches the disciples as a whole and the consequences of this confession.[126]

Finally, in early Christianity the confession of sins occurs in relation to the community. Such a confession of sins may be referred to
in Acts 19:18, and is more probably treated in James 5:16 and 1 John
1:9. The individual confesses her sins in and before the community.
In the community people confess their sins to each other. The confession of sins occurs in the public space of the community. In the
community "the reinstallation in the fellowship of the community"[127] occurs.

What Is Testified to and What Is Confessed

Witnessing and confessing have a propositional content. They occur
for the sake of their content: what is testified to and what is confessed. Both a testimony and a confession are about something. A
witness makes a statement. In that statement she claims that what
she testifies to is true. She does so by putting forward her own
person as a pledge of the truth of her testimony. According to K.
Hemmerle, testimony is the "assertion of truth in the giving of oneself."[128] The action of the witness is aimed at bringing to bear the
full weight of what is testified to, which is not accessible except by
way of the person of the witness. To this extent Hemmerle is right
when he says, "Testimony is not presence of the witness, but presence of what is testified to. But this presence of what is testified to
occurs precisely with and through the I-self of the human being."[129]

The earliest Christian witnessing has Jesus Christ as its central
content. This is already made clear by the New Testament material.
In the great majority of passages in the New Testament that talk
about witnessing, Jesus Christ is its object. The earliest Christian testimony is first of all testimony to the resurrection of Jesus. The "central statement of the biblical witness" is "Jesus Christ is risen, he is
truly risen!"[130] On the basis of their encounter with the risen Christ,
the apostles and disciples bear witness that the one who was crucified is alive, that they have seen and heard him, that they have
become his eyewitnesses and "earwitnesses." Due to their experiences as witnesses and to the charge that they received from Christ
to be witnesses, they are enabled and called to communicate that
content authentically. They bear witness to what they have seen and
heard and what they have experienced through, with, and in Christ.

For this reason the content of their witnessing cannot be only Jesus' resurrection. Instead, their witnessing encompasses his whole communicative praxis as well as his person. Because of their specific competence and qualification, the earliest Christian witnesses authentically make known who Jesus was, is, and will be.

The content of the testimony of the apostolic witnesses is initially their experience as witnesses, their *"expérience originaire"*[131] of the risen Christ, who shows himself as living to them. The apostles and disciples experience themselves as addressees of the action of the risen and exalted Lord. They recognize in him Jesus the Christ who by God's action was delivered from death and raised on high to God. They recognize in him Jesus the Christ who comes to them out of God's glory and acts effectively among them. At the same time they recognize in him the one who as the earthly Jesus called them into community with himself, whose life they shared, and in whose communicative praxis they took part as they followed him. They recognize in him the one who, in his praxis of the rule of God, revealed God to them as the One in whose liberating rule they had lived in living with Jesus. They recognize the risen Christ as the one whose shameful end on the cross they experienced.

The central content of their witnessing is that with Jesus' execution his action, what he bore witness to, his testimony, and he himself were not destroyed, but rather were definitively confirmed and delivered. Their witnessing aims at making public Jesus' person and praxis, God's action in him, and Jesus' eschatological action as "the one ordained by God as judge of the living and the dead" (Acts 10:42). This is the content of their witnessing. In order to communicate this content, the earliest Christian witnesses tell Jesus' history and theirs with him, so that it might become manifest to others as God's history with Jesus and with them. To this end they carry out action filled with Jesus' Spirit.

Confession and witness agree in having Jesus as their primary content. Confession has its origin with those who were the first to confess Jesus Christ and the first to declare themselves for Jesus Christ. This occurs in the early Christian community in the context of baptism, in regular worship, in persecution, and in the struggle against heresy. On each occasion Jesus is the content of early Christian confession. Sometimes the confession of Christ includes that of the Father, and thus has a binitarian structure. A trinitarian confessional statement, however, does not yet appear in the New Testament.[132]

Jesus Christ is made known above all in regular worship. The community acclaims him as Lord. In confessing that Jesus is Lord it places itself under Jesus' lordship or rule.[133] The confession of the one *Kyrios* is sometimes joined to the confession of the one God, the Father of Jesus Christ. To be sure, the early Christian community's confession in worship refers primarily to Jesus, whom the community in its confession recognizes, acknowledges, and praises as its Lord. In the community's confession in worship it declares itself for Jesus.

The early Christian baptismal confession—of which there is admittedly only sparse evidence in the New Testament—likewise has the person of Jesus for its content. The person being baptized declares herself for Jesus as the "Son of God" (Heb 4:14) or as the "Lord" (Eph 4:5). In doing so she makes the community's confession her own, in order from then on to declare herself for Jesus in common with the community.

In the context of persecution, Jesus again stands at the center of the confession. This is enunciated in a paradigmatic way in the saying concerning those who declare themselves for Jesus and those who deny him (Luke 12:8-9). Jesus' disciples are to declare themselves for him before human beings so that he will declare himself for them at the last judgment. In the context of the struggle against heresy, Jesus is again the content of the community's authentic witness, which serves as a measuring rod for membership to the community. In opposition to the anti-Christian teachers of false doctrine, in the Johannine letters the Christian community establishes the confession "Jesus is the Christ" as the standard of orthodoxy. In this way it emphasizes that the earthly Jesus, who came in the flesh, is the Christ, the Son of the heavenly Father.

Only the early Christian confession of sins does not have Jesus for its content. One need not look far for the reason. In the confession of sins the point is to confess one's own sins, in and before the community in order to obtain forgiveness from God.

Testimonies and Confessions

Witness and confession are further characterized by their textuality. Both are textually mediated. People bear witness and make confession in and with the help of texts: namely, testimonies and confessions. Of course, both are distinguished in a characteristic way precisely with regard to their textuality. Every act of confession is necessarily carried out in an explicitly linguistic manner and thus is verbally articulated. This is not the case with witnessing. Witnessing can also occur nonverbally. Admittedly, even then it is embedded in a context of linguistically mediated interaction and, in order to be understood as testimony, it must be interpreted and "read" as such.

From the perspective of a textual theory that conceives of texts as texts-in-function, and on that basis determines what type of texts they are, it is impossible to show that testimony is its own type of text, or to assign it unequivocally to one such type. Different types of texts can function as testimonies; that is, they can be produced, used, interpreted, and received as testimonies. This can be made clear both with reference to the apostolic testimony and with reference to the other texts in and with which people bear witness.

Claude Geffré sees in the New Testament texts concerning the resurrection "two fundamental literary genres: testimony and narration."[134] In my opinion, though, testimony does not form its own literary genre. Instead, various types of texts, including narrative ones, function as texts of testimony. The earliest witness of Christians to Jesus' resurrection is articulated, on the one hand, in the form of a participial predication about God or in the form of a one-place resurrection formula constructed as a declarative statement, as well as in extensions of this formula all the way to the confessional formula of 1 Cor 15:3-5. On the other hand, the earliest witness of Christians to Jesus' resurrection comes to expression in narrative texts of the Easter stories. In their present form these narratives represent a later development of the resurrection testimony.[135]

But the narratives of resurrection appearances should be taken as testimonies. They are about the first witnesses' experiences as witnesses, and about the first witnesses' charge to be witnesses. The narratives of resurrection appearances witness to Jesus' resurrec-

tion, and do so with the intention of making the risen Christ known
to others and of winning them for Jesus. The fact that the apostolic
testimony to Jesus' resurrection comes to expression in "confessional formulas" indicates that the former is directed toward the
latter. A testimony becomes a confession when it articulates, in binding form, the agreement of the community of believers concerning
what is thematized in the confession.

Apostolic testimonies are texts that render the experience of the
earliest apostolic witnesses in the form of statements by them as witnesses. In the early church these initially oral testimonies were not
only memorized—very soon they were also put in fixed written
form. As writings of testimony they were handed on, received, interpreted, and explicated, in order to extend the chain of witnessing. This extension occurs in the kergymatic, missionary testimony
of Christians.

While the action of witnessing occurs either verbally or nonverbally, confession is necessarily carried out in an explicitly linguistic
form. Confession is the binding, public, communal act of putting
faith in words. Confession is made with the mouth (cf. Rom 10:9).
Every act of confession implies an admittedly qualified "confession
of the lips."[136] It is articulated in a verbal confessional text, which
initially is an actually spoken text but then can become a written
confession.

The confession of the early church initially occurs in an exclusively oral manner. In short, compact texts of oral speech, the early
Christian community gathered for worship confesses Jesus as *Kyrios*
and declares itself for him as its Lord. In doing so it used two types
of texts: the homology and the hymn.[137] The foundational confessional text, used in the regular worship of the early Christian community, is "Jesus is Lord" (1 Cor 12:3).

The New Testament material makes isolated references to the
baptismal confession of the early church, but it contains no confessional text used in baptism itself. In view of this fact we cannot say
anything certain about the textual form of the early church's baptismal confession. From the Letter to the Hebrews, though, we can
conclude that in the text of baptismal confession, spoken either

before or during the celebration of baptism, the person being baptized most likely confessed Jesus as the Son of God.

The question of which texts the early church used for its confession in the context of persecution must remain open. This is because although we find references to such confessions in the New Testament, we do not find any corresponding confessional texts. On the basis of the saying about declaring oneself for Jesus or denying him, it is nevertheless clear that the confession in question was a confession of Jesus and was made in public. In that confession, "a final word is spoken, beyond which nothing more can be said."[138]

With regard to confession in the context of the struggle against heresy, we can extract elements of confessional texts from the Johannine letters. They show that the texts "Jesus is the Son of God" and "Jesus is the Christ" are the basic confession that serves as the criterion for differentiating and separating right belief[139] from false belief and thus as the criterion for membership in the community.[140]

The fact that confession in worship is linguistic and textual is obvious. In worship, confessional texts are put into words "with the mouth" and are articulated *expressis verbis*. It is likely that fixed texts have existed for the baptismal confession since the early days of Christianity, although not of course always in verbally identical form.

Situations of Testimony and of Confession

As communicative actions, witness and confession are situationally defined. People bear witness and make confession in specific situations of action. The original situation of testimony and confession possesses a paradigmatic value. In the case of witnessing, the original situation is the experience of the earliest Christian witnesses in their encounter with the risen Christ. In this situation they have an experience as witnesses that will fundamentally define their life from then on. In their act of witnessing they give expression to this "original experience," an "experience of something new."[141] The apostolic witnesses experience themselves as involved in an event that breaks through their previous horizon and fundamentally changes it. Inasmuch as the earliest witnesses experience themselves as the first addressees of the risen Christ's action, and thus of God's action, they have an experience of that which is new, an experience that radically breaks through their understanding of reality and of themselves, and thus also their understanding of their own situation of action. This experience opens up to them a new reality, a new self-understanding, a new view of their action and of their situation of action. In their witnessing as a christopractical action, they respond in accordance with that experience. In kerygmatic-missionary situations of action, the earliest witnesses communicate to others their experience as witnesses. They put Jesus Christ and his gospel into words in the places and the contexts into which they are led by their existence as missionary witnesses.

The earliest witnesses' experience with Jesus is likewise articulated in situations in which, as his disciples and in his Spirit, they turn their energies to other human beings, stand by them and stand up for them. In such situations of the action of service, they witness to Jesus' praxis of solidarity and thus to his person, in whom God's prevenient goodness and God's liberating rule have dawned. Where the earliest Christian witnesses speak out in the name of Jesus and of God against abuses, developing relations of domination and injustices in the Christian communities, as well as against social, religious, and political injustice, they bear witness in situations of prophetic action to Jesus' prophetic praxis. Where in their existence as witnesses they suffer in their own bodies persecution, imprisonment, and violent death, they bear witness of the action of suffering to Jesus' person and passion. They follow in the way of his suffering, and with the story of their own suffering they point to the story of Jesus' suffering.

Like witness, confession also occurs in specific situations of action. It is also related to its original situation, although of course in a different way. The confession made in the original situation of confession is retained as a text beyond that situation. For this reason it serves as a confessional text in analogous contexts. Confession occurs, particularly in the ritualized situation of action of worship, inasmuch as what was once confessed by others is repeatedly confessed, and inasmuch as, with the help of a traditional confessional text, confession is made anew. The consensus that was once attained is continually repeated and appropriated, until it is in a given case extended by means of a new consensus.

In early Christianity, confession occurs in the contexts of baptism, regular worship, persecution, and the struggle against heresy. In these situations of action a definitive "yes" and "no" are spoken in confession. In the gathering for worship, the community acclaims Jesus as *Kyrios* and declares itself for him as its Lord. In baptism the person being baptized makes her confession before the community. In doing so she repeats the confession of the community and makes it her own. In the struggle against heresy the Christian community, over against anti-Christian teachers of false doctrine, declares itself for Jesus, the Son of God. In the situation of persecution, the issue is that the hard-pressed itinerant prophets publicly declare themselves for Jesus and not deny him. With one exception no specific situations can be given for the early Christian confession of sins. The exception is the probable late New Testament situation of anointing the sick, part of which was a confession of sins on the part of the sick person before the elders.[142] In general the confession of sins of course most likely occurred in and before the community in the context of worship.

We thus can see that in early Christianity, confession takes place with reference to two situations. This double situational reference will remain determinative for confession in its development in the history of the church and of dogma. On the one hand, confession occurs in regularly recurring situations of action in worship. In these situations the more or less formalized confession of the community is articulated, received, and handed on. On the other hand, confession is required in particular, dramatically acute situations of action in which, as in the case of persecution, the confession or denial of Jesus is at issue, or in which, as in the case of the struggle against heresy, the identity and integrity of the Christian community are at stake. The history and praxis of Christian confession unfold between these two poles: regular confession in a context of ritual communication, and confession that occurs in a precarious situation of action in view of and in response to specific challenges.

Goals of Witness and Confession

Finally, the actions of witness and confession can be placed in relation to each other with regard to their structure of action, their intentions, and their goals. In my opinion they differ essentially in the fact that, while witness aims at persuading, in the act of confession a shared persuasion, an already achieved consensus, is articulated. Friedhelm Krüger underlines and further specifies the claim that confession "seeks consensus" when he says that "confession wants to draw others into itself, into agreement, and thus to make them confessors."[143] Eberhard Jüngel has the same thing in view when he sees confession "as an act of the individual directed toward achieving agreement."[144] In my judgment, though, confession is characterized precisely by the fact that it is not a mere aiming at agreement, but rather brings an already achieved agreement to expression, carrying out this agreement and appropriating it. To confess is to achieve consensus. Confession can be made only on the basis of an agreement manifested textually in the text of the confession.

By contrast, in my opinion witness aims at agreement. The act of bearing witness occurs with the intention of reaching an understanding with the recipient of the testimony, with the intention of persuading her of what is being attested. This view is contradicted by Karl Barth and Jean-Pierre Jossua, according to whom the act of bearing witness occurs disinterestedly and without intention, pursuing no goal of any sort.[145] I agree with Jossua's intention of emphasizing the disinterestedness of witness over against all forms of proselytizing. This understanding of witness is valid insofar as witnessing must not instrumentalize others, in the sense of strategic action. My concern, though, is to underline witness's communicative orientation toward others, its interest in them and its intention of making something visible and understandable to them. To this extent I understand witness as directed toward persuasion, and regard it as oriented toward reaching understanding and guided by an interest in arriving at an agreement with its addressees concerning that to which it attests.

The witness of the earliest apostolic witnesses seeks to communicate to other human beings the reality of the risen Christ that has been revealed to the witnesses. Their witness seeks to make known to others Jesus' person and praxis, his action and God's action in him. Their witnessing seeks to win others for Jesus and to invite them into the christopraxis of discipleship. In accordance with Jesus' charge to his witnesses, their witnessing aims at drawing attention in their own praxis to Jesus' gospel and to Jesus in such a way that in their praxis Jesus and his gospel will be brought near to the witnesses' addressees and will be made visible to them in a persuasive way, so that the addressees will be convinced[146] about Jesus and will convert to him and declare themselves for him. It is the intention and the concern of the apostles and the disciples, in the power of the Holy Spirit, to open people's eyes to that which Jesus was, is, and will be, to convince them about Jesus and to lead them to faith in him.

In contrast to witness with its goal of persuasion, confession puts into words an already achieved shared conviction. Confession articulates an agreement. Confession is made only on the basis of an agreement, which manifests itself in the text of the confession and which is verbalized in the act of confessing. Accordingly, confession seeks to bring a consensus to expression in a binding way. In confession this consensus is carried out, made present, and appropriated as valid.

The consensual moment is already at work in confession within worship. Already in the earliest Christian communities, confession is directed toward putting a commonality into words. This commonality consists in the shared knowledge, acknowledgment, and praise of the community's Lord Jesus Christ, as that knowledge, acknowledgment, and praise are carried out in the assembly gathered for worship. Inasmuch as the worshiping assembly declares itself for its Lord, the community is constituted as a community of confession and gives expression in a public and binding manner to the commonality and unity attained by placing itself under the lordship of Jesus. The baptismal confession made before the community has as its goal the appropriation of the community's faith, which the person being baptized makes his own in order from that time onward to declare himself for Jesus in common with the community. In the struggle against heresy the community declares itself for Jesus as God's Son, in opposition to the anti-Christian teachers of false doctrine. In doing so the community confirms over against the heretics its shared conviction of faith and its unity. The declaration for Jesus made in persecution aims at definitively articulating the confessor's communion with Jesus. Only the confession of sins is not an expression of a commonality, but it has a commonality as its goal. This is clearly expressed in the ancient church's reconciliation as reconciliation with God and with the church—a reconciliation that brings about peace with the church. To that extent the confession of sins seeks to restore the endangered or broken community with God and with the church.[147]

As communicative actions of Christians, both witness and confession are rooted in the communicative praxis of the disciples and of the earliest Christian communities. Like the gospel and the communicative praxis of Jesus, both have a communicative structure. As will be developed in more detail in chapter 3, both are complementary as well as basic actions of faith in which Christian faith is articulated, in which Jesus stands at the center, and in and with which christopraxis occurs.

3. SYSTEMATIC-PRACTICAL PERSPECTIVES

TRUTH AND PRAXIS

The Communicative and the Theological Theory of Truth

The communicative theory of action sketched in chapter 1 proved to be theologically fruitful and relevant insofar as it engages in a reconstruction of, and a reflection upon, the basic structures of human praxis, and thereby among other things develops a communicative understanding of truth that is both helpful and challenging to theology.

Conversely theology, precisely by making the instruments of the communicative theory of action its own, at the same time advances its own claim to truth over against the communicative theory of action. Theology explains and defends its claim to truth in both conversation and critical debate with the consensus theory of truth. Christian faith asserts the contents of its communicative praxis as true. Moreover, it asserts that truth itself has a practical dimension, insofar namely as truth can and must be done. If such an assertion appears to the communicative theory of action to be obsolete and a premodern confusion of validity claims, a theological theory of action must explain its assertion. It must advance reasons for that assertion and, if the case arises, introduce those reasons into the discourse about what should count as true. One of the important ways in which a theological theory of action does this is by making use of categories and concepts of the communicative theory of action. At the same time, a theological theory of action appropriates the instruments of the communicative theory of action critically, and where necessary extends them.

The communicative theory of action itself helps to clarify the relation between truth and praxis. First, the communicative theory of action points out the connection between truth, truthfulness, rightness, and comprehensibility—the four validity claims that are raised together in every speech act, with one of them being highlighted in each particular case. Second, the communicative theory of action relates the validity claim of truth to the community of communication and to the consensus of all. Whether the claim is rightly raised depends on their potential agreement. The communicative theory of action thus understands truth as something communicative, which is jointly sought and consensually found in communicative praxis. Third, the communicative theory of action brings out the fact that the validity claim of the truth of statements is a claim that is explicitly raised in a particular use of language: namely, the constative use of language, and more precisely in constative speech acts. In them a claim is raised whose explicitly performative formulation, "I hereby assert that . . . ," at the same time makes clear that in raising this claim with words, something is being done: namely, the speech act of assertion is being carried out.

Nevertheless, the assertion that truth is to be done and can be done remains troublesome both to speech act theory and to the communicative theory of action. At the outset I used the Gospel of John to introduce this troublesome biblical assertion. In order to allow it to become productive, I will in the following discussion return once again to the Bible and initially sketch the broad features of the biblical understanding of truth. In particular I will give attention to the most systematically reflected understanding of truth, the Johannine understanding. Against the background of Jürgen Habermas's consensus theory of truth, and of its critique and further development especially in Karl-Otto Apel's transcendental-pragmatic theory of truth, all of which were treated in chapter 1, I will then attempt to point out dimensions of a theological theory of truth. In doing so I will be taking up the challenge directed by Walter Kasper against the "forgotten status of truth in systematic theology."[1] According to Kasper, for theology today, "on the basis of Scripture and tradition, and in conversation with philosophy, a renewal and a deepening of its understanding of truth, as well as a broadening of that understanding in the sense of greater catholicity, is necessary."[2]

The Biblical Understanding of Truth

In his Rector's Address of 1927 in Marburg on the subject "What Is Truth? Concerning the Historical Concept of Truth," Hans von Soden took the Johannine scene of Jesus before Pilate as the point of departure for a contrast between the Greek and the Hebrew conceptions of truth: "What is truth?" contrasted with "I am the truth." According to von Soden, "in Jesus and Pilate two different concepts of truth, two concepts of truth and reality confront each other: that of the Jews and that of the Greeks, that of the Oriental and that of the Hellenistic spirit."[3] In von Soden's view, the Greeks take *alētheia* to be an actual state of affairs and its accurate recognition or statement. For the Hebrew *'emeth*, the concrete meaning of its linguistic root, which in the verbal form means to support, to carry, to hold fast, or to make fast, is decisive. According to von Soden, *'emeth* means solidity and durability, dependability and inviolability. On that basis it comes "to mean, on the one hand, the faithfulness of persons, and on the other hand, the truth of statements."[4] In von Soden's view it is characteristic of truth in the Hebrew sense that it is done or occurs. Truth designates a behavior both of God and of human beings that fulfills an expectation and a claim, a behavior that justifies a trust. "Truth is not something that somehow lies under things or behind them, and that would be found by penetrating into their depth, into their inside. Rather, truth is what will become clear in the future."[5] Von Soden's opposition between the biblical and the Greek understandings of truth—which, he admits, exhibit some common features—can be found in variant forms up to the present day.[6]

In his investigation of the Hebrew concept of truth in the Greek linguistic region[7] of the Septuagint, Klaus Koch names five characteristics of the Hebrew word *'emeth*. To these he contrasts five characteristics of the Greek concept of *alētheia*. Koch argues that, from the two, the Septuagint produces a hybrid with a strong Greek coloring. According to Koch, *'emeth* is as both statement and announcement characterized first by its future orientation. This is shown in the prophets' dispute over the question of who is the true and who is the false prophet. The conflict between Jeremiah and Hananiah, described in Jeremiah 28, is paradigmatic in this regard. "Whether the prophet has been sent in truth, in *'emeth*, by Yahweh is known by whether the word spoken by the prophet comes to pass."[8] Second, *'emeth* is a matter of reflection and meditation. Finding out what *'emeth* is and what it is not is decisive for human existence. *'Emeth* is to be sought with the whole heart (1 Kings 2:4; 3:6; Ps 15:2). Third, *'emeth* in Koch's view also means trust. For him, *'emeth* and *'emunah* are closely related not only linguistically, but in terms of their subject matter. Fourth, *'emeth* is not only to be known; above all, it is to be done. "Truth is every deed that creates something dependable in which other human beings can trust."[9] In this sense Jacob as he is dying asks his son Joseph, "Promise that you will act toward me with steadfast love and with *'emeth*, and will not bury me in Egypt" (Gen 47:29). Fifth, in Koch's reading, when *'emeth* is said of God, it refers to all that God has created and continually creates anew. "The works of [God's] hands are *'emeth*" (Ps 111:7-8; cf. 115:1-3).

By contrast, in Koch's view it is characteristic of the Greek concept of truth, first, that it applies not to the future, but rather to what is timelessly valid. Second, it is a matter of critical knowledge. Third, along with the future aspect the moment of trust also falls away. Fourth, although action follows from the right knowledge of truth, for Greek understanding truth cannot be done. Fifth, although in Greek there is also a search for a highest truth, this truth is to be found in the eternally unchanging structures of being. Koch then demonstrates by means of examples how in the Septuagint the Greek understanding of truth infiltrates the Hebrew concept of truth and makes static ontological statements out of the dynamic historical statements of the Hebrew text.

James Barr takes the methodological approach that guides the positions we have discussed so far and semantically dissects it with the knife of linguistic analysis. Yet even if we take our point of departure from the semantic function exercised by the words *'emeth* and *alētheia*, the Hebrew and the Greek understandings are by no means equivalent. We need to exercise caution about basing too strong a theological claim on etymology, for "those who suggest that the 'Hebrew background' is the key to *alētheia*, here speak as if a sentence like 'I am the truth' were quite normal in Hebrew speech."[10]

Diethelm Michel appropriates Barr's methodological postulates for his investigation of "truth" in Hebrew.[11] By means of this investigation he uncovers and analyzes five ways in which *'emeth* is used. In Michel's view, *'emeth* serves first to designate the correctness of statements. It occurs most frequently in this context. Second, *'emeth* is to be understood, according to Michel, in the sense of genuineness. Third, it designates the truth of the divine word of promise. Fourth, it is applied to the divine commandments, which are *'emeth* because Yahweh causes the promises and threats connected with them to come to pass. Fifth, *'emeth* designates human action, namely the fulfilling of the commandments.

In all cases, including examination of the connection of *'emeth* with *ḥesed*, *shalom*, and so forth, Michel comes to a conclusion that he himself finds "surprising": namely, "that all occurrences can be understood on the basis of the concept of according [*Stimmen*] or agreeing [*Übereinstimmen*],"[12] and that in no passage is it necessary "to understand *'emeth* as a personal property (unlike *'emunah*!). On the contrary, *'emeth* seems to be related throughout to a verbal element (statement, promise, commandment)."[13]

Michel has introduced a necessary corrective to extravagant claims that the Hebrew concept of truth is personal and historical and definitely does not mean propositional truth. Yet his solution is not wholly satisfying, above all because of the indeterminacy of the concept of agreement. I concur with H. Wildberger that "by no means are all occurrences of *'emeth* to be understood on the basis of the concept of according or agreeing," and that, where *'emeth* is predicated of persons and of God, "the meaning of 'dependability' passes over into that of 'faithfulness.' "[14]

It is no accident that in the New Testament the question "What is truth?" is located in the Gospel of John. This Gospel is concerned with truth in a way in which none of the other New Testament writings are, and in my opinion the Johannine understanding is also central to the reflection of fundamental theology. The concept of *alētheia* is hardly present in the Synoptic Gospels. It appears occasionally in the Pauline writings.

Paul speaks of the "truth of the gospel" (Gal 2:5, 14), saying that the Galatians are to uphold this truth. For the sake of this truth he had to oppose the "false believers" (Gal 2:4) and Cephas (2:14). He admonishes the Galatian community to obey the truth (5:7). Paul says of himself that he is openly teaching the truth (2 Cor 4:2; cf. 7:14). He makes it clear to the Corinthians that the truth of his apostolic proclamation will ultimately prevail: "For we cannot do anything against the truth, but only for the truth" (2 Cor 13:8). In Romans Paul talks about people who "by their wickedness suppress the truth" (Rom 1:18): "they exchanged the truth about God for a lie" (Rom 1:25). Besides Rom 1:25, Rom 3:7 and 15:8 also talk about the *alētheia tou theou*, which here means God's faithfulness. In Rom 3:4, the *theos alēthēs* and the *pistis* of that God stand over against the *apistia* of some human beings, who have not remained faithful to God.

The Pastoral Epistles understand *alētheia* essentially in the sense of orthodoxy and as right doctrine (1 Tim 6:5). The Christian should exert himself to prove himself before God as a person who openly and clearly professes the *logos tēs alētheias*, true doctrine (2 Tim 2:15; cf. 3:8; 4:4).

With John *alētheia* becomes a central concept of Christian theology. In the Johannine writings the New Testament concept of truth receives its most comprehensive and its theologically richest development. With Ignace de la Potterie[15] and against Rudolf Bultmann, I am convinced that truth in John does not mean "God's reality"[16] or "God's very reality revealing itself—occurring!—in Jesus."[17] Instead, truth in John is defined christologically from the very beginning: "Truth . . . is not identified with God, but with Christ and with the Spirit."[18] The point of departure for the Johannine understanding of truth is the basic principle that Jesus Christ is the truth in person. De la Potterie further accentuates this christological definition by emphasizing, along with John 1:17, that grace and truth came through Jesus Christ, and that in this verse *egeneto* describes a "historical happening, an event of the past."[19] With regard to John 1:18, de la Potterie says concisely, "Only the incarnate word was full of truth. The incarnate word alone was the revelation."[20]

The christological definition of the Johannine concept of truth, developed by de la Potterie at monumental length, is also highlighted by other scholars.[21] Their presentations are in part very detailed, but if we summarize them and de la Potterie's argument, we can in my opinion note four basic features of the Johannine understanding of truth:

(1) Jesus speaks the truth (8:40, 44; 16:7). He bears witness to the truth (18:37). For that he has come into the world. Jesus bears witness not to something in the sense of a propositional truth, although his testimony has a propositional content. He bears witness to the truth that he himself is in person. "I am the way, and the truth, and the life" (14:6). In him shines the *doxa* or teaching whose truth can be seen and heard, the *doxa* that gives itself to be known "in the insistent word of its appearance."[22]

(2) The truth that both is spoken by Jesus and becomes visible in his activity and in his person is critical. It unmasks the devil as a liar and puts the devil's "children" on trial. The truth brings about crisis, differentiation, and separation. The truth uncovers lies as such, denounces them and liberates from them. For "the truth will make you free" (8:32).

(3) The truth made manifest in Jesus Christ remains with those who are Jesus' own. It does so through Jesus' Spirit, the *pneuma tēs alētheias* (14:17). The Spirit of truth, who proceeds from the Father and enters into the disciples, bears witness with them to Jesus (15:26-27). The Spirit of truth will stand by them and will "guide [them] into all the truth" (16:13). This last promise highlights the eschatological dimension of truth.

(4) Truth in John's sense is practical. It must be done. "But those who do what is true come to the light, so that it may be clearly seen that their deeds have been done in God" (3:21; cf. 1 John 1:6). The doing of the truth is "an act of letting the truth demonstrate itself through the truth to the point of becoming a deed. The doing of the truth is the active acceptance and preservation of the offerings of truth."[23] In my opinion truth must not only become a life-determin-

ing norm—it can and must be done as such. The doing of truth indicates the genesis of faith itself. For John faith is itself a work, a
praxis. "Praxis for him is above all the work of faith itself. Doing the
truth is coming gradually to faith."[24] Precisely this shows the practical dimension of truth. Doing truth means orthopraxy.[25] The truth
that Jesus Christ is, is done in christopraxis.

Dimensions of a Theological Theory of Truth

In his overview of "The Understanding of Truth in Theology,"
Walter Kasper notes that a theological engagement with the current
philosophical theories of truth is hardly taking place. In Kasper's
view, Helmut Peukert is a laudable high-level exception. "Overall,
however, [Peukert] remains under the sway of the consensus theory
of truth of J. Habermas and K.-O. Apel. He broadens this theory, but
does not come to a genuinely theological approach of his own to the
question of truth."[26] According to Kasper, the consensus, the correspondence, and the coherence theories of truth belong together
for the theological concept of truth. Dietrich Ritschl likewise points
out that correspondence truth, coherence truth, and consensus
truth play a role both in the life of believers and in theology. From
Ritschl's perspective, we should not give priority to one of these
models from the outset for theological reasons.[27] Claude Geffré conceives of the truth of theology as truth that is defined by Jesus' self-
revelation, belongs to the order of testimony, is radically historical, is
an expression of ecclesial consensus, and is practical.[28] Over against
the inadequate correspondence theory of traditional fundamental
theology, and in view of the weaknesses of a fundamental theology
that argues in terms of a coherence or evidential theory, Francis
Schüssler Fiorenza introduces praxis and consensus as warrants into
the reflective equilibrium of a founding of fundamental theology
that does not fall prey to a false foundationalism.[29]

I shall attempt to pick up the search for an integrative understanding of theological truth indicated by these persons and positions and
to advance that search in the sense of a theological theory of action.
I shall do so by bringing together de la Potterie's explanation of the
four dimensions of Christian truth with Apel's sketch of an integrative theory of truth.

Ignace de la Potterie recognizes in the Christian understanding of truth a synthesis of the dimensions of the historicity, the transcendence, and the interiority of truth.[30] The first dimension, that of the historicity [*Geschichtlichkeit*] of truth, lies in the occurrence [*Geschehen*], in the reality of the revelation that has occurred in Jesus Christ. In de la Potterie's view the second dimension lies in the "openness to transcendence."[31] In this opening Christian truth goes beyond history and opens a way of access to communion with God. As the third dimension of truth, which is a dimension of truth's historicity, de la Potterie names its eschatological goal.[32] Fourth and finally, he addresses (with regard to John 3:21! and Søren Kierkegaard) the interiority of truth. His existentially determined and narrowed reception of philosophical positions makes its mark here in particular. He considers neither the approaches of the philosophy of praxis nor those of the theory of intersubjectivity.

In my opinion an integrative (fundamental-) theological theory of truth would have to proceed in such a way that it explained the four dimensions of Christian truth in a comprehensive theory. This theory would have to join Apel in giving the elements of correspondence, evidence, coherence, and consensus their due. From my perspective, the framework of a theological theory of action presents itself for this purpose. In this framework the propositional, revelatory, systematic, and practical structure of theological truth could be appropriately developed.

First, a theological theory of truth implies the dimension of correspondence, insofar as a theological theory of truth is concerned with historical states of affairs that it asserts as facts.[33] Central among the assertions of a fundamental-theological theory of truth is the assertion that Jesus is the truth in person. This assertion contradicts the consensus of contemporary philosophical theories of truth, since this consensus is oriented to statements. Over against Habermas, a theological theory of truth must make clear that this assertion does not present an unacceptable confusion of validity claims, that on the contrary this assertion bursts the boundaries of a purely propositional understanding of truth. In trying to make this clear, a theological theory of truth would in my opinion do well to take over Habermas's differentiation of the four validity claims, and to bring to bear in a critical response to his work its own claims to truth, rightness, truthfulness, and comprehensibility. A fundamental-theological theory of truth must bring the dimension of correspondence to expression in such a way that it explains both that theory asserts something and what it asserts: namely, what it asserts as in fact having occurred or occurring. Central among the factual assertions of theology are those of the factual character of Jesus' person and praxis, of his death on the cross, of his resurrection, and of his presence in the community gathered in his name. Of course, that all this is fact is not to be demonstrated in terms of the correspondence theory alone. Rather, to that end we need to lay claim to the dimension of evidence.

Second, a theological theory of truth implies the dimension of evidence, in which reality is discovered and made manifest and emerges in its "nonconcealment." A theological theory of truth is concerned with the determinate reality of God that is made clear and is seen and understood as such in Jesus' person and praxis. In Jesus' person and praxis that reality reveals itself, discloses itself, makes itself clear and persuasive, and in doing so shows itself as revelation. Such a reality must first of all be narrated[34] and attested. It is only accessible in narration and attestation in which the witnesses vouch for the truth of their testimony with their own existence. In their own action they make accessible, show, and make visible the truth of their testimony.

Third, a theological theory of truth implies the dimension of coherence. A theological theory of truth cannot simply depend on facts or pieces of evidence. It must integrate these into a coherent interconnection. Of course, this coherence can never be more than provisional, subject to the eschatological reservation. Theology must systematically unfold the truth of Christian faith and show the interconnection of its individual assertions. These assertions have their specific value only within the horizon of the "whole" of faith and of that "whole" at which faith aims. Theology must not present the "whole" (which, as factual, can be true or false)[35] in the sense of totalizing forms of thought. Only within the horizon of hope can it anticipate the "whole." To that extent every theological theory of truth must remain critical in the face of the necessary systematic claim of theology. Every theological theory of truth must hold to the knowledge that such "systems" are only provisional, revisable, and in need of revision.

Fourth, a theological theory of truth must reflect the practical dimension of truth: not its interiority (de la Potterie), but its intersubjectivity. On the one hand, that has to happen in a consensus theory of truth that takes up and integrates the elements of correspondence, evidence, and coherence. The initial steps of such a theory have been worked out, using the "sense of the faithful" (*consensus fidelium* or *consensus ecclesiasticum*) as a starting point.[36] On the other hand, the truth with which theology is concerned needs to be proven and verified in individual, collective, and ecclesial praxis.

A theological theory of truth needs to demonstrate that the theological claims to truth are "redeemed" in Christian and ecclesial praxis. It needs to show that the consensus of the church comes to expression in a binding way in the act of confession. It needs to show that the truth of faith is proven and verified in being narrated, attested, and confessed. It needs to show that the truth sought by theology must finally and ultimately be done in ecclesial praxis.

The standard for a theological theory of truth remains the fact that Jesus is the *autoalētheia*,[37] the discerning, critical, uncovering, and unity-creating truth in person. This truth shows itself, and it must be attested and pointed to. This truth makes sense, so it must be coherently formulated. This truth binds human beings together and is articulated in the church's confession. This truth must be done. In Jesus Christ a theological theory of truth has its *krisis*. In christopraxis it has its practical counterpart.

FAITH AND ACTION

The question concerning the relation between faith and action is a central question not only of the theological theory of action. The way in which this question is answered makes it possible to recognize that certain fundamental theological choices have been made. These choices determine: (1) what Christian faith is primarily seen as being; (2) whether and how it is seen as belonging together with praxis, and what form of praxis it is seen as belonging with; (3) what theology's self-understanding is. The question concerning the relation between faith and action thus proves to be a central theological question in various respects.

First, it touches on epistemological, hermeneutical, and practical aspects of the relation between faith and reality. Second, it marks the location occupied by praxis in each particular conception of faith. Conversely, it marks the relation to faith of the praxis that is thus at least implicitly envisioned. Third, the question concerning the starting point, the status, and the scope of theology is also raised. The manner in which the relation between faith and action is thematized uncovers the overall approach *in nuce*. The questions of what faith, what action, and what theology are, are decided by the manner in which the relation between faith and action is thematized.

In an objectivistic view of faith as a system of objects of belief (*credenda*) that are authoritatively presented to the faithful by the magisterium and that the faithful must appropriate, praxis scarcely comes into view. Praxis appears only, if at all, in the perspective of the agreement between the objects that are presented and those that are adopted. Interestingly, the objectivistic position shares with the subjectivistic conception of faith the systematic excision or diminution of praxis. In one form of the subjectivistic conception, faith is understood as a disposition, particular to each person, which the individual must acquire toward that reality which is absolutely determinative. Or the subjectivistic conception may understand faith as a system of subjective attitudes and dispositions that opens up reality in a particular perspective. In both these understandings of faith, the interconnection between faith and action again does not become clear. Even where faith is seen as a view of reality and an attitude toward reality that are integrated into a specific form of life, a practical deficiency remains.

Over against both an objectivistic and a subjectivistic analysis of faith, a theological theory of action sets forth the intersubjective character and the communicative structure of faith, and comes to understand faith as a communicative praxis.

In the following discussion I will sketch steps toward such an understanding. The discussion will first turn to reflections of theological ethics, and then to reflections of practical theology. Finally, I will sketch what it means to conceive of faith itself as a communicative praxis that is articulated and carried out in actions of faith.

Reflections of Theological Ethics

In the 1970s in German-language moral theology a widespread controversy arose concerning the foundations and the basic orientations of theological ethics. This controversy was ignited by Alfons Auer's work *Autonomous Morality and Christian Faith*.[38] In this dispute about foundations, the position formulated by Auer and accepted by the majority of moral theologians was that of an autonomous morality in the Christian context. The opposing position was that of an ethics of faith. This controversy is instructive with regard to the question concerning the relation between faith and action insofar as the issue in this controversy is the role played by Christian faith in relation to the ethical action of Christians. In the view of the proponents of an autonomous morality, reason provides the norms for the action of the Christian, as well as for the action of every other human being. The action must derive its binding character from rational, communicable insight. According to this approach, arriving at concrete material norms is not faith's responsibility. Instead, faith creates a new horizon of meaning for autonomous ethical action. This horizon has a stimulating, criticizing, and integrating effect.[39]

By contrast, the proponents of an ethics of faith want to lift up concrete, binding contents of ethical obligation from faith.[40] They understand the required ethical action of Christians as action done from faith in the sense that concrete ethical norms are to be derived from faith. These norms are to be distinguished by a specific Christian quality that differentiates them from norms that hold for human beings in general.

From the perspective of a theological theory of action, both positions share a common deficiency: they separate faith and action. The one side places autonomous ethical action in a horizon of faith as a second, supplemental step. The other side goes to such lengths to play up the prevenient character of faith as something presupposed that action becomes a preprogrammed derivative of faith.

Neither position attains to an integrative view of faith and action. With neither of them is faith seen as action.[41]

Further developing the autonomous position, in the last few years various efforts have been made to use the theory of action to provide a foundation and development for theological ethics. Thus Gerhard Höver has presented "Approaches to Reorienting Moral Theology by Means of the Theory of Action."[42] He seeks to overcome an ahistorical objectivism by reflecting upon the temporality and the temporal form that are constitutive of human action, and thus of ethical action. In conversation and in critical engagement with Neoscholastic moral theology, he elaborates objective reference, circumstances, and intentions as fundamental anthropological components of ethical action. According to Höver, their unity becomes visible only by means of means-end relations. Picking up on the Aristotelian tradition of the practical syllogism, as well as on Immanuel Kant's transcendental concept of action, Höver explains (in deliberate differentiation from Habermas's theory of action)[43] the presuppositions and basic elements of a transcendental logic of action. He relates ethics and philosophical theory of action to each other, and distinguishes them in the sense that the latter analyzes the elements and structures of ethical action, while *eo ipso* normative ethics reflects the basic structures of ethical action. Ethics grounds ethical action with regard to its ethical character, its temporality and temporal form, its capacity for truth, and thus its content of meaning. Particularly relevant for the philosophical theory of action in Höver's view are human action's ethical character, temporality, and manner of being carried out. Höver defines the basic structure of human action philosophically as "action's own proper teleology."[44]

Höver conceives of moral theology as interpretation of the faith in the medium of ethics, with such interpretation having to be articulated in the context of the ethical rationality of modernity. In my opinion, Höver's work contains above all important reflections on temporality and the temporal form of action. These reflections are significant for a theological theory of action. But in his reflections upon the basic structure of ethical action, he does not take into consideration the relation to faith. Moreover, what he offers for reorienting moral theology by means of the theory of action remains determined by an overly narrow, teleological understanding of action. To be sure, his understanding of action overcomes objectivism, but it does not take note of the constitutively intersubjective dimension of human action. Höver thus attains neither to an intersubjective understanding of action nor to a practical and communicative concept of faith.

Klaus Demmer, in his *Methodology for Moral Theology*,[45] characterizes moral theology as a hermeneutical theory of action and as a theory of norms. He underlines this discipline's focus on the theory of action. He does this in contrast to that understanding of the discipline which confines itself to normative discourse and thus to questions of grounding. According to Demmer, moral theology focuses on the theory of action insofar as moral theology is engaged primarily in a systematic consideration of the ethical significance contained in God's action in Jesus Christ—action that makes it possible to see God's salvific action in and upon human beings. In Demmer's view, moral theology is an ecclesial science practiced within the church as a community of communication and consensus. The reference point of moral theology is the *consensus fidelium*. Moreover, moral theology is a communicative and integrative science that takes into account the fact that the believer goes beyond the boundaries of the explicit community of faith and enters "into universal ethical communication."[46] Demmer conceives of moral theology as a science of faith. He takes faith as *fides quae* (the "faith that" or a body of beliefs) and lays out its relation to reason. In Demmer's view, faith is essentially the enabling of action. Faith provides the motivations and intentions for the action of Christians. These motivations and intentions have their intellectually mediated result in goals of action, and thereby open up the horizon of meaning of Christian action.

In a work with the title *Living the Truth: A Theory of Action*,[47] Demmer develops his conception of moral theology as a theory of action with a hermeneutical and life-historical orientation. Such a conception conceives of the moral theologian as a thinker of existence who ponders how God becomes effective in the history of her life. At the same time this moves her "to introduce her own biography into the general discourse . . . as a healthy corrective."[48] Initially, she (1) sketches the theological (taking "theology" in the sense of "moral theology") framework of an existential-historical and theological-anthropological form of thought, (2) uncovers the basic elements of a theological anthropology, and (3) relates God's action and human action to each other within the framework of a theology of providence that has been given a pedagogical and life-historical bent. Then follows a foundational reflection upon the constitutive elements of both the person and the ethical personality, of both truth and truthfulness. Moral theology is presented as a school of truthfulness that understands itself as reflective life history. In this perspective, the moral theologian becomes the ecclesial thinker of existence.

In addition, truth and truthfulness are treated in turn as basic ethical dispositions that are shaped by life history as their interpretive framework. Responsibility must be assumed for them in key situations, and they are injured and corroded in power calculations, in the refusal of solidarity, and in deceitful life. Finally, Demmer sketches the basic features of a personalistically and hermeneutically conceived metaphysics of ethical action. Starting with conscience as the source of ethical action, this metaphysics explains the dimensions of fundamental or life decision all the way to the structure of the individual decision.

In my opinion Demmer's position, presented as a "theory of action," remains below the level of a theological theory of action. First, he opposes the hermeneutically conceived theory of action to the theory of norms, instead of conceiving and developing the latter as a part of the former. Second, he looks at faith only as *fides quae*. He does not consider its constitutively practical and communicative structure, which is revealed from the perspective of *fides qua* ("the faith by which"). Third, he identifies action as disposition. His approach ends up with a personalistic metaphysics of action without giving attention to the explicitly postmetaphysical theoretical work on the theory of action, including discourse ethics.

In my opinion, a theological ethics should be conceived, within the framework of a theological theory of action, as an ethical theory of the Christian-communicative praxis of faith.[49] This ethical theory is carried out in conversation and in critical engagement with discourse ethics. Both with the help of discourse ethics and over against discourse ethics, this theory puts forward the basic structures of Christian-communicative praxis. Taking as its point of departure Jesus' praxis of God's rule and the communicative praxis of the disciples and communities of Jesus Christ, this theory elucidates the biblical foundations of Christian-communicative praxis and identifies and explains them as the communicative-ethical praxis of faith, as christopraxis. In doing so this theory at the same time attains to an integrative understanding of faith and action, understanding them both as being exhibited and developed communicatively and practically.

Reflections of Practical Theology

In practical theology, reflections and analyses using the theory of action have been undertaken both with regard to the scientific-theoretical foundation of practical theology and within the framework of its individual domains and disciplines. Going through the history of practical theology's self-understanding, Norbert Mette has made the proposal of conceiving it as "an explicitly theological theory of communicative action."[50] This theory takes on the task of "using an investigation of the concrete requirements of Christian action to explicate the foundational statements, acquired within the framework of fundamental theology, concerning the structure of Christian action."[51] Practical theology undertakes this explication on the basis of both a communicative theory of action and the systematic-theological reflection upon action—a reflection that in turn is determined by praxis. Practical theology conceived in this way understands itself as an approach that overcomes the constrictions of an institutionally oriented functional theory of ecclesial praxis, and engages in reflection upon concrete forms in which Christian praxis is carried out. This occurs in a theory of pastoral action. Such a theory is a politico-theological theory of action, and is *eo ipso* organized in an interdisciplinary manner.

Johannes van der Ven has put forward an *Outline of an Empirical Theology*, in which he conceives of hermeneutical-communicative praxis as the basis of empirical theology, which at the same time presents itself as normative reflection upon this praxis. This praxis is normatively reflected in the eschatological perspective of Jesus' praxis, a perspective articulated in the symbol of the *basileia*. According to van der Ven, the meaning implied in the symbol of the *basileia* for concepts such as inspiration, orientation, and motive for action can be clarified by means of the normative principles of freedom, equality, universality, and solidarity. In this context "faith in God as hermeneutical-communicative praxis [forms] the direct object,"[52] the goal and the condition of empirical theology, which is unfolded in a five-phase cycle.[53]

The biblical foundations of a practical-theological theory of action are likewise set forward by Ottmar Fuchs. In his systematizing summary of the collection that he edited containing "Contributions to the Founding of Practical Theology as a Theory of Action,"[54] he conceives practical theology in the paradigm of a biblical-critical science of action, and sees it as oriented toward the praxis of liberation.

Moreover, within the framework of practical theology are many and various examinations, informed by the theory of action, of individual themes and domains.[55] Rolf Zerfass elucidates ecclesial proclamation from the perspective of the theory of action. He points to communication free of domination as the utopian-critical standard for a proclamation that seeks to correspond to Jesus' proclamation and to the message of the gospel.[56]

Zerfass characterizes "evangelistic proclamation"[57] as a praxis that, like Jesus' praxis of proclamation, develops out of its specific contexts of action and at the same time breaks them open by announcing God's rule. Such proclamation is related to the present situation of its addressees. It uncovers this situation and aims to change it so that new spaces for life arise for its addressees, whom it invites to *martyria* (martyrdom), *diakonia* (service), and *koinōnia* (community) in following Jesus. Zerfass likewise presents a communicative understanding of the church's worship and defines liturgy as

> a communicative action . . . into which the individual Christian is taken with his hopes and disappointments, with the contradictory

experiences of his existence with its deadly limitations. . . . He sees himself invited to trust the experience that has found expression in the language of the liturgy, and to join himself to the Eucharist acted out there.[58]

Diaconal action has been variously analyzed as a communicative praxis of faith engaged in solidarity and grounded in Jesus' helping action.[59] Zerfass emphasizes that diaconal action itself constitutes an internal moment of proclamation and belongs together with *martyria* and *koinōnia*. In Zerfass's view, *martyria*, *diakonia*, and *koinōnia* must "also not be thought of as sectors, as juxtaposed fields of action of ecclesial activity. Rather they are three sides of the same subject matter. It is only by means of them that what Jesus is all about presents itself spatially (three-dimensionally) and asserts its historical reality."[60]

I see precisely this danger, that ecclesial praxis falls apart into sectors, in the conception of the *Handbook of Practical Theology*.[61] According to one of its editors, it "follows, on the basis of the church as it is lived day by day," a "situational-pragmatic"[62] approach. In a differentiated matrix it correlates goals (obligations) with domains (dimensions) of church-forming action. It names as goals of action: (a) proclamation and communication, (b) formation and socialization, (c) pastoral care and *diakonia*, (d) administration and organization. The domains of action presented and treated in the individual volumes are: I. Field of Praxis: Theory; II. Field of Praxis: The Individual/The Group; III. Field of Praxis: Communities; IV. Field of Praxis: Society and the Public Sphere. The intersection of a goal of action with a domain of action gives rise to specific fields of action. Each of them exhibits a number of possible situations of action. This procedure results in a topography of church-forming action and reveals an abundance of fields and situations in which actions are done at the "workplace 'church.' "[63]

In this procedure a multitude of actions also come to light, but the question is not posed about what makes them church-forming actions or actions of faith. It is questionable whether actions of faith can be divided among fields and situations and correlated with them. Moreover, the field and the situation do not suffice to qualify them as actions of faith. On the one hand, such actions need not appear only in ecclesial fields of action. On the other hand, actions that are obviously structured in very different ways emerge in all fields of praxis: liturgical actions, administrative actions, therapeutic actions, publicistic actions, and so forth. Another possibility would be to seek the qualification as an action of faith with regard to the goals (obligations) in view of which such actions are undertaken. But then faith would again become the horizon within which and toward which actions occur.

In view of the difficulties that a situational-pragmatic approach has in characterizing the contents and the structure of specific actions, it is advisable to choose another means of access. Over against an approach oriented toward functions or sectors, it is my opinion that we should on the one hand point out the internal connection between faith and action, and on the other hand ascertain specific actions of faith. This occurs when faith itself is conceived as a communicative praxis that on the basis of its biblical foundations is exhibited in a systematic-practical manner in various dimensions.

Faith as Communicative Praxis

In his practical fundamental theology, Johann Baptist Metz has outlined the practical concept of faith that is determinative for the approach taken by a theological theory of action. He proposes the following definition of the faith of Christians: "The faith of Christians is a praxis in history and society that is to be understood as hope in solidarity in the God of Jesus as a God of the living and the dead who calls all people to be subjects in God's presence."[64] As discussed in chapter 1, Helmut Peukert has explained the politico-theological understanding of Christian faith as praxis on the basis of reflections shaped by the theory of action. In doing so he has also attained to insights of decisive importance with regard to the analysis of the Christian praxis of faith. Of the understanding of Christian faith as a communicative praxis, he says pointedly, "Faith is in itself a praxis which, as praxis and thus in concrete communicative action, asserts God for others and seeks to verify this assertion in action. Faith is thus the living out of human existence in its most extreme possibilities."[65]

Taking recourse to what has been said earlier concerning the basic structure of communicative action, concerning the communicative structure of the gospel, and concerning the communicative praxis of Jesus and of his disciples and communities, faith can be conceived as a communicative praxis.[66] As such it is at the same time intersubjective, propositional-performative, textual, situational, and intentional. In its nucleus the propositional content of Christian faith is the person and praxis of Jesus as well as God's action in him. Faith is about what occurred in and with Jesus, in his communicative action in God's name, through his praxis of the rule of God, with him and his claim to make present the reality of God and of the *basileia*—even and precisely in view of his shameful death. In addition, faith is about what occurred in Jesus in his death and in his resurrection through God's action in him, definitively confirming Jesus' praxis and his person and delivering him. Furthermore, faith is about the praxis of Jesus' disciples, the praxis of the early Christian communities and of the church, who point to Jesus' person and praxis, who are grounded therein, who in christopraxis take up Jesus' action and advance it in Jesus' Spirit.

Inasmuch as Christians relate to Jesus' person and praxis, they do something—in their situations and contexts, by means of various texts, and with regard to their intentions and goals—that constitutes their faith. What they do, in which contexts, with which texts, with what intention, and in which actions—in my opinion that can be clarified on the basis of the New Testament material with the two concepts of witnessing and confessing. Witnessing and confessing represent complementary and at the same time basic communicative actions of faith. Christian faith is articulated in them and practiced by means of them. In and with them, Christian faith is done as christopraxis.

ACTIONS OF FAITH—ACTIONS OF THE CHURCH

Starting from the communicative actions of the disciples and communities of Jesus Christ, on the one hand, and with regard to an understanding of faith in terms of the theory of action, on the other hand, we can explain witnessing and confessing as two actions of faith. Both are grounded in the Bible, assume their place in the historical development of the church, of theology, and of dogma, are ecumenically relevant, and possess both a systematic-theological and a practical value. In my opinion they represent communicative actions of faith, are related to each other in a complementary way, and demonstrate themselves to be basic actions of faith, in and with which christopraxis occurs on the part of various subjects in their particular situations of action. On the basis of the biblical material, I differentiate between kerygmatic-missionary witness, diaconal witness, prophetic witness, and witness by suffering. I likewise differentiate between confession in worship, instructional confession, and situational confession. The following discussion shall ponder both these actions of faith and exhibit them in their communicative structure.

Witnessing as an Action of Faith

Kerygmatic-Missionary Witnessing. Christians are "pupils of the biblical witnesses."[67] They are so in four respects. First, as kerygmatic-missionary witnesses they make known the gospel of Jesus Christ and in their action of proclamation point toward Christ's person.

Kerygmatic-missionary witnesses put themselves at the disposition of Jesus Christ as Christ's messengers. They invite others to share the gospel communicated by them. Their missionary existence as witnesses aims at winning human beings for Jesus. In this missionary existence they intervene in the life of human beings, direct themselves toward them, and communicate the gospel to them as something new. In their christopraxis, kerygmatic-missionary witnesses allow the gospel to speak. They also bring what is attested in the gospel to its addressees. Christian testimony is essentially missionary. This holds true even when the previous praxis of Christian mission and the imperialistic-Eurocentric understanding of mission at work in it are to be called into question.[68] Through her praxis, the kerygmatic-missionary witness wants to convince human beings about Jesus Christ. "Witnessing and mission as service to the word of testimony" are an "essential living out of the church's life."[69]

Not only those who hold office in the church, but all Christians who make the communication of the gospel their own and who make its content accessible and visible in their praxis are bearers of kerygmatic-missionary witness. The content of Christians' kerygmatic witnessing is the gospel of Jesus Christ. This is true whether or not those doing the witnessing are persons officially responsible for the church's proclamation. In the act of witnessing, Christians are to transmit and make known the gospel of Jesus Christ to other human beings, in order to confront them with Jesus and to invite them to follow him. Such explicit communication of the gospel has its foundation and its standard in the apostolic witness. This is so inasmuch as the former, like the latter, attempts to awaken in others an interest in Jesus' person and praxis, Jesus' action, and God's action in him, and seeks to bring others to participation in the Jesus-like praxis that is made visible in their own act of witnessing. Kerygmatic-missionary witnessing makes the contents of the gospel accessible and transparent in the praxis of the witnesses, so that "attention is drawn to Jesus Christ in such a way that he can present himself—which means presenting himself in his perspectives—and in doing so can stand in for others and thus can become relevant in this context."[70]

Like the apostolic testimony, the kerygmatic-missionary testimony is textually mediated. It is carried out in an explicitly verbal manner. The communication of the gospel occurs in a multiplicity of texts. It cannot be tied down to particular types of texts.

In addition, the witnessing of Christians occurs in specific situations. The kerygmatic-missionary situation is one of the paradigmatic locations in which witnessing as a Christian action of faith is carried out. This action can be done in all sorts of situations, wherever Christians—individuals, groups, communities, local churches, and the universal church—point in their praxis to Jesus Christ, his action, and his person as normative, living, and present. Accordingly, Christian witnessing is always occurring in new situations. Indeed it aims at articulating that to which it bears witness and at bringing it into new situations. In precisely this way it is oriented toward innovative action. It aims at changing situations, at transforming them in accord with Jesus and with christopraxis.

Inasmuch as such witnessing goes to meet others, it appears on the scene "seeking to win them over: that is, asking and calling for their agreement."[71] As testimony to the rule of God that has dawned with Jesus, a domination-free and liberating rule that even liberates from death, it seeks to reach an understanding with its addressees. Kerygmatic-missionary witnessing perverts itself when, instead of building upon communicative praxis marked by invitation, it builds upon colonial subjugation, strategic indoctrination, and techniques of repression. Kerygmatic-missionary witnessing aims at convincing human beings concerning the person of Jesus and his communicative-liberating praxis of the *basileia*. It aims at inviting them to join in this praxis made possible by God's action. It invites them to christopraxis.

Diaconal Witnessing. The second respect of witnessing, diaconal witnessing, takes place where human beings give of themselves to others, stand up for them, stand by them in their distress and help them. It occurs where human beings stand in solidarity with the needy, the suffering, and the oppressed, and in so doing carry on Jesus' solidarity and act in Jesus' Spirit. According to Karl Barth, a basic form of testimony consists in the fact "that I give assistance to my neighbour as a sign of the promised help of God."[72] For Barth the comprehensive concept of Christian neighbor-love is the concept of the witness. Anyone who performs this service of a witness to others becomes a diaconal witness to Jesus Christ. In her *diakonia*—be it in the realm of social services or be it political[73]—the witness makes the structure of Jesus' action her own, lives from Jesus' solidarity and community with the poor, the disenfranchised, and the weak, and in her own action calls attention to Jesus' praxis and person.

As the essential element of testimony within the church, Jean-Pierre Jossua names the help that believers mutually render to each other in full equality and reciprocity.[74] Inasmuch as Christians give of themselves to others, stand up for them, stand by them in their distress, help them, and stand in solidarity with them, they bear witness to Jesus' praxis of solidarity. Their diaconal witnessing points to Jesus' person and praxis, even where this is not explicitly verbalized. Diaconal witnessing may explicitly talk about Jesus' praxis of solidarity and community as its content. Or the act of witnessing may occur in such a way that the ground for the action comes explicitly into view only when the witness is asked.[75] In any case the act of witnessing has Jesus' praxis of solidarity and community at least implicitly as its content. "In the sense of Jesus' encompassing charge to bear witness," diaconal witnessing works "to bear witness to the love of Jesus Christ on the fronts of bodily distress, affliction of the soul, and socially unjust relations."[76]

Depending on the situation, diaconal witnessing occurs in a more verbalized manner, more by gestures, or more nonverbally. Jesus' person and praxis are not necessarily articulated in words. Rather they form the foundation on which, and the horizon within which, this action occurs in Jesus' Spirit. Diaconal action can be asked about its foundation and its horizon, and is ready to respond to such questioning. Diaconal action is textual in the sense that in it one can read answers to the questions: Whence does it derive? Where is it grounded? What does it attest? and To what purpose does it occur?

Diaconal witnessing is clearly directed toward others. The diaconal witness goes to meet human beings, though not primarily to convince them, but rather to stand by them in their distress, to stand up for them, and to help them. Diaconal witnessing's praxis of solidarity aims at easing the suffering of human beings, of liberating them, through political action and through action in the realm of social service, from their distress, their affliction, and the injustice perpetrated against them. Inasmuch as the witness enters into relationship with his addressees, diaconal witnessing aims at enabling and building up relationships of solidarity. Precisely without consciously intending to have a persuasive effect, such praxis may have an appealing character and may persuade human beings concerning the Jesus-like praxis of universal solidarity.

Prophetic Witnessing. The third respect of witnessing, prophetic witnessing, occurs where, in the name of Jesus and of the God of Jesus Christ, human beings protest against the dominant relations, where they intervene and take God's side in God's "case" against the world or "idols."[77] Such witnessing, which criticizes injustice, denounces oppressive relations of domination [*Herrschaft*], and confronts them with God's promised liberation and God's liberating rule [*Herrschaft*—see chap. 2, n. 49], is the praxis of prophetic witnesses.

The content of witness "begins with the content of ancient prophecy: the denunciation of a situation of sin and the proclamation of a new order."[78] The prophetic witness places the dominant relations before God's court of judgment, appears on the scene as God's plaintiff against injustice, and proclaims along with God's protest God's promise of a new, just, and humane order. Prophetic witnesses exhibit this new thing symbolically in their action and anticipate it as Jesus did in his prophetic praxis of solidarity. In doing so they demonstrate that they are innovative agents whose protest, objection, and accusation are embedded in a new, humanizing praxis. Anyone who acts prophetically bears witness to the person and praxis of Jesus, which denounce every form of oppression and exploitation and confront all injustice with God's liberating rule. Anyone who acts prophetically acts in Jesus' Spirit. Prophetic witnesses to Jesus Christ today are both individuals and groups, initiatives, communities, and local churches who fight injustice and oppression and who commit themselves to the survival of all persons and to all persons having a life worthy of human beings.

Prophetic witnessing contains criticism of the dominant relations; protest against political, social, economic, and religious injustice; and insistence on a just and human ordering of life. The "denunciation of a situation of sin" and the "proclamation of a new order"[79] occur in the name of Jesus and of the God of Jesus Christ. To that extent prophetic witness has as its more or less explicit content, along with the unjust relations to be denounced, Jesus' prophetic praxis and the God of Jesus Christ, in whose name prophetic witnessing brings its charge. Prophetic witnessing has as its object God's "case" against the "world," inasmuch as prophetic witnessing (1) confronts oppressive relations of domination with the liberating rule of God that has come in Jesus' person and praxis; (2) points to God's promised liberation; and (3) anticipates that liberation by following the prophet Jesus in its own prophetic praxis. "In its prophetic language, then, religion places the world on trial."[80]

Prophetic witnessing places the "world" before God's court of judgment and files charges against it. At the same time prophetic witnessing sues for justice for the victims.

As a rule, prophetic testimony is made with language. Prophetic witnesses present their critique of oppressive relations of domination in texts of accusation. In these texts they protest in the name of Jesus and of the God of Jesus Christ against injustice, and combine with their protest the promise of a new, just order. In accusation and announcement they allow God's liberating rule to speak. They do this both *expressis verbis* in their verbal action and their prophetic texts, and in nonverbal, prophetic symbolic actions. The nonverbal prophetic witness is interwoven with the verbal. Together with the verbal witness, it is "read," interpreted and understood as a text of testimony.

Along with all the criticism and accusation, prophetic witnessing shows an orientation toward others: on the one hand, toward those for the sake of whom the prophetic witness denounces the dominant relations, and on the other hand, toward those whom she attempts, with her action, to dissuade from continuing to maintain those relations. Both through her praxis of solidarity with the victims of injustice, oppression, and exploitation and through her accusation of those who are responsible for the victims' state, the prophetic witness aims at dissuading the oppressors from their unjust action and at winning them for the building up of the human order promised by God.

Witnessing through Suffering. This fourth form of witnessing occurs where, on account of their faith, human beings take upon themselves persecution, imprisonment, torture, and death. Inasmuch as they are following Jesus on his path of suffering, they point with their suffering to his suffering, and in doing so make Jesus and his passion present and visible. Witnessing through suffering culminates in martyrdom. The martyr is the witness par excellence, who with his death perfects and seals his witness to Jesus Christ in the testimony of blood. Not only in the early church have there been those who witness through suffering. Persecution, suffering, and violent death were and are experiences of Christians in all periods of

the church's life. The contemporary relevance of witnessing
through suffering shows itself in the persecution of Christians and
churches in various parts of the world. Today "a historico-cultural
change in the type of martyrdom and in the profile of the martyrs"
is to be observed, a "change from 'heroic' martyrs to 'anonymous'
martyrs, from the strictly individual testimony of blood to a sort of
collective martyrdom, in which the individual names recede."[81]

Today those who witness through suffering are both individuals
and groups, communities, indeed entire local churches,[82] who are
persecuted on the basis of the praxis of faith. In persecution they
follow Jesus and attest to the presence of his person, praxis, and passion. With their suffering and dying, those who witness through suffering bear witness to the fact that Jesus' passion continues, that
Jesus lies in agony until the end of the world.[83]

Witnessing through suffering mostly does not verbalize its contents. The witness's own suffering becomes transparent to Jesus'
passion. The witness's suffering says that in following Jesus in his
sufferings, she is making Jesus' passion her own. In martyrdom the
witness becomes like her suffering Lord and makes him visible in
her own flesh. Witnessing through suffering is that communicative
action of Christians in which, in enduring persecution, suffering,
and violent death, a specific content is not put into words, sentences, and utterances, or at least not primarily, but instead shows
itself in bodily form, in the witness's own tortured flesh. That this
body points to the suffering Jesus becomes clear from the context,
on the basis of the ground of the persecution and suffering.

To be sure, the ground of the persecution can be explicitly thematized in interrogation, in a trial, or elsewhere. But it can also be
silently presupposed. Precisely in the case of witnessing through
suffering, a silent testimony is made in which the tortured body of
the persecuted "speaks"—speaks about what has been done to her.
The act of following Jesus in his sufferings has been written into the
"texture" of the tormented victim and can be read there. At the
same time, this texture represents a testimony for the prosecution
against the persecutors.

Finally, witnessing through suffering is also an action toward
others: toward the persecutors, torturers, and executioners. The

person who witnesses through suffering aims at dissuading them from their abominable deeds. The body of the person marked by torture "speaks" not only of what has been done to him; it also speaks to those who torture him. The person who witnesses through suffering places his persecutors before the alternative of either losing their human face or breaking out of the deadly machinery of persecution. In the face of the destruction that threatens him, he makes a final offer to his persecutors, an offer put forward with ultimate existential seriousness. He offers them the chance to let themselves be persuaded. He himself becomes a witness in blood and thereby attains agreement with the action of Jesus Christ, an agreement that stands in opposition to the consensus of his persecutors. In doing so, he shows that his executioners are in the wrong, unmasks their action as murderous, and makes their untruth obvious.

Confession as an Action of the Church

Confession in Worship. The structure of confession laid down in early Christianity unfolds in the historical development of the church and of dogma. Confession's connection with the community emerges in particular in the act of confession in worship. This holds true especially for the confession of faith, in which the community holds onto the central elements of its shared faith and brings them to expression. As early as the second century, with the concept of the "rule of truth or of faith," the connection with the faith of the whole church comes into play. The authentic faith of the church articulates itself in the church's confession in worship. The Council of Nicea initiated a process of giving fixed form to the confession of faith in texts that were approved by synods and councils, and which had a binding character. In this process, the church as a whole increasingly becomes the subject of the act of confession. But confession continues to occur in the worship of the community. In this worship the confession of faith has its location as the "developed 'Amen' of the community," responding to the gospel.[84]

In the confession of faith that occurs in worship, the community confesses in a public and binding manner the fact that it belongs in a consciously appropriated way to God's history with human beings. The community confesses God's deeds, God's action in creation, God's action in Jesus Christ, God's action of raising Jesus, God's action in the Spirit in the church, and God's eschatological action, in anticipation of which the community acts. In worship the community confesses in the creed the holiness, catholicity, unity, and apostolicity of the church. In doing so the community, amidst the real divisions of the Christian church, makes an important confession of the unity of Christians in the one church of Jesus Christ.

Already in the early church, the confession of faith in worship was increasingly differentiated and refined in the course of the ecclesial struggle against heresy. The entirety of ecclesial doctrine, addressed in the concept of the *regula fidei* or rule of faith, was initially put into words in freely formulated texts whose words were not fixed. With the councils of Nicea, Constantinople, and Chalcedon, it was then given a fixed formulation with a binding character in the text of the creed approved by the councils. In the East the Nicene Creed soon became the text of the confession of faith to be prayed in every worship service. In the West it only gradually established itself as the creed for the mass, and it has continued to be used, along with the Apostles' Creed, until the present day as the text of the confession of faith in worship.

The baptismal confession is the personal confession of the person being baptized, who confesses her faith after renouncing the powers of evil. At the same time she confesses the faith of the church. By making her baptismal confession before the community, she makes its faith her own and confesses with the community the triune God.

Most likely there were fixed texts for the baptismal confession from the early period of Christianity, although they were not verbally identical in all places. Beginning in the fourth century two forms of texts were developed for this confession. One form, that of a declarative text, was employed within the framework of baptismal preparation. The text of the confession used in the baptismal act itself was formulated in an interrogative manner.

After the Council of Chalcedon the Nicene Creed, which was probably already being used in the East, became the confessional text employed in baptism in the Constantinopolitan church. The Apostles' Creed,[85] which arose out of the ancient Roman confession, was used in the Western church beginning in the Carolingian period. Either in declarative form or in the form of baptismal questions, it has continued in use up to the present day in both the Catholic church and the churches of the Reformation.

The confession of sins likewise has an ecclesial connection. This connection is visible particularly in the public penance practiced in the ancient church. The fact that the community as well as the individual is a subject of the act of confessing sins shows itself both in the general confession of sins at the beginning of the celebration of the Eucharist and in the general absolution. By contrast, in private confession the ecclesial dimension of penance and of the confession of sins recedes. After having been buried for centuries, this dimension was rediscovered only by the Second Vatican Council.

The confession of sins is also made in the form of verbally articulated texts. Most likely the general confession has been carried out in the form of specific, preformulated texts since the early church. Beginning with the second century, such texts also became available for the general absolution and the confiteor.[86]

On the one hand, confession occurs in regularly recurring situations of action in worship. It is thus a part of the performance of a ritual action.[87] On the other hand, confession is required in particular, dramatically heightened situations of action in which the identity and the integrity of the Christian community are at issue. The history and praxis of Christian confessing and confession unfold between these two poles.[88] The one pole is that of the regular act of confessing as the act of repeating, receiving, and passing on the formulaic confession in ritualized situations of action. The other pole is that of the act of making a particularly relevant confession in an explosive situation of action and in the face of specific challenges to which the confession responds.

In the liturgical act of confessing, the accent lies less on the reference to the situation than on the repetition and appropriation of the ecclesial consensus grounded in the original situation of the church. From the time of the ancient church, in the confession of faith in worship the church's shared faith has been confessed before God, before one another, and in public. The creed is a "bond of communion with all the other believers."[89] It aims at formulating and at holding fast to the central elements of the faith shared in the faith community of the church. While the confession of faith authoritatively puts into words the agreement in faith in communion with God and with each other, this agreement is repeated and appropriated in the baptismal confession. In this confession the person being baptized joins her voice to the church's confession, repeats it, and makes it her own in her own act of confessing.

Instructional Confession. With the advent of synodical and conciliar confessions, an instructional confession emerges. In contrast to confession in worship, whose point of reference is the community, instructional confession has the church as its subject. On the one hand, the bearers of such confessions are local churches, which at synods and councils of particular churches confess the faith of the church in an instructional way in the face of specific challenges. On the other hand, beginning with the Council of Nicea the church as a whole emerges as the subject of such confession. At an ecumenical council the church as a whole formulates the confession of the church as the "result of a binding consensus."[90] In doing so the church in its magisterial office lays down what is to be believed and confessed. The synodical and conciliar confessions bring to expression the doctrine of the church, demarcated over against heterodox views and directed toward unity in belief. Until the end of the Middles Ages, however, this doctrine of the church was articulated in a plurality of confessions, until the Catholic church of the Council of Trent put an end to the "legitimate pluralism of confessions."[91]

The confessional writings of the Reformation bring forth a new form of instructional confession. The Lutheran confessional writings, such as the Confessio Augustana, initially raise a claim concerning the whole church. Then they are related to the Lutheran church as a whole. The situation is different with the Reformed confessional writings. In accordance with the Reformed understanding of the church, which sees the universal church as being realized in the visible local community,[92] the subject of the Reformed confessional writings is the community of believers. Within a bounded time and location, this community spontaneously brings the gospel of Jesus Christ to expression in what is for the time being a definitive form.

Beginning with the fourth century, the synodical and conciliar confessions[93] put the faith into words in the form of binding Christian doctrine. The first fourth-century instance is the anti-Arian confession of the Synod of Antioch from the year 325, which presents in three sections of extensive detail that which is to be believed (*credendum*).

With the Nicene Creed a unified formula that is binding for the whole church arises for the first time. As a conciliar, instructional confession, this unified formula has as its content the ecclesial doctrine formulated in opposition to Arian heterodoxy. What we call the Nicene Creed—the creedal text ratified at Nicea and revised at Constantinople—puts forward the contents of the church's confession with several marked differences from the original confession of Nicea. Above all, the third article is expanded considerably. The Chalcedonian Definition gives a precise, antimonophysitic specification to the christological statements.

The synodical and conciliar confessions of the Middle Ages accept the earlier confessional statements and occasionally expand them with regard to individual aspects. The confession of the Catholic church then experiences an essential, substantive supplement in the Council of Trent with the Professio Fidei Tridentina of 1564.

In the confessional writings that arise in the churches of the Reformation, the faith of the church is unfolded in a new form of instructional confessing. The Lutheran confessional writings initially understand themselves as expositions of the faith of the Catholic church. According to its self-understanding, the Confessio Augustana is directed toward maintaining the unity of the church. In its orientation toward the church as a whole, the Confessio Augustana contains the basic doctrines of the whole church as well as questions concerning worship and church order.[94]

The Confessio Augustana is conciliatory, concerned with preserving the threatened unity of the church. By contrast, Philipp Melanchthon's 1531 Apology of the Augsburg Confession elaborates in detail

the doctrinal differences between Lutherans and adherents of the
old belief, arranging those differences in sharp antitheses.

With the *Book of Concord* of 1580, a *corpus doctrinae* or body of
doctrine arises for Lutheranism as a whole. This concludes the con-
fession-forming phase of the Lutheran Reformation.

The numerous Reformed confessional writings, which from the
beginning understand themselves as referring to a bounded time
and location, develop the basic contents of Reformed doctrine in definitive form. These confessional writings start with Ulrich Zwingli's
A Short Christian Introduction of 1523, his Berne Theses of 1528,
and his *Fidei ratio* of 1530, and extend up to the diverse confessional texts of today.[95]

For instructional confession, a decisive role is played from the
outset by confessional texts that are given a fixed written form, approved by synods and councils, and thus given a binding formulation. After all, the issue is demarcating and validly defining authentic
ecclesial doctrine against heterodox views. These written texts preserve, however, a relation to the spoken word, insofar as they not
only are read aloud when they are officially approved, but also
sometimes enter into the worship service.

Instructional confession makes use of a set of theological concepts on which a synod or a council has agreed. This is true both
with regard to the ecclesial doctrine that is to be defined and with
regard to the false doctrine that is to be rejected. The doctrinal confession approved by a synod or a council represents a substantive
and textually binding agreement. This agreement is to be received as
such, and in a given case is to be expanded and further defined.

With the confessional writings of the Reformation, a new type of
confessional text arises. This new type understands itself as an
answer, given in a specific situation in authoritative form, to God's
Word. It is ordered around God's Word, subordinate to that Word,
and at the same time draws a boundary over against false doctrine.
Confessional writings are doctrinal texts. They contain the obligatory doctrine of the church. They are not destined for use in worship, and indeed cannot be prayed at all. They sometimes assume a

considerable length, and are conceived from the beginning as written texts.

In instructional confession, the intention of giving a lasting and binding formulation to an achieved ecclesial consensus is obvious. Synodical and conciliar confessions arise in order to give lasting formulation to ecclesial agreements in situations of dogmatic conflict, and thereby to define ecclesial doctrine and to secure the unity of the church. To that extent, synodical and conciliar confessions are formulas of unity. They pursue the goal of consensually defining the contents and the boundaries of the church's confession, and thus of consensually defining the foundations of ecclesial unity.

The confessional writings of the Reformation preserve the intention and the claim of the synodical and conciliar confessions of being authoritative agreements. They underline the moment of consensus that is formulated in a binding and obligatory way in the confessional writing that has been presented and approved.

Situational Confession. In the twentieth century a new type of confession and a new form of confessing have arisen. I call it situational confession. What is at issue is an act of confessing in an explosive situation in which a position is taken and a side is chosen unambiguously. This act of confessing is characterized by a new understanding of the way in which truth and praxis, situation and doctrine are bound together. Such confessing occurs where the church is compelled to confess in a specific historical and political context, where the church must say "yes" or "no," where a decisive consensus is required of the church for the sake of its own identity, integrity, and mission. In my opinion, we see situational confessing in the three confessional texts that I will address briefly in the following paragraphs: the 1934 Barmen Theological Declaration of the First Confessional Synod of the German Evangelical Church, the 1975 confessional text "Our Hope" of the Synod of the Dioceses of the Federal Republic of Germany, and the Kairos Document of South African Christians, presented in 1985.[96]

Situational confessing always has an ecclesial subject, be it a local church or a regional church. Even the universal church of Jesus

Christ could see itself compelled, in the face of global challenges in an intensified worldwide situation, to confess the faith of the church in a situational manner. This would have to happen in an ecumenical council of all Christians, as the conciliar process seeks to attain.[97]

In situational confessing, what are at issue are specific questions of faith, with regard to which the church must take an unambiguous position in a specific situation, in the face of concrete challenges that particularly concern the church's ethical and political actions. The contents of situational confessing are not the whole of faith. Instead, in each particular case situational confessing thematizes specific contested aspects, with regard to which the church is compelled to come to a binding agreement for the sake of its being the church.

In the case of the Barmen Theological Declaration, the concrete challenge is the heresy and the heretical praxis of the "German Christians." In the face of these challenges, the Barmen Declaration confesses for the sake of the unity of the church six articles of "evangelical truths" (art. 2.1), along with the corresponding renunciations.

The synodical confession "Our Hope" confronts the contemporary social situation with the central confessional statements of the church's creed, and accentuates these statements with regard to the concrete sociopolitical situation. "Our Hope" directs attention to the ecumenical action with which the Catholic church in the Federal Republic of Germany is, in the praxis of following Jesus, particularly commissioned to engage: action in the *oikumenē* of Christians, of Christians and Jews, of the North and the South, and of creation.

The Kairos Document criticizes the "state theology" that gives theological sanction to the status quo, as well as the "church theology" that is ineffectual in the face of the status quo. In opposition, the text puts forward a biblically founded prophetic theology that combines social analysis and orientation toward liberating praxis. In the Kairos Document the confessing movement of South African Christians declares itself decidedly for the liberating God of the Bible and that God's Son, Jesus Christ. On this basis it renounces apartheid and the system based on it.[98]

Situational confession takes different textual forms. The Barmen Theological Declaration has the form of a "doctrinal text" that exhibits "all the classic features of a confession."[99] This text actualizes the confessions of the Reformation with regard to a specific explosive situation. With regard to the contemporary false doctrine of the "German Christians," the text expounds fundamental "evangelical truths" on the basis of the Holy Scriptures. This confessional text thus clearly highlights the situational frame of reference for its action.

The synodical confession "Our Hope" possesses a textual form that is hard to define. From the point of view of its shape, extent, and thematic content, it is comparable to a confessional writing of the Reformation. But it combines a style peculiarly its own with situational concreteness and an orientation to praxis. "Our Hope" is less a "doctrinal text" than a "confessional text . . . that wants to instigate testimony."[100] The binding character of the synodical confession does not rest in its text and its formulations as something to be accepted precisely as written. Its binding character rests in the fact that the Catholic church in the Federal Republic of Germany has approved "Our Hope" as its situational confession and has thereby committed itself to do what is expressed in the text.

In the Kairos Document we encounter an understanding of confessing and of confession that is articulated in texts, but that relativizes the significance of those texts in comparison with the praxis of confessing.[101] The Kairos Document conceives itself in the sense of a contextual theology. This agrees with an approach to confession and a view of confession that are becoming increasingly widespread in the theologies and churches of the Third World.[102] The Kairos Document understands itself as provisional, incomplete, and open to revision at any time. Its practical choice is unequivocal, as is the obligatory character at which it aims for the action of the church. Yet as clearly unequivocal as they are, the Kairos Document just as clearly is not bound to its text as formulated. Here we see at work an understanding of confession that sees the unity of the church as being given in the church's unequivocalness not in doctrinal matters, but in praxis, in deeds rather than in texts.[103]

The Barmen Theological Declaration articulates the authentic confession of the church in a dramatically accentuated situation in which "the Christian church faces the demand that it deny the exclusive claim of its God and accept alongside its God other powers that are repugnant to its God."[104] Such a situation of confession was a given for the Christian church in South Africa in the face of a state that, while understanding itself as Christian, lent constitutional status to the racism of apartheid in a constitution that began with a confession of faith.[105] The response required of the church in this situation could consist only in a binding consensus that apartheid was sin and heresy and that the church must resist it.

It seems not to be the case that Christians in Germany are faced with the demand that they deny the exclusive claim of their God and accept alongside their God other powers repugnant to their God. From this point of view, was the situation one that made a synodical confession compelling and necessary? The text indeed makes clear that the church in Germany is confronted with a creeping "denial" of God and of Jesus Christ that threatens the church's identity and integrity. The text makes clear that the church is confronted with the replacement of its identity and integrity by the "powers" of apathy, consumerism, the delusion of innocence, and the delusion of control. The Synod made its situational confession in the face of these powers and with regard to challenges that the German church faces on the basis of its history (of guilt) and its contemporary entanglement in guilt.

The act of situational confession expresses an agreement achieved by the church with reference to a specific, explosive situation of action and with reference to a question that clamors for a decision. Such an agreement is limited from the outset by the situation to be judged, the matter to be decided, and the action of the church required with regard to them. New dramatic situations thus require a new act of situational confession.

Basic Actions of Faith

As a communicative praxis, being a Christian is carried out in a basic way in the act of bearing witness. In and with this action, Christians, communities, local churches, and the universal church point to

Jesus Christ. In doing so they enter into relation with Jesus Christ, through the mediation of his earliest apostolic witnesses, and make his person and praxis accessible and visible. As pupils of the biblical witnesses, they continue the action of the biblical witnesses. By continuing that action, they follow the biblical witnesses into the life of following Jesus. They point to Jesus in their own christopraxis as its ground, content, and goal.

Christians are essentially witnesses who recognize and acknowledge that the earliest witnesses are credible and that what the earliest witnesses attest is true. Christians receive the testimony of the apostles and disciples in the church as a community of testimony. In the church they carry this testimony onward and bring it to bear in creative and innovative ways in new situations of action. This occurs with the intention of reaching an understanding with the recipients of the testimony concerning what is being attested. It occurs with the intention of persuading human beings and of winning them for Jesus and his praxis of the rule of God. Bearing witness thus also has an ecclesial function. Bearing witness indicates the location of the church, makes its task clear, and designates the way in which the church, through the mediation of the earliest witnesses and those of the church's own history, points to Jesus Christ and makes him publicly present as the ground and the goal of its existence.

Bearing witness is a foundational action of the faith of individuals, groups, communities, local churches, and the universal church. In this action all of these point in all sorts of places and in all sorts of situations to Jesus Christ, the witness to God's rule, whose testimony God has demonstrated to be true. They do this by communicating in their own testimony Jesus' testimony and that of his apostles and disciples. They point to Jesus Christ by vouching for the truth of their testimony with their own existence. They point to Jesus Christ inasmuch as their action shows to the recipients of their testimony the relevance of that testimony, with the intention of convincing, inviting, and winning those recipients for that to which and to whom they bear witness.

Bearing witness is an action of Christians in which the communicative and practical structure of faith is realized in perspectives of kerygmatic mission, of *diakonia*, of prophecy, and of suffering. It is a basic action of faith oriented toward what is new about the gospel, toward new relationships of solidarity and a new, humane order of living together. To that extent, bearing witness is an innovatively organized action of faith.

Confessing is that action, oriented by memory, in which the community of believers completes, makes present, repeats, and appropriates an agreement. To confess means to achieve consensus. Confession can be made only on the basis of an agreement that is manifested in a binding manner in the confession (confessional text) and that is verbalized in the act of confession. Confession is the fundamental ecclesial action. It makes the church a community of faith and confession. The subject of this action is first of all the church, which in the act of confession formulates a consensus in the sense of an understanding reached concerning itself. The process of reaching this understanding includes the drawing of boundaries. The church binds itself to this consensus unless and until it is superseded by a new, more far-reaching consensus.

"Confession is the binding public registration of the fact of belonging to God in Jesus Christ."[106] Since New Testament times, the object of the confession of the church was and is God's action in Jesus Christ. With their confession the early Christian communities declared themselves for Jesus Christ and identified themselves as Christians. At the same time they thereby registered and confirmed their community and unity with each other.

Confession is located in the church and proves to be a fundamental ecclesial action. It identifies the church as the church of Jesus Christ, as the community of sisters and brothers with Christ and each other. Confession is done at various places: in worship in the baptismal confession, the confession of faith, and the confession of sins; in synodical and conciliar doctrinal confessions; in the Reformation confessional writings; in situational confession.

In the face of vexing problems that threaten a life of human dignity and even survival itself on the earth, the church today faces the question whether the confession of Jesus Christ does not imply reaching a binding understanding concerning such basic questions. The church faces the question whether such problems do not prove to be confessional questions, in the face of which the church is compelled to respond with a clear "yes" or "no." Concerning what things must the church today reach an understanding for the sake of its unity, identity, and integrity as the church of Jesus Christ, in order not to deny its Lord? This is one of the burning ecumenical questions.[107]

In his 1932 lectures on "The Essence of the Church," Dietrich Bonhoeffer maintained that "the first confession of the Christian community before the world is deeds. Deeds interpret themselves. When deeds have become a power, then the world will ask for verbal confession as well."[108] I agree with Bonhoeffer's concern, but not with his distinction between confession in word and confession in deed. In the act of confession the distinction between word and deed collapses. Confession is a basic ecclesial praxis. In the act of confession the church acts by enunciating, in a binding manner before God, each other, and the general public, that which fundamentally determines its christopraxis. Confession is a basic action of faith on the part of the church.

COMMUNIO AND COMMUNITY OF COMMUNICATION

Since the Second Vatican Council, theological reflection upon the church has spoken increasingly of the church's community character. In Counter-Reformation and Neoscholastic theology beginning with Robert Bellarmine, the church was understood primarily as society (*societas*) and as body or as the mystical Body of Christ (*Corpus Christi Mysticum*). The purpose of this understanding was to highlight the church's visibility and hierarchical structure in opposition to Reformation ecclesiology. Since Vatican II, an understanding that goes back to the early centuries of the church has been acquiring increasing prominence. This understanding underscores the communitarian character and the relational aspect of ecclesial reality, in contrast to the ideas of society and of Body of Christ with their one-sidedly institutional orientation.[109] Since Vatican II, the concept of community has been moving increasingly into the center of ecclesiological reflection. Today, talk of the church as community is everywhere. The church is characterized as a community of faith and of hope, as a community of tradition and of interpretation, as a community of action and of life, as a eucharistic community and as a conciliar community. The *communio*-ecclesiology is even characterized as "the central and fundamental idea of the Council's documents."[110]

In the following discussion I will initially assemble several ecclesial and theological statements about the church as community. I will then articulate the characteristics of the church as a community of communication. Finally, I will sketch a christopractical understanding of the church as *communio*.

Church as Community

The documents of Vatican II speak in various places and ways of the church as *communio*, although from the texts of the Council themselves the idea of *communio* could not be regarded as foundational for the Council. The "Dogmatic Constitution on the Church," which defines the church fundamentally as "mystery" (chap. 1) and as "people of God" (chap. 2), characterizes the church under the first of those headings as "the community of faith, hope and charity."[111] The church is simultaneously a "visible assembly" and a "spiritual community."[112] In the chapter on the church as the people of God, the church is called a "priestly community,"[113] in which the priesthood of all believers and the hierarchical priesthood are correlated with each other. The document further notes that "within the Church particular Churches hold a rightful place." These latter constitute an "assembly of charity," over which the Chair of Peter presides. This assembly is bound together by a "close communion with respect to spiritual riches." It is to this communion that "the members of the People of God are called."[114] The bishops teach "in communion with the Roman Pontiff" and "are to be respected by all as witnesses to divine and Catholic truth."[115]

The "Decree on Ecumenism" states that the Holy Spirit, "dwelling in those who believe, pervading and ruling over the entire Church . . . brings about that marvelous communion of the faithful and joins them together so intimately in Christ that He is the principle of the Church's unity."[116] At the same time, the Decree acknowledges that within the one church, "quite large Communities became separated from full communion with the Catholic Church."

Through belief in Christ and through baptism the adherents of those communities stand in "a certain, though imperfect, communion with the Catholic Church." In any case they, too, have "access to the community of salvation."[117] Having been baptized, they are oriented toward the complete profession of faith as well as "toward a complete participation in eucharistic communion."[118]

The "Decree on the Church's Missionary Activity" deals with the building up of the Christian community (§§15-18). The Decree also explains the correlation of particular churches with the whole church and emphasizes young churches' "communion with the church universal."[119]

The "Pastoral Constitution on the Church in the Modern World" was of fundamental importance both for the self-understanding of the Council and for the Council's pope, John XXIII.[120] That text places the community of the church in the context of human community (part 1, chap. 2), of political community (part 2, chap. 4), and of the community of nations (part 2, chap. 5). Along the line of the integrated understanding of *communio* indicated by the "Pastoral Constitution in the Modern World," one should also mention the postconciliar pastoral instruction "Communio et Progressio." This text reflects upon Christ in the context of *communio* and communication, calling Christ the "Perfectus Communicator."[121] On that basis "Communio et Progressio" arrives at an ecclesiology that is communicative in its basic conception.[122]

Recent works and proposals of ecclesiology provide evidence that the concept of community in ecclesiological terminology is open to various interpretations. Hans Zirker elucidates the church on the basis of its functions as a community that moves toward understanding, a community of tradition, and a community of action.[123] Jesus' proclamation was already aimed at reaching an understanding. After Easter Jesus' history is both ascertained and mediated in the early Christian communities, which reach an understanding both about ecclesial action and about the "agreement made concerning action."[124] On the basis of the early church's way of learning and of reaching an understanding, Zirker explains three ways of intrachurch communication. In Zirker's view, multichannel exchange in mutual participation and reciprocal responsibility particularly corresponds to the self-understanding of the early church, summed up in the key concept of *koinōnia*. By contrast, the emphasis on the binding character of a central agent of decision transports the ecclesial community "into a juridical form" that formulates the primacy of the Bishop of Rome "according to the notions and in the concepts of dominating power."[125] Zirker recognizes a third way in the synodical process of reaching understandings. The principle of this process is to secure unity through the coming together of the many, and to do so by means of a shared process of developing a common mind.

Second, Zirker treats the church as a community of tradition. Here the basic form of cultural life is constituted both by verbally mediated traditions and by traditions preserved in patterns of action. The church needs to receive and appropriate the tradition that, as the normative content of faith, underlies the church. At the same time, this reception and appropriation presuppose an interpretive participation.

Finally, Zirker expounds the fact that (and the extent to which) the church is a community of action. For Zirker, action is the "answer, consequence, and expression of faith."[126] The church as community of action articulates and realizes itself in a fundamental form in the liturgy. As further fields of ecclesial action, Zirker analyzes proclamation and teaching, mission, diaconal social service, and political action.

Under the programmatic title "The Communion of Saints," Miguel M. Garijo-Guembe in his ecclesiology introduces the concept of *communio* as one of the fundamental concepts concerning the essence of the church. With reference to *Lumen Gentium*, he treats the church as a "communion of believers: that is, as *koinōnia* and the people of God."[127] Again on the basis of *Lumen Gentium* he emphasizes that the church is consummated in the celebration of the Eucharist. In this celebration "the essence of the church [is represented] on the level of the symbolic and the sacramental" through "participation (= communion)."[128] As a further aspect of *communio* he elucidates the conception of the whole church as the *koinōnia* of local churches. The basis for this conception was laid in the early church. It was central in the ancient church and has been preserved in the Eastern church. Garijo-Guembe elucidates this conception, in order finally to explain both the "unity of the church as the *koinōnia* of churches and the role of Rome within this conception."[129]

Taking as his point of departure Habermas's theory of action, and with a regard for the ecclesiology of Vatican II, Paul Lakeland understands and analyzes the church as a community of communicative action.[130] In opposition to the ecclesial fundamentalism of a Catholic "ecclesiolatry"[131] that asserts itself as immune to questioning, Lakeland conceives of the church as a community of interpretation. He requires that an authentic ecclesiology be "reflection on the fact of the praxis of the believing community," rather than "reflection on this or that idea of the church."[132]

On the basis of the communicative theory of action, Lakeland discerns indications of systematically distorted communication in the church. As such he regards both sexism and clericalism in the Catholic church. Starting from the distinction between hidden and open strategic action, he wants on the one hand to understand success-oriented evangelism as appropriate open strategic action of the church. In my opinion this is problematic. On the other hand, he rightly conceives of covert strategic action as a deception of the addressees that contradicts the church's message and intention. Lakeland highlights the fundamental equality of all believers before God and emphasizes the conception of the pilgrim people of God as the primary understanding of the church in Vatican II. In Lakeland's view, this understanding is both biblically and historically grounded. It relativizes the church and relates it to Christ, the "light of all nations."[133] Without erasing a necessary institutional element, this understanding of the church is "communitarian rather than institutional."[134] Lakeland then turns to the communicative praxis of the people of God and describes ecclesial communities such as base communities and women-church as forms of praxis of an ecclesiology of the people of God.[135]

Finally, the church is seen as a community of communication in various works that theologically take up and process Habermas's and Apel's conception. Appealing especially to Habermas and Peukert, Barbara Kappenberg engages in reflections concerning the "possible foundation of the church as a successful community of communication, or as the phenomenon of successful, ideal communication on the basis of the Judeo-Christian tradition."[136] Hans-Joachim Höhn analyzes the church as "the system of meaning of the proclamation of faith—a system that precedes and transcends individuals—as well as the system of action of the praxis of faith, as that system arises out of the interactions of individuals."[137] Höhn elaborates *diakonia, martyria, koinōnia,* and *leiturgia* as the basic ways in which the praxis of faith is carried out. He presents them as basic ways in which communicative action is carried out. In Höhn's view, *diakonia* represents a community action oriented toward need; *martyria,* a consciousness-transforming community action; *koinōnia,* a socially integrative community action; and *leiturgia,* a metacommunicative community action. Peter Hofmann, in his fundamental theological reception and critique of Apel's transcendental philosophy of the community of communication, speaks of the church as an "ideal-real community of communication."[138] As discussed above, Wolfgang Pauly understands the church as a conciliar, universal community of communication.

Characteristics of the Church as a Community of Communication

We can regard the church as a community of communication in which, in their communicative action, various subjects, in their specific contexts and by means of appropriate texts and other media, hand on and receive specific contents, holding onto them, making them present, rendering them comprehensible, and creatively advancing them, all with regard to the goals of the subjects involved. At the same time, in a certain respect the church itself is the subject, location, medium, and goal of the communicative action of Christians. The church as a community of communication serves in a double sense the communication of the gospel or the communication of Christ. Jesus Christ is communicated in the church and through the church's mediation. At the same time, Jesus Christ himself acts communicatively in the church.[139] In the church it is not only diverse subjects who have the task—be it connected with a specific office or universal to all Christians—of carrying out the communication of Christ. The church itself is the subject of this communication. The church in its various forms goes about performing its task. These forms at the same time represent forms of the realization of the church as a community of communication.

Siegfried Wiedenhofer has recently articulated four structurally necessary fundamental forms of the church. On the one hand, he conceives of these forms as "basic forms of human sociality . . . transformed by faith." As basic forms of human sociality they are irreducible to each other. "On the other hand, for the same reason they also cannot be isolated, [so] that each is thus dependent upon the others and defined by the others."[140] As these fundamental forms Wiedenhofer distinguishes (1) the house church, base community, and personal community; (2) the local community, or community under the leadership of a pastor; (3) the episcopal local church; (4) the worldwide church. Wiedenhofer investigates each of the forms with regard to its contribution of the ecclesial transmission of faith. He understands this transmission as an interactive structure of processes of tradition, and correlates its form to the four forms of the church. This correlation occurs in the following way. Wiedenhofer explains the daily praxis of faith as the dominant form of the first, communal worship as the dominant form of the second, and "authentic proclamation and authoritative decision as the dominant form of the tradition of both particular churches and the church as a whole."[141]

Within Protestant ecclesiology Wolfgang Huber had already distinguished four social forms of the church: the local worshiping community, the initiative group, the regional church, and the ecclesial confederation as an ecumenical community extending across confessional and regional borders. Huber recognizes "basic forms of the church" in all four levels, insofar as all four arise out of basic impulses of ecclesial life: "the gathering for worship, life together in a committed form of life, mutual support, and the desire for the most comprehensive community possible."[142]

In my opinion, the distinction between four fundamental forms in which the church manifests and articulates itself as subject represents a fundamental ecclesiological insight with important consequences. Wiedenhofer makes this distinction out of the necessity of differentiating the ecclesial transmission of faith. For that reason Wiedenhofer applies the distinction to the Christian ecclesial tradition's forms and processes of reception and appropriation. By contrast, by viewing the initiative group as a form of church, Huber's division attaches ecclesiological importance to the innovative moment. As instances of this form Huber numbers religious orders as well as all those groups who "want to have their entire form of life defined by their faith, and who thereby exercise an 'innovative' influence . . . upon the church."[143]

I see both in Huber and in Wiedenhofer a problematic tendency functionally to differentiate the four forms of the church and to divide up among them the fundamental ways of carrying out the life of the church. By contrast, from the perspective of the theological theory of action I think that it is necessary to highlight what is common to all four levels and to identify it as the communication of Christ. We must explain this shared communication of Christ by means of the basic actions of faith, in order to go on from there to investigate which forms of bearing witness and of confessing are primarily realized or need to be realized in which forms of church.

In its four basic forms, the church is a subject of the communication of Christ. The first of these forms is the house church, base community, personal community, initiative group, or "community engaged in following Christ"[144] in which Jesus Christ is attested and confessed on the level of interpersonal interaction. The second form is the local worshiping community, in which the acts of bearing witness and of confessing occur on the level of the *ekklēsia* gathered in one place. The third form is the regional church as a communion of groups and communities that is led by a bishop, and that is "representatively joined together into the unity of the regional church by the College of Presbyters, and above all by the bishop."[145] The fourth form is the whole church as the universal church of Jesus Christ, represented by the College of Bishops together with the Bishop of Rome.

The church is first a subject in the communion of its various subjects in the one community of communication that is the church. The church is a community and creates community to the extent that the church's various subjects and forms mutually acknowledge, support, and strengthen each other for the building up of the body of Christ. The ecclesial community of communication is endangered wherever specific forms in which the church is realized as a community of communication—be those forms centralized and monolithic or particularistic and contextual—neglect, curtail, or "excommunicate" other forms. The ecclesial community of communication is endangered wherever the process whereby diverse subjects reach an understanding is monopolized or systematically restricted to certain pathways and thus distorted. When the ecclesial community of communication is thus endangered, it has a pressing need for a change, wrought with the help of conciliar discourse, in the existing conditions by which understanding is reached.

Second, the church is not only a subject, but also a location of the communication of Christ. The church is this location in each of the forms in which the church is realized in the multiplicity of its contexts and situations of action. As discussed above, these contexts and situations of action include proclamation and worship, *diakonia* and prophecy, as well as suffering in solidarity with the suffering Jesus. In this suffering with Jesus the "pathic structure"[146] of Christian ecclesial existence comes to expression. On all levels of the church as a community of communication, Christ is attested and confessed in numerous locations and in a multiplicity of contexts. Ecclesial communication must not be without location or context. It must be contextualized. It must enter into the situation of its subjects and become inculturated or incarnate in that situation.[147] It must do so in order to open up, clarify, and change that situation, making the situation a location of its christopraxis. The ecclesial community of communication is threatened in its unity, identity, and integrity at those places where it does not embed itself in a location, concretize itself right at that place, and tie together its various locations. The ecclesial community of communication is threatened where it does not, through its situations of action and its contexts, make itself visible and clearly comprehensible as the location of the communication of Christ.

Third, the church is a content of the communication of Christ, insofar as Jesus gathered human beings in the praxis of the rule of God and the early Christian communities experienced and knew them-

selves as called together as *ekklēsia* by the risen Christ. The church
bears witness to and confesses Christ as present in it and, through
the Spirit, active in it. The church thus also identifies itself as a community that in its witness and confession brings to expression its
community with Christ and the community among its members. Accordingly, it is logical that the church as object of the communication of Christ enters as it does into the formulation of the creed, in
and with which the church confesses itself to be one, holy, catholic,
and apostolic, and identifies itself as a "communion of saints."[148]

The four attributes of unity, catholicity, apostolicity, and holiness
characterize the facticity and the counterfactual "promise"[149] of the
church. In this facticity and counterfactual promise the church is,
fourth, a medium of the communication of Christ. In the church's
sacramental, missionary, and diaconal action, in its action of solidarity, the church mediates Christ, communicates Christ, and as the
body of Christ participates in Christ.

Finally, the church is also in a certain sense a goal of the communication of Christ. The church conceives of itself as a form of the
realization of Jesus' intentions—albeit a provisional form. The
church must of course always keep present to consciousness, and at
the same time be prophetically and critically reminded, that the
church itself is not the light of the world. Instead the church remains related to Christ as the *lumen gentium*, a light to the nations,
and has the purpose of pointing to Christ and of exhibiting Christ in
its christopraxis.

The church is a community of christopractical communication. As
such it is a community of communicative praxis in which christopraxis happens and ought to happen in both anamnestic and innovative perspectives in missionary, diaconal, and prophetic action, in
the interaction of worship, in synodical or conciliar interaction, and
thus in a binding process of reaching an understanding. Through the
person and praxis of Jesus, through God's action in him, through the
action of the disciples and of the early Christian communities, and
through the church's own binding process of reaching an understanding, the church's communicative action down through history
is both normatively preestablished and to be confronted situation by
situation.

Christopractical *Communio*

An understanding of the church as *communio* makes a lot of sense for the theory of action. Moreover, it is theologically fruitful, ecclesiologically important, and practically relevant. Such an understanding has a solid biblical foundation in the Pauline conception of *ekklēsia* as *koinōnia*, specifically as *koinōnia* with Jesus Christ (1 Cor 1:9) through shared participation in the body of Christ. It is from this shared participation that *koinōnia* in the body of Christ proceeds (1 Cor 10:16-17).[150] As "communion of the Spirit" (2 Cor 13:13) of Jesus Christ, *koinōnia* in the body of Christ is directed toward comprehensive community and realizes itself in the *koinōnia* that the apostle has with his communities, community members have with one another, and communities entertain with one another through "giving to each other and receiving one from each other a share"[151] in their spiritual and material goods. The collection of the Pauline communities for the community in Jerusalem thus becomes an "expression of *koinōnia* of the church as a whole."[152]

As communion with Jesus Christ "that comes into being by Jesus Christ grounding and granting this communion,"[153] *koinōnia* in the New Testament understanding is christologically founded and is grounded in the communicative praxis of Jesus Christ. As communion among those who participate in Christ and who through Christ have become the body of Christ, this communion is at the same time practically oriented. As "communion in his sufferings" (Phil 3:10), it includes an element of suffering. Finally, it has an ecclesial dimension insofar as it defines the relation of communions and communities among each other and their connection with each other in mutual responsibility and care.

An understanding of the church as a *communio* of communions, communities, and regional churches is not only biblically grounded, but also governing for the ancient church and determinative for the Eastern church up to the present day.[154] We could understand the church as a communion of regional and particular churches, and as a conciliar communion of different churches, all on the way to the unity of the church that is both given in Christ and enjoined by

Christ. It is this unified church that would carry through in binding agreement the unity and community confessed in the creed. Such an understanding of the church is as ecumenically possible as it is of great consequence for the praxis of the church.[155]

The *communio*-ecclesiology that I am proposing understands and explains the concept of *communio* as a theological qualification of the church as a community of communication. This ecclesiology takes the person, praxis, and presence of Jesus as its point of departure. It conceives of the church as the people of God communicating and interacting with one another in the acts of bearing witness and confessing.[156] This ecclesiology is simultaneously fundamental, conciliar, and practical. Such a christopractical understanding of *communio* is anything but christomonist, insofar as it does not propagate a "pyramidal and clerical ecclesiology"[157] that culminates in Christ and in the pope as Christ's representative and the bearer of Christ's power. Instead this understanding of *communio* elucidates the church from the perspectives of its various subjects and their communicative, contextual, and conciliar praxis. Such an understanding is *eo ipso* oriented toward the process of reaching an understanding. It is directed toward community in mutual recognition and reciprocal responsibility. It takes into consideration the contribution that the individual members of Christ's body make with regard to the whole people of God "in responsible ways that are perfectly apostolic, that are perfect examples of brotherhood and solidarity, and yet are different from each other."[158] A *communio*-conception with these contours does not elevate the (Catholic) church from among other (church) communions. Nor does it seek to distance church communions from other *communitates*. In the sense of the Vatican II document *Gaudium et Spes* it relates ecclesial *communitas* and *communio* to social and political *communitates* on the local, regional, national, and international levels. Consequently, such a *communio* cannot be primarily occupied with itself and concerned about itself. Its urgent concern is rather the kerygmatic-missionary, diaconal, prophetic, empathic, and suffering communication of the *communio* of Christ to all human beings and the sharing of that *communio* with them.

Compared to such a *communio*-understanding, the *communio*-conception put forward by the Synod of Bishops of 1985 is defensive, oriented toward the internal affairs of the church, and has a marked tendency toward ecclesial self-centeredness.[159] This conception represents a selective appropriation of the Second Vatican Council and is structured in such a way that "the theological importance proper to the people of God is not given its due weight"[160] or is consciously repressed. On the basis of the "conflicted ecclesiology of Vatican II,"[161] a procedure of this type is admittedly justified in appealing to the Council and in supporting itself with the Council's words about the *communio hierarchica*.[162] It can invoke in particular a text that understands itself as a clarification of the concept of *communio* and that argues in a way that is nothing less than christomonist, conceiving the collegiality of bishops as "hierarchical communion with the head of the College and its members."[163] In picking up the Pauline model of the body of Christ this argument semantically insinuates that the Bishop of Rome is to be identified with the head of the church, indeed as the head of the church. This would attribute to him a position that according to the New Testament belongs to Christ alone.

In contrast to a narrowly christomonist understanding of *communio*, a christopractical understanding grasps the church as a community of communicative action. Christ is communicated in the interaction of the subjects and forms of this community in reciprocal understanding and support, in action and reflection that are related back to each other. Such a christopractical view of *communio* recognizes above all in the church as a community of communication a community of equals who all together belong to the people of God. As members of the body of Christ they are united and are bound together in a eucharistic and conciliar community, in which they are connected with Christ and with each other and aim at the goal of universal understanding and solidarity. At the same time such a *communio* needs a structure that secures and enhances communication and interaction at the levels of the local community, the local church, and the universal church. It also needs a legal order that makes possible and ensures mutual understanding and responsibility through binding consensus.[164]

The theological statement that the church is a *communio* must become visible in the church's structure and praxis, and must verify and prove itself in that structure and praxis. This occurs inasmuch as the church, as a community of testimony and confession, convincingly bears witness to Jesus Christ and, on the basis of mutually attained conviction, confesses Jesus Christ.

CHRISTOPRAXIS IN THE HORIZON OF UNIVERSAL SOLIDARITY

The concept and the praxis of solidarity are relevant for both the communicative and the theological theories of action. The theological theory of action is constituted precisely on the basis of the paradox of anamnestic solidarity and confronts the communicative theory of action with the perspective of universal solidarity. The concept of solidarity is both a limit concept and a foundational concept of communicative ethics. For Habermas, solidarity means that resource in the lifeworld without which even modern societies cannot get along, and which must assert itself against the two other forces of money and administrative power. Solidarity, which grows out of the mutual recognition of subjects, and life together in solidarity are the narrative foundation of interaction and the goal of communicative ethics.[165]

According to Apel, in view of the stage at which human history has arrived, discourse ethics is to be conceived as a macro-ethically oriented ethics of responsibility. At this stage of history for the first time the task is "to assume responsibility in solidarity for the global consequences of the collective activities of human beings, and to organize this responsibility itself as a collective praxis."[166] In Apel's view, discourses are characterized precisely as a medium of cooperative organization of responsibility in solidarity. In the horizon of a world that is becoming increasingly interwoven and at the same time is obviously divided, communicative ethics also implies "international solidarity with the oppressed,"[167] and contains the teleological perspective of a "universal historical solidarity."[168]

Solidarity becomes central for a theological theory of action that operates at the level of fundamental theology and that is carried out as reflection on Christian ecclesial praxis in the context of the sciences, society, and the one world. In interdisciplinary conversation with the human sciences and philosophy, theology can learn both the fact that and the extent to which solidarity constitutes and gives direction to human life together. In critical engagement with social movements, theology can ascertain the status of solidarity in political praxis. With regard to the arising global society, theology can develop as theology that thinks both contextually and globally, as theology of a world that is split into poor and rich and that is crying out for solidarity.[169]

Solidarity is not a concept with Christian origins. It arose out of the judicial domain, and in the nineteenth century advanced to a position as one of the guiding concepts of the labor movement. Both political theology and the theology of liberation give it theological weight.[170] Recently it has moved into the center of papal social teaching. In the following pages I will pursue the theme of solidarity in the beginnings of the labor movement and the church's social teaching, in order to show how solidarity can be conceived in the sense of a theological theory of action as universally oriented christopraxis.[171]

Solidarity as a Guiding Term of the Labor Movement

Before the labor movement unified itself under the slogan of solidarity, it had come together under another guiding concept, which it had borrowed from both Christianity and the bourgeois revolution. This was the idea of brotherhood, one of the key terms of the French Revolution of 1789. *Brotherhood* designated one of the goals of bourgeois democracy as it sought after *liberté, egalité,* and *fraternité.* In the labor movement, brotherhood became the point of orientation of the social emancipation of the proletariat. Until 1848 the concept served both to designate a series of associations of workers and to specify the goal of their common struggle.

In 1837 the English "Working Men's Association" speaks of the spirit of brotherhood shared by workers in all lands. One year later the same organization declares in a "Message of the Working Classes of Europe": "Fellow producers of wealth! seeing that our oppressors are thus united, why should not we, too, have our bond of brotherhood and holy alliance?"[172] The demand for brotherhood as the principle of the unification in both spirit and action of the laboring class on the national and international levels had strong religious and Christian connotations. In his 1841 book *De la vie sociale*, the French communist Richard Lahautière derived brotherhood from the teaching of Jesus. Wilhelm Weitling and other utopian communists saw brotherhood as grounded in early Christianity.

In 1849 *The Brotherhood*,[173] the organ of the German Labor Brotherhood, published "Ten Commandments of Workers." The tenth was "You shall love your neighbor as yourself. Only thus will you succeed in escaping servitude. Only thus can you be truly free, for freedom and equality proceed only from a third—brotherhood."[174]

Karl Marx and Friedrich Engels initially supported the idea of brotherhood, but soon they rejected it and replaced it with other concepts, among them the concept of solidarity. In 1844 Marx expressed himself full of admiration for the brotherhood that he found among French workers. In an 1845 report on a London festival of workers from various nations, Engels emphasized their spirit of brotherhood. But already in 1846 he complained in a letter about the "sighing about brotherliness."[175]

When Marx and Engels became members of the Federation of the Just, it had the motto "All human beings are brothers!" In a short time the two of them succeeded in transforming the Federation of the Just into the Federation of Communists, which took shape under the new slogan "Workers of the world, unite!" Marx and Engels increasingly rejected the idea of brotherhood. In their view it veiled and perpetuated the existing class oppositions instead of uncovering them and inspiring the proletariat to fight against them. In an article on the June Revolution of 1848 in France, Marx wrote that "*fraternité*, the brotherhood of antagonistic classes, one of which exploits the other" is in truth "civil war."[176] A little later he wrote concerning "the Class Struggles in France, 1848 to 1850":

> The phrase which corresponded to this imaginary abolition of class relations was *fraternité*, universal fraternisation and brotherhood. This pleasant dissociation from class antagonisms, this sentimental

reconciliation of contradictory class interests, this visionary elevation above the class struggle, this *fraternité* was the real catchword of the February Revolution.[177]

Marx and Engels were not entirely successful in eliminating the concept of brotherhood from the vocabulary of the labor movement. They themselves later used the concept on occasion in connection with the International. In the Communist Manifesto, however, they abandoned this terminology and put in its place the central concept of class struggle. Nor is there any mention of solidarity in the Communist Manifesto. Nevertheless, the appeal here to coalitions, associations, and the increasingly broadly extended unification of workers implies the dimension of solidarity on the national and international levels.[178]

Solidarity is not only an idea or a principle. It is, as Marx and Engels develop it, an expression of the actual relations of the existing class struggle. On the one hand, an association of workers in solidarity is grounded in given class relations and is to that extent objective. On the other hand, such an association is a consciously undertaken intersubjective activity, the intersubjective anticipation of a form of life, "an association, in which the free development of each is the condition for the free development of all."[179] Moreover, the association in solidarity of the laboring class is socially productive: "In revolutionary activity the changing of oneself coincides with the changing of circumstances."[180]

As class solidarity, the solidarity of the proletariat includes the overcoming of competition of workers among themselves, their joining together for unified action, and their self-organization as a class. This is at the same time a reaction to the unification of the bourgeoisie. Such class solidarity must be international, since according to Marx and Engels the bourgeoisie also develops internationally with the "world market." On that basis Marx and Engels make clear that "united action, of the leading civilized countries at least, is one of the first conditions for the emancipation of the proletariat."[181]

In 1850 the Universal Society of Revolutionary Communists was constituted. In its founding document it accepted six articles. The first article names as the "aim of the association . . . the downfall of all privileged classes." The second article focuses on international solidarity as the means for attaining this goal: "To contribute to the realisation of this aim, the association will form ties of solidarity between all sections of the revolutionary communist party, causing national divisions to disappear according to the principle of republican fraternity."[182]

The "Provisional Rules of the Working Men's International Association" of 1864 conclude that the emancipation of the laboring class has "hitherto failed from the want of solidarity between the manifold divisions of labour in each country, and from the absence of a fraternal bond of union between the working classes of different countries."[183] In *Der Vorbote*, the organ of the German section of the International, its editor Johann Philipp Becker explained that the International Working Men's Association wanted "above all to unite the existing societies of workers . . . to ensure their existence and development through the exercise of systematic overall obligation (solidarity)." Becker calls the solidarity of the working class "brotherhood of deeds" and contrasts it with the bourgeois "brotherhood of words."[184] After presenting the work of the individual sections of the International, the "Third Annual Report of the International Working Men's Association" comes to the conclusion that it has presented "facts that demonstrate incontrovertibly that society consists but of two hostile classes—the oppressors and the oppressed—and that nothing short of a solitary union of the sons of toil throughout the world will ever redeem them from their present thraldom."[185]

Since the days of the First International the demand for solidarity of workers on the national and international levels has been a constitutive moment of the labor movement.[186] It remains such even after the collapse of "really existing" socialism, because and inasmuch as really existing capitalism has by no means been disposed of in the process. Solidarity has also become the perspective of other social movements, such as that of the Third World.[187]

Solidarity as a Theme of Christian Doctrine

Even if the "solidarism" of a Heinrich Pesch, a Gustav Gundlach, and an Oswald von Nell-Breuning decisively influenced Catholic social teaching, the concept of solidarity hardly plays a role in the teaching of the Catholic church before the Second Vatican Council.[188] Even in the texts of the Council we find only occasional references, albeit significant ones. For example, the "Decree on the Apostolate of the Laity" says that "among the signs of the times, the irresistibly increasing sense of solidarity among all peoples is especially noteworthy. It is a function of the lay apostolate to promote this awareness zealously and to transform it into a sincere and genuine sense of brotherhood."[189] According to this decree, the task is to convert (*convertere*) the sense of solidarity into brotherhood. The "Pastoral Constitution on the Church in the Modern World" includes a section titled "The Incarnate Word and Human Solidarity."[190] "Gaudium et Spes" also talks about the growing "sense of international solidarity."[191] The text also says that it is a task of Christians in international organizations to "help to form an awareness of genuine universal solidarity and responsibility."[192] The concept of *universalis solidarietatis* here designates the necessity and urgency of a global solidarity "to construct a peaceful and fraternal community of nations."[193] In the same sense the "Decree on the Church's Missionary Activity" appeals to the laity "that there may appear in their way of life a new bond of unity and of universal solidarity, drawn from the mystery of Christ."[194]

Solidarity is mentioned in John XXIII's encyclical "Mater et Magistra"[195] and in his encyclical on peace "Pacem in Terris."[196] The theme of solidarity receives pronounced value within church teaching for the first time in Paul VI's encyclical "The Development of Peoples." John Paul II, the ally and helper of the Polish labor movement Solidarnosc, makes the theme of solidarity the focus of papal social proclamation.[197] His encyclical on human work, "Laborem Exercens," contains a section titled "Worker Solidarity." This section recognizes "the call to solidarity and common action addressed to the workers" as a "reaction against the degradation of the human subject of work, and against the unheard of accompanying exploitation in the field of wages, working conditions and social security for the worker."[198] Solidarity assumes center stage in papal social teaching in the encyclical "Sollicitudo Rei Socialis," which John Paul II published in 1987 on the twentieth birthday of "Populorum Progressio." One of the German editions bears the well-phrased title: "Solidarity—the Answer to the Misery in Today's World."[199]

In agreement with "Populorum Progressio," this social encyclical underlines the "duty of solidarity"[200] as a moral obligation to global responsibility with regard to the relations between poor and rich countries and with regard to the misery in the countries of the Two-Thirds World. In particular, the division of the world into two antagonistic blocks, a capitalist liberalism and a Marxist collectivism, involves for both the tendency to imperialism and to neocolonialism, and "deadens the impulse toward united cooperation by all for the common good of the human race."[201] Instead of moving toward a just and peaceful future, it seems that "in today's world, including the world of economics, the prevailing picture is one destined to lead us more quickly towards death."[202] On the other hand, "Sollicitudo Rei Socialis" points to some signs of hope, including the growing conviction of "a radical interdependence and consequently of the need for a solidarity which will take up interdependence and transfer it to the moral plane."[203]

The central chapter 5 sees the contemporary world as a world subject to "structures of sin"[204] and engaged in idolatry. The encyclical longs for an urgent change of human relationships to each other and to self, with regard to human communities, and with regard to nature. Wherever reciprocal dependence is recognized, "the correlative response as a moral and social attitude, as a 'virtue,' is solidarity." The encyclical explicitly differentiates solidarity from every feeling of vague sympathy and from every superficial emotion. It understands solidarity as a firm and continual resolve to engage oneself for the "common good . . . because we are all really responsible for all."[205]

According to "Sollicitudo Rei Socialis," the praxis of solidarity within each society becomes effective "when its members recognize one another as persons." This papal teaching document particularly emphasizes the solidarity of the poor among themselves, which includes both mutual assistance and public manifestations that denounce current injustice and give expression to the just demands of the poor. According to John Paul, on the level of international relations "interdependence must be transformed into solidarity, based upon the principle that the goods of creation are meant for all." Solidarity, the text continues, "helps us to see the 'other'— whether a person, people or nation—not just as some kind of instrument, with a work capacity and physical strength to be exploited at low cost and then discarded when no longer useful, but as our 'neighbor,' a 'helper' (cf. Gen 2:18-20)." The pope considers it necessary that mutual distrust be transformed into collaboration. "This is precisely the act proper to solidarity among individuals and nations." Where solidarity occurs, the path to peace and justice is open. On that basis John Paul can say, *"Opus solidarietatis pax*, peace as the fruit of solidarity."[206] Furthermore, the encyclical talks explicitly about global solidarity, saying that "an essential condition for global solidarity is autonomy and free self-determination. . . . But at the same time solidarity demands a readiness to accept sacrifices necessary for the good of the whole world community."[207]

Although the most recent[208] social encyclical, "Centesimus Annus" in 1991, makes cursory reference to solidarity, the text does not contain perspectives that give further systematic development to the theme.

At the conclusion of this brief synopsis of the theme of solidarity in ecclesial teaching,[209] I would like to point to a highly significant declaration of the Pontifical Commission Iustitia et Pax on the theme "The Church and Racism."[210] This document, which bears the subtitle "Towards a More Fraternal Society," explains solidarity as something that goes beyond brotherhood. First the declaration highlights the importance of respecting the differences between peoples, cultures, and human communities, as well as the significance of brotherhood—a significance that goes beyond such respect. Then the text continues: "Recognition of fraternity is not enough. One must go on to effective solidarity between all, in particular between rich and poor."[211]

Ecclesial and Universal Solidarity as Christopraxis

In the course of the Industrial Revolution of the eighteenth and nineteenth centuries, the labor movement constituted itself as an oppositional power to the existing class relations. It organized itself both nationally and internationally with the goal of powerfully op-

posing the current exploitation of the proletariat, struggling against
the refusal to provide the basic necessities of life and against the sup-
pression of the rights of the proletariat, overcoming the dynamic of
workers being played off against each other, and together achieving
the collective interest. Inasmuch as the labor movement stepped forward to struggle in solidarity with each other for their own liberation, the movement had in view the anticipation of a new form of
social life in which there would be a free association of all, an association characterized by solidarity rather than slavish oppression.
This is the teleological perspective of international solidarity.

The strength of the Marxian and internationalist conception lies
in the fact that it takes sides. Its strength lies in the fact that it discerns concrete subjects and gives a central place to the organizational question. Solidarity understood along Marxist lines is
essentially class solidarity. This also brings to light its problematic
character. Solidarity understood along Marxist lines proceeds from
the assumption, grounded in a philosophy of history, that the proletariat is the subject of the liberation of all. The Marxist conception
lays claim to an objectivity founded in actually existing class relations. But this objectivity is not present in Western capitalism, miti-
gated as it is by the social welfare state. Nor was it present in the
state socialism of the East. Moreover, we must ask whether the concept of class solidarity is not ultimately particularistic.

By contrast, contemporary papal social teaching is universally directed from the very beginning. I see its strength in the distinction
between various dimensions of solidarity on the subjective, intersubjective, societal, international, and global levels. It makes clear
that in a fundamental way solidarity both is grounded in the recognition of the other and aims at that recognition. Admittedly, beyond
these analytical beginnings the qualities of papal social teaching are
chiefly those of moral appeal. It refers to the moral duty of solidarity
and introduces solidarity as a virtue, rather than submitting it to a
stringent analysis with the tools of the human and social sciences
and reflecting upon it theologically. To be sure, there are references
to grounding solidarity in the theology of creation ("Sollicitudo Rei
Socialis," §39), in the Trinity (ibid., §40), and in an ecclesiology of
communio (ibid.). What is lacking, though, is a systematic theologi-

cal foundation. Papal social teaching rightly emphasizes the necessity and the urgency of universal solidarity, but papal social teaching does not go far enough. On the one hand, it neglects to develop the ecclesial dimension of solidarity. On the other hand, it does think of solidarity in a way that is radically universal: namely, in a way that transcends the present generation and the present world.

A church that has been internationally organized for centuries longer than the labor movement and that encompasses persons of various classes, peoples, and cultures must wrestle with the question of its own international solidarity, directed both externally and internally. So far papal social teaching has not articulated this kind of ecclesial solidarity. This solidarity first becomes a theme for a church that no longer conceives of unity in a monolithic and Eurocentric way, but sets out on the road to a "culturally polycentric global church."[212] This kind of truly catholic global church brings into view the solidarity of God's people with each other, the solidarity of the various members of the one body of Christ in communal christopraxis.

The insight into the necessity of ecclesial solidarity entails first of all the insight that the church itself is divided. It is divided not only into confessions and denominations, but also between North and South. In view of this division the church must take a side. It must act in accordance with the partiality of Jesus and of God. Ecclesial solidarity is often mobilized by means of diaconal, prophetic, empathetic, and even suffering support and help for persecuted Christians and churches in other countries. At a basic level it is guided by the knowledge and the recognition that the "others"—Christians, ecclesial bodies, and churches—belong to the one body of Christ. This type of ecclesial solidarity grows as christopraxis out of the experience of belonging together, out of the experience of sharing the one bread and wine. Such solidarity contradicts eo ipso every form of paternalism. It works against every type of racism, sexism, and imperialism. It excludes every attempt—be it pastoral, organizational, financial, or theological—to decide other people's futures for them.

The orientation of ecclesial solidarity is both international and universal. It is of decisive importance that ecclesial solidarity is embedded in universal solidarity. What this really means has so far not been thought through with sufficient radicality in church teaching. Universal solidarity is not only geographically universal, but temporally universal. Universal solidarity is concerned with the future of the yet unborn and with the future of the world. Picking up on Walter Benjamin, Helmut Peukert has shown that such solidarity falls into self-contradiction if it does not include the victims of history, those who have been annihilated in the past. Universal solidarity includes anticipatory and anamnestic solidarity. Such solidarity can be conceived only theologically. The theological theory of action is a fundamental-practical, postidealist theology[213] that does just that. As such the theological theory of action of course does not triumphalistically exalt itself over a conception that is able to locate the weak messianic power of solidarity only[214] of human beings. Instead of seeking to outdo this concept of solidarity by means of idealist metaphysics, the theological theory of action points to what its own tradition holds fast as a fundamental memory: the testimony that the action of the biblical witnesses elucidates and makes persuasively visible, and that must be proven and verified in the christopraxis of faith.

Solidarity is fundamentally neither a virtue nor a principle, but a social praxis of subjects and collectives. The solidarity of the oppressed in their struggle for liberation necessarily looks different from that of the rich with the poor. The latter entails, first of all, repentance. Solidarity of this type is tied to the knowledge, the recognition, and the confession of one's own guilt. This dimension of solidarity is clearly enunciated in the Final Report of the European Ecumenical Assembly, "Peace with Justice."[215] This document expresses not only the international, global dimension, but also the ecological dimension as "solidarity with all of God's creation."[216]

Universal solidarity as anticipatory and anamnestic christopraxis is grounded in the partiality and praxis of Jesus Christ, in Christ's resurrection in the bread and wine of Christ's body shared in solidarity, in the community of Christ's church, in the expectation of the resurrection of the dead and the second coming of Christ. Universal solidarity grounded in this way becomes the central category for a particular kind of fundamental theology. A fundamental theology of this type assures itself of its own location and interest contextually, while at the same time being globally oriented. It is carried out in an interdisciplinary manner in conversation with the other sciences. It studies what constitutes solidarity, how solidarity arises and develops, and how solidarity both has been and is being learned and realized. It productively engages social movements in a critical manner. It has an ecumenical and global orientation, but at the same time learns from church teaching and inspires church teaching and praxis by its own reflection and critique.

Solidarity is fundamentally both human and theological. Human identity is constituted by the recognition of the other and of others as persons who have the same rights, needs, and necessities of life. Solidarity must be learned in a process that transcends existing relations and aims at contextually and globally oriented, communal, and universal attention, respect and responsibility. In addition repentance is required:

> Today repentance and return to God means seeking a way . . . into a society in which human beings possess equal rights and live in solidarity with each other, . . . into a multiplicity of cultures, traditions and peoples, . . . into a renewed community of men and women in church and society, in which women bear at all levels an equal share of responsibility with men, and in which they can freely introduce their gifts, insights, values and experiences, . . . into a society in which the creation of peace and the peaceful resolution of conflicts is sought out and maintained, and into a community of peoples who in solidarity contribute to the good of others, . . . into a community of human beings with all creatures, in which the rights and integrity of all creatures are respected, . . . into a community that is aware that it needs constant forgiveness and renewal, and that praises God for God's love and gifts.[217]

ABBREVIATIONS

BBB - Bonner biblische Beiträge
BevTh - Beiträge zur evangelischen Theologie
CD - K. Barth, *Church Dogmatics*, ed. G. W. Bromiley and T. F. Torrance
(Edinburgh: T. and T. Clark, 1936-77)
CS - Communicatio Socialis
DocVatII - W. M. Abbott and J. Gallagher, eds., *The Documents of Vatican
II* (New York: Herder and Herder; New York: Association, 1966)
FRLANT - Forschungen zur Religion und Literatur des Alten und Neuen
Testaments
FZPhTh - Freiburger Zeitschrift für Philosophie und Theologie
HThK - Herders Theologischer Kommentar zum Neuen Testament
MECW - K. Marx and F. Engels, *Collected Works* (London: Lawrence and
Wishart, 1975-82)
NHThG - P. Eicher, ed., *Neues Handbuch theologischer Grundbegriffe*
(Munich: Kösel, 1984-85)
NTA - Neutestamentliche Abhandlungen
QD - Quaestiones Disputatae
SBB - Stuttgarter biblische Beiträge
SBS - Stuttgarter Bibelstudien
ThRv - Theologische Revue
ZKT - Zeitschrift für Katholische Theologie
ZNW - Zeitschrift für die neutestamentliche Wissenschaft

NOTES

Introduction: Contours of a Theological Theory of Action

1. "Science" can be a misleading translation of the German *Wissenschaft*, since "science" often has the limited reference of the "natural sciences." The German word does not give preference to that particular branch of knowing, to that particular *scientia*, but refers equally to chemistry and philosophy, physics and art history—*Trans.*

Chapter 1. The Approach of a Communicative Theory of Action

1. J. Habermas, *The Theory of Communicative Action*, trans. T. McCarthy, vol. 1, *Reason and the Rationalization of Society* (Boston: Beacon Press, 1983), 287.

2. Cf. J. L. Austin, *How to Do Things with Words*, 2nd ed., ed. J. O. Urmson and Marina Sbisà (Cambridge, Mass.: Harvard Univ. Press, 1962); E. Arens, *The Logic of Pragmatic Thinking: From Peirce to Habermas*, trans. D. Smith (Atlantic Highlands, N.J.: Humanities Press, 1994), 50-55.

3. Habermas, *Theory of Communicative Action*, vol. 1, 293.

4. Ibid., 307.

5. J. Habermas, "Erläuterungen zum Begriff des kommunikativen Handelns," in *Vorstudien und Ergänzungen zur Theorie des kommunikativen Handelns* (Frankfurt am Main: 1984), 596.

6. Ibid., 599.

7. Habermas, *Theory of Communicative Action*, vol. 1, 138.

8. Ibid., 94.

9. Ibid., 9.

10. Ibid., 18.

11. Ibid., 42.

12. Ibid., 222.

13. Ibid., 242; cf. E. Arens, "Kommunikative Rationalität und Religion," in E. Arens, O. John, and P. Rottländer, *Erinnerung, Befreiung, Solidarität: Benjamin, Marcuse, Habermas und die politische Theologie* (Düsseldorf: 1991), 145-200, 169ff.

14. J. Habermas, *Moral Consciousness and Communicative Action*, trans. C. Lenhardt and S. Weber Nicholsen (Cambridge, Mass.: MIT Press, 1990); J. Habermas, *Erläuterungen zur Diskursethik* (Frankfurt am Main: Suhrkamp Verlag, 1991); K.-O. Apel, *Diskurs und Verantwortung* (Frankfurt am Main: 1990).

15. Habermas, *Erläuterungen zur Diskursethik*, 11-12.

16. Ibid., 11.

17. Ibid., 12.

18. Habermas, *Theory of Communicative Action*, vol. 1, 42. On the concept and status of the ideal speech situation, cf. the section below entitled "Truth and Consensus."

19. Habermas, "Wahrheitstheorien," in *Vorstudien*, 127-83, 177.

20. Cf. R. Alexy, "Eine Theorie des praktischen Diskurses," in W. Oelmüller, ed., *Normenbegründung—Normendurchsetzung* (Paderborn: 1978), 22-58; Habermas, *Moral Consciousness*, 87-92.

21. J. Habermas, "Discourse Ethics: Notes on a Program of Philosophical Justification," in *Moral Consciousness*, 89.

22. Ibid., 63.

23. Ibid., 65.

24. Ibid., 92-93.

25. Apel, *Diskurs und Verantwortung*, 121.

26. Ibid., 116.

27. Ibid.

28. Cf. ibid., esp. 103-53, 179-216; K.-O. Apel, *Towards a Transformation of Philosophy*, trans. G. Aday and D. Frisby, International Library of Phenomenology and Moral Sciences (London: Routledge and Kegan Paul, 1980); H. Peukert, *Science, Action and Fundamental Theology: Toward a Theology of Communicative Action*, trans. J. Bohman (Cambridge, Mass.: MIT Press, 1984), 182-93; H. Peukert, "Intersubjektivität—Kommunikationsgemeinschaft—Religion," in M. M. Olivetti, ed., *Intersoggettività—Socialità—Religione*, Archivio di Filosofia 54 (Padua: 1986), 167-78; cf. E. Arens, "Befreiungsethik als Herausforderung," in *Orientierung* 55 (1991): 193-96.

29. J. Habermas, "What Is Universal Pragmatics?" in *Communication and the Evolution of Society*, trans. T. McCarthy (Boston: Beacon Press, 1979), 63.

30. Cf. J. Habermas, "Vorbereitende Bemerkungen zu einer Theorie der kommunikativen Kompetenz," in J. Habermas and N. Luhmann, *Theorie der Gesellschaft oder Sozialtechnologie—Was leistet die Systemforschung?* (Frankfurt am Main: 1971), 101-41; Habermas, "Wahrheitstheorien."

31. Habermas, "Wahrheitstheorien," 136.

32. Habermas, "Vorbereitende Bemerkungen," 122.

33. Ibid., 136.

34. Ibid., 137.

35. Ibid., 139.

36. Ibid., 140.

37. A. Beckermann, "Die realistischen Voraussetzungen der Konsenstheorie von J. Habermas," in *Zeitschrift für allgemeine Wissenschaftstheorie* 2 (1972): 63-80, 67; cf. K. Füssel, "Die sprachanalytische und wissenschaftstheoretische Diskussion um den Begriff der Wahrheit in ihrer Relevanz für eine systematische Theologie" (doct. diss., University of Münster, 1975).

38. Beckermann, "Voraussetzungen der Konsenstheorie," 80.

39. O. Höffe, "Kritische Überlegungen zur Konsenstheorie der Wahrheit," *Philosophisches Jahrbuch* 83 (1976): 313-32, 327; cf. G. Skirbekk, "Rationaler Konsens und Ideale Sprechsituation als Geltungsgrund? Über Recht und Grenze eines tranzendentalpragmatischen Geltungskonzepts," in W. Kuhlmann and D. Böhler, eds., *Kommunikation und Reflexion: Festschrift für K.-O. Apel* (Frankfurt am Main: 1982), 54-82, 72ff.

40. L. B. Puntel, *Wahrheitstheorien in der neueren Philosophie* (Darmstadt: 1978), 164.

41. Ibid., 163.

42. Cf. N. Rescher, *The Coherence Theory of Truth* (Oxford: Clarendon Press, 1973).

43. Cf. Puntel, *Wahrheitstheorien*, 200-204, with reference to B. Blanshard, *The Nature of Thought* (New York: Macmillan, 1940); cf. H. Kraml, "Konvergenz der Wahrheitstheorien als Wahrheitstheorie," in *ZKT* 101 (1979): 443-53.

44. Cf. Puntel, *Wahrheitstheorien*, 192-96; cf. Rescher, *Coherence Theory*, 169-75.

45. Puntel, *Wahrheitstheorien*, 211; ellipses in original.

46. Ibid., 215.

47. Kraml, "Konvergenz der Wahrheitstheorien," 453.

48. Cf. J. Habermas, "A Reply to My Critics," trans. T. McCarthy, in J. B. Thompson and D. Held, eds., *Habermas: Critical Debates* (Cambridge, Mass.: MIT Press, 1982), 239, 274, 275.

49. Habermas, *Theory of Communicative Action*, vol. 1, 42.

50. Habermas, "Reply to My Critics," 273ff.; J. Habermas, "Ein Interview mit der *New Left Review*," in *Die neue Unübersichtlichkeit: Kleine politische Schriften V*, Edition Suhrkamp 1321 (Frankfurt am Main: Suhrkamp Verlag, 1985), 213–57, 227ff.; K.-O. Apel, "Fallibilismus, Konsenstheorie der Wahrheit und Letztbegründung," in Forum für Philosophie Bad Homburg, ed., *Philosophie und Begründung* (Frankfurt am Main: 1987), 116–211, 151ff.; A. Wellmer, *Ethik und Dialog* (Frankfurt am Main: 1986), 72ff.

51. Cf. K.-O. Apel, "C. S. Peirce and Post-Tarskian Truth," in E. Freeman, ed., *The Relevance of Charles Peirce* (La Salle, Ill.: 1983), 189–223; Apel, "Fallibilismus."

52. See also Peukert, *Science, Action and Fundamental Theology*.

53. Subtitle of the German edition of Peukert's *Science, Action and Fundamental Theology*; the English edition replaces it with "Toward a Theology of Communicative Action."

54. Peukert, *Science, Action and Fundamental Theology*, 211.

55. Ibid., 213; cf. J. Habermas, *Texte und Kontexte* (Frankfurt am Main: 1991), 143. Cf. T. Pröpper, *Erlösungsglaube und Freiheitsgeschichte*, 2nd ed. (Munich: 1988), 165–71.

56. Peukert, *Science, Action and Fundamental Theology*, 214; cf. Habermas, *Texte und Kontexte*, 147–48.

57. Peukert, *Science, Action and Fundamental Theology*, 214; cf. Habermas, *Texte und Kontexte*, 142.

58. Peukert, *Science, Action and Fundamental Theology*, 215. With regard to Peukert's approach, cf. the works named in E. Arens, "Kleine Bilanz der bisherigen Peukertrezeption," in H.-U. von Brachel and N. Mette, eds., *Kommunikation und Solidarität* (Freiburg: 1985), 14–32; as well as in E. Arens, "Theologie nach Habermas," in E. Arens, ed., *Habermas und die Theologie*, 2nd ed. (Düsseldorf: 1989), 9–38. Cf. also O. John, "Fortschrittskritik und Erinnerung," in Arens, John, and Rottländer, *Erinnerung, Befreiung, Solidarität*, 13–80, 22ff.; P. Rottländer, "Philosophie, Gesellschaftstheorie und die Permanenz der Religion," ibid., 81–144, 105ff.

59. Cf. the following articles by H. Peukert: "Sprache und Freiheit: Zur Pragmatik ethischer Rede," in F. Kamphaus and R. Zerfass, eds., *Ethische Predigt und Alltagsverhalten* (Munich: 1977), 44–75; "Kontingenzerfahrung und Identitätsfindung," in J. Blank and G. Hasenhüttl, eds., *Erfahrung, Glaube und Moral* (Düsseldorf: 1982), 76–102; "Fundamentaltheologie," *NHThG*, vol. 2, 16–25; "Was ist eine Praktische Wissenschaft?" in O. Fuchs, ed., *Theologie und Handeln* (Düsseldorf: 1984), 64–79; "Enlightenment and Theology as Unfinished Projects," in D. S. Browning and F. Schüssler

Fiorenza, eds., *Habermas, Modernity, and Public Theology* (New York: Crossroad, 1992), 43-65.

60. Cf. the following articles by H. Peukert: "Die Zukunft der Bildung," *Frankfurter Hefte-extra* (1984): 129-37; "Kritische Theorie und Pädagogik," *Zeitschrift für Pädagogik* 39 (1983): 195-217; "Tradition und Transformation—Zu einer pädagogischen Theorie der Überlieferung," *Religionspädagogische Beiträge*, no. 19 (1987): 16-34; "Praxis universaler Solidarität," in E. Schillebeeckx, ed., *Mystik und Politik: Theologie im Ringen um Geschichte und Gesellschaft: Johann Baptist Metz zu Ehren* (Mainz: Matthias-Grünewald, 1988), 172-85; " 'Erziehung nach Auschwitz'—eine überholte Situationsdefinition?" *Neue Sammlung* 30 (1990): 345-54; "Basic Problems of a Critical Theory of Education," *Journal of Philosophy of Education* 26 (1993); "Present Challenges to the Educational Theory of Modernity," *Education* 47 (1993): 7-24.

61. J. Habermas, "The Unity of Reason in the Diversity of Its Voices," in *Postmetaphysical Thinking: Philosophical Essays*, trans. W. M. Hohengarten (Cambridge, Mass.: MIT Press, 1992), 145; Habermas, *Texte und Kontexte*, 110-56. Cf. Arens, "Kommunikative Rationalität und Religion," in Arens, John, and Rottländer, *Erinnerung, Befreiung, Solidarität*, 188ff.

62. Peukert, "Sprache und Freiheit," 66.

63. Cf. Arens, "Theologie nach Habermas," 9-38.

64. Cf. H.-J. Höhn, *Vernunft—Glaube—Politik: Reflexionsstufen einer christlichen Sozialethik* (Paderborn: 1990), esp. 140-70; H.-J. Höhn, "Vernunft—Kommunikation—Diskurs: Zu Anspruch und Grenze der Transzendentalpragmatik als Basistheorie der Philosophie," *FZPhTh* 36 (1989): 93-128, 124ff.; H.-J. Höhn, "Sozialethik im Diskurs: Skizzen zum Gespräch zwischen Diskursethik und Katholischer Soziallehre," in Arens, ed., *Habermas und die Theologie*, 187-98.

65. Höhn, *Vernunft—Glaube—Politik*, 147.

66. Here Höhn appeals to Peukert among others; cf. Höhn, *Vernunft—Glaube—Politik*, 151ff. Cf. Peukert, *Science, Action and Fundamental Theology*, 202-10, as well as Habermas's response in "Reply to My Critics," 246-47, which Höhn likewise cites.

67. Höhn, *Vernunft—Glaube—Politik*, 158.

68. Ibid., 167, n. 52. One finds a similar use of metaphysics and the theory of meaning to superelevate the transcendental pragmatics of K.-O. Apel in P. Hofmann, *Glaubensbegründung: Die Transzendentalphilosophie der Kommunikationsgemeinschaft in fundamentaltheologischer Sicht* (Frankfurt am Main: 1988); cf. H. Verweyen, *Gottes letztes Wort: Grun-*

driss der Fundamentaltheologie (Düsseldorf: 1991), 179–81, as well as my review in *ThRv* 87 (1991): 46–48.

69. Cf. C. Kissling, "Die Theorie des kommunikativen Handelns in Diskussion," in *FZPhTh* 37 (1990): 233–52, 249–50.

70. Cf. W. Pauly, *Wahrheit und Konsens: Die Erkenntnistheorie von Jürgen Habermas und ihre theologische Relevanz* (Frankfurt am Main: 1989).

71. Ibid., 151.

72. Ibid., 188.

73. Ibid., 196.

74. Ibid., 328.

75. Ibid., 339.

76. Cf. esp. Pauly's reflections on Habermas's reception of Jewish mysticism (ibid., 317–27), and the similarly situated positions of R. J. Siebert (*The Critical Theory of Religion* [New York: Mouton, 1985]) and J. Glebe-Möller (*A Political Dogmatic* [Philadelphia: Fortress Press, 1987]); cf. Arens, "Theologie nach Habermas," 11ff., 22–23.

Chapter 2.   Biblical Foundations of a Theological Theory of Action

1. O.-H. Pesch, "Evangelium/Gesetz," *NHThG*, vol. 1: 317–32, 318.

2. Cf. E. Güttgemanns, *Offene Fragen zur Formgeschichte des Evangeliums* (Munich: 1970).

3. Cf. R. Feneberg and W. Feneberg, *Das Leben Jesu im Evangelium*, QD 88 (Freiburg: 1980).

4. Cf. D. Dormeyer, *Evangelium als literarische und theologische Gattung*, Erträge der Forschung 263 (Darmstadt: 1989).

5. Cf. R. Reck, *Kommunikation und Gemeindeaufbau: Eine Studie zu Entstehung, Leben und Wachstum paulinischer Gemeinden in den Kommunikationsstrukturen der Antike*, SBB 22 (Stuttgart: 1991); cf. my review in *ThRv* 87 (1991): 397–98.

6. On the history of the formation of pragmatic theory, cf. my exposition in E. Arens, *The Logic of Pragmatic Thinking: From Peirce to Habermas*, trans. D. Smith (Atlantic Highlands, N.J.: Humanities Press, 1994). The basic insights are summarized in E. Arens, *Bezeugen und Bekennen: Elementare Handlungen des Glaubens* (Düsseldorf: 1989), 16ff.

7. The German plays upon the verb *handeln* ("to act"), which in the form *handeln von* means "to be about"—*Trans.*

8. This is the fundamental insight of speech act theory as it has been developed by John L. Austin and John R. Searle, and received and further developed by Jürgen Habermas and Karl-Otto Apel. Cf. J. L. Austin, *How to Do Things with Words*, 2nd ed., ed. J. O. Urmson and Marina Sbisà (Cambridge, Mass.: Harvard Univ. Press, 1962); J. R. Searle, *Speech Acts: An Essay in the Philosophy of Language* (London: Cambridge Univ. Press, 1969).

9. G. Friedrich, "εὐαγγελίζομαι etc., "*Theological Dictionary of the New Testament*, vol. 2, ed. G. Kittel, trans. and ed. G. Bromiley (Grand Rapids, Mich.: Eerdmans, 1964), 721-37, 721-22.

10. Cf. T. Söding, *Glaube bei Markus: Glaube an das Evangelium, Gebetsglaube und Wunderglaube im Kontext der markinischen Basileiatheologie und Christologie*, 2nd ed., SBB 12 (Stuttgart: 1987), 234-35.

11. P. Stuhlmacher, "The Pauline Gospel," trans. J. Vriend, in P. Stuhlmacher, ed., *The Gospel and the Gospels* (Grand Rapids, Mich.: Eerdmans, 1991), 149-72, 163.

12. This is the decided position of H. Frankermölle, "Jesus als deuterojesajanischer Freudenbote? Zur Rezeption von Jes 52,7 und 61,1 im NT, durch Jesus und in den Targumin," in H. Frankermölle and K. Kertelge, eds., *Vom Urchristentum zu Jesus: Festschrift für Joachim Gnilka* (Freiburg: 1989), 34-68.

13. Reck, *Kommunikation*, 165-66.

14. Cf. H. Frankermölle, *Biblische Handlungsanweisungen: Beispiele pragmatischer Exegese* (Mainz: 1983), 50-75. With regard to Mark's narrative strategy and his guiding of the reception of his text, cf. R. Zwick, *Montage im Markusevangelium: Studien zur narrativen Organisation der ältesten Jesuserzählung*, SBB 18 (Stuttgart: 1989).

15. G. Friedrich, "εὐαγγελίζομαι etc.," 730.

16. Reck, *Kommunikation*, 168; cf. 168-78.

17. H. Merklein, "Zum Verständnis des paulinischen Begriffs 'Evangelium,' " in Katholisches Bibelwerk, ed., *Dynamik im Wort: Lehre von der Bibel, Leben aus der Bibel* (Stuttgart: 1983), 217-33, 231.

18. The German word is *Reich*, which is also the word translated as "reign" in the phrase "reign of God"—*Trans.*

19. P. Dschulnigg, *Sprache, Redaktion und Intention des Markusevangeliums*, SBB 11 (Stuttgart: 1984), 387-88.

20. H. Frankermölle, *Evangelium: Begriff und Gattung*, SBB 15 (Stuttgart: 1988), 151.

21. F. Prast, *Presbyter und Evangelium in nachapostolischer Zeit*, Forschung zur Bibel 29 (Stuttgart: 1979), 105, n. 283.

22. S. J. Schmidt, *Texttheorie* (Munich: 1973), 145.

23. This nice formulation is from J. R. Donahue, *The Gospel in Parable: Metaphor, Narrative, and Theology in the Synoptic Gospels*, 2nd ed. (Minneapolis: Fortress Press, 1989).

24. In my opinion it is not only the beginning of the Sayings tradition that is to be placed during Jesus' lifetime—thus rightly H. Schürmann, "Die vorösterlichen Anfänge der Logien-Tradition," in H. Schürmann, *Traditionsgeschichtliche Untersuchungen zu den synoptischen Evangelien* (Düsseldorf: 1968), 39–65. The tradition of deeds would also begin with Jesus' public activity, insofar as word got around of his sovereign, provocative, liberating, and scandalous action, and people told each other stories about Jesus' authoritative praxis. Cf. F. Mussner et al., "Methodologie der Frage nach dem historischen Jesus," in K. Kertelge, ed., *Rückfrage nach Jesus*, QD 63 (Freiburg: 1974), 118–47, 120ff. On the Jesus phenomenon becoming language, cf. P. G. Müller, *Der Traditionsprozess im Neuen Testament* (Freiburg: 1982). Müller, though, sees only the *homo loquens* (the person speaking) Jesus of Nazareth at the origin of the process of tradition (113ff.) and does not view him more comprehensively as *homo agens* (the person doing).

25. On the letter as a means of communication in antiquity and with Paul, cf. Reck, *Kommunikation*.

26. Frankermölle, *Evangelium*, 31.

27. R. Zwick claims that the gospel form "in its basic narrative layout" is beholden to Jesus' parables (Zwick, *Montage im Markusevangelium*, 626); cf. 626ff., at the end of his "Studies on the Narrative Organization of the Earlier Jesus Narrative." Arguing against this position is Frankermölle, *Evangelium*, 200. According to G. Theissen, the "miraculous story" of the Gospel of Mark develops out of the "compositional structure of the miracle stories" (G. Theissen, *The Miracle Stories of the Early Christian Tradition*, trans. F. McDonagh, ed. J. Riches [Edinburgh: T. and T. Clark, 1983], 215); cf. Dormeyer, *Evangelium*, 145–46. On the narrative genre cf. also F. Hahn, ed., *Der Erzähler des Evangeliums*, SBB 118/119 (Stuttgart: 1985).

28. B. Gerhardsson, "The Path of the Gospel Tradition," trans. J. Vriend, in Stuhlmacher, ed., *The Gospel and the Gospels*, 75–96, 88.

29. Cf. for example the diverse ways of specifying the goal set by the Gospel of Mark: as missionary in Dschulnigg, *Sprache*; as pastoral in E. Best, *Mark: The Gospel as Story* (Edinburgh: T. and T. Clark, 1984); as antiheretical in T. J. Weeden, *Mark: Traditions in Conflict* (Philadelphia: 1971).

30. With regard to the following discussion, cf. Arens, *The Logic of Pragmatic Thinking*, as well as the references to secondary literature given

there. Cf. also J. Gnilka, *Jesus von Nazaret: Botschaft und Geschichte*, 2nd ed., HThK, supp. vol. 3 (Freiburg: 1990); G. Stemberger, *Pharisäer, Sadduzäer, Essener*, SBS 144 (Stuttgart: 1991); J. D. Crossan, *The Historical Jesus: The Life of a Mediterranean Jewish Peasant* (San Francisco: Harper & Row, 1991).

31. J. Neusner, *The Rabbinic Traditions about the Pharisees before 70*, vol. 3 (Leiden: 1971), 300.

32. Cf. M. Hengel, *The Zealots: Investigations into the Jewish Freedom Movement in the Period from Herod I until 70 A.D.*, trans. D. Smith (Edinburgh: T. and T. Clark, 1989), 86–88, 227, 377.

33. Cf. J. Maier and K. Schubert, *Die Qumran-Essener* (Munich: 1973).

34. Cf. R. Pesch, *Jesu ureigean Taten?* QD 52 (Freiburg: 1970); Theissen, *Miracle Stories*, 277ff.; M. Smith, *Jesus the Magician* (New York: Harper & Row, 1978).

35. Cf. the account by Tacitus, reported by Gnilka (*Jesus von Nazaret*, 129), of two healings performed by the Roman Caesar Vespasian in Egypt. Gnilka's commentary is that "the action issues in a public theatrical display. The story is told *ad gloriam Caesaris*" (ibid., 130).

36. Cf. L. Schottroff and W. Stegemann, *Jesus and the Hope of the Poor*, trans. M. J. O'Connell (Maryknoll, N.Y.: Orbis, 1986), 7–13.

37. Cf. G. Baumbach, *Jesus von Nazareth im Lichte der jüdischen Gruppenbildung* (Berlin: 1971), 32–48.

38. Hengel, *Zealots*, 339.

39. Cf. G. Vermes, *Jesus the Jew* (London: Philadelphia: Fortress Press, 1973), 42–57.

40. K. Müller, "Jesus und die Sadduzäer," in H. Merklein and J. Lange, eds., *Biblische Randbemerkungen: Schülerfestschrift für Rudolf Schnackenburg zum 60. Geburtstag*, 2nd ed. (Würzburg: 1974), 3–24, 7.

41. K. Schubert, *Jesus im Lichte der Religionsgeschichte des Judentums* (Vienna: 1973), 52.

42. J. Neusner characterizes the Pharisees before 70 as a "table-fellowship-sect" (Neusner, *Rabbinic Traditions*, vol. 3, 305-6).

43. Cf. M. Hengel, *The Charismatic Leader and His Followers*, trans. J. Greig (New York: Crossroad, 1981), 50–57.

44. Cf. E. Schillebeeckx, *Jesus: An Experiment in Christology*, trans. H. Hoskins (New York: Crossroad, 1979), 218–29.

45. Cf. G. Theissen, *Sociology of Early Palestinian Christianity*, trans. J. Bowden (Philadelphia: Fortress Press, 1978), 8–16.

46. M. Trautmann, *Zeichenhafte Handlungen Jesu*, Forschungen zur Bibel 37 (Würzburg: 1980), 228.

47. Theissen, *Sociology of Early Palestinian Christianity*, 17.

48. E. Schüssler Fiorenza, *In Memory of Her: A Feminist Theological Reconstruction of Christian Origins* (New York: Crossroad, 1983), 140.

49. When the author uses the German word *Herrschaft* in a clearly negative sense, as here, it is translated as *domination*. When the author does not particularly or clearly intend a negative sense, *Herrschaft* is translated as *rule*, most notably in the compound *Gottesherrschaft*, "God's rule"— Trans.

50. Cf. S. Applebaum, "Economic Life in Palestine," in *The Jewish People of the First Century* (Philadelphia: Fortress Press, 1976), 631-700.

51. Cf. H. Merklein, *Die Gottesherrschaft als Handlungsprinzip*, 3rd ed. (Würzburg: 1984), 48ff.; P. Hoffmann and V. Eid, *Jesus von Nazareth und eine christliche Moral*, 3rd ed., QD 66 (Freiburg: 1979), 31ff.

52. Cf. R. Meyer, "Der *Am ha-Ares*: Ein Beitrag zur Religionssoziologie Palästinas im ersten und zweiten nachchristlichen Jahrhundert," *Judaica* 3 (1947): 169-99, 196-97.

53. Cf. R. Zerfass, "Herrschaftsfreie Kommunikation—eine Forderung an die kirchliche Verkündigung," in W. Weber, ed., *Macht—Dienst— Herrschaft in Kirche und Gesellschaft* (Freiburg: 1974), 81-106.

54. D. Bonhoeffer gives this basic feature a rich and concise formulation when he says that "Jesus is there only for others" (D. Bonhoeffer, *Letters and Papers from Prison*, 3rd ed., ed. E. Bethge, trans. R. Fuller, rev. trans. F. Clarke et al. [London: SCM Press, 1967], 209).

55. E. Schüssler Fiorenza, *In Memory of Her*, 143.

56. The German word *Gottesdienst* translates literally as "service of God," but it is also used more narrowly in the same sense as "worship service" in English—*Trans*.

57. H. Braun, *Jesus of Nazareth: The Man and His Time*, trans. E. Kalin (Philadelphia: Fortress Press, 1979), 63.

58. Cf. Merklein, *Gottesherrschaft*; H. Merklein, *Jesu Botschaft von der Gottesherrschaft*, SBS 111 (Stuttgart: 1983).

59. Cf. U. B. Müller, "Vision und Botschaft: Erwägungen zur prophetischen Struktur der Verkündigung Jesu," *Zeitschrift für Theologie und Kirche* 74 (1977): 416-48.

60. H. Flender, *Die Botschaft von der Herrschaft Gottes* (Munich: 1968), 48.

61. Merklein, *Gottesherrschaft*, 218.

62. Hoffmann and Eid, *Jesus von Nazareth*, 50.

63. Cf. Merklein, *Gottesherrschaft*, 119.

64. Cf. Schillebeeckx, *Jesus*; Hoffmann and Eid, *Jesus von Nazareth*, 53.

65. With regard to the following discussion, cf. Arens, *The Logic of Pragmatic Thinking*; E. Arens, "Metaphorische Erzählungen und kommunikative Handlungen Jesu," *Biblische Zeitschrift* 32 (1988): 52-71, and the literature examined in that article. Cf. also K. Erlemann, *Das Bild Gottes in den synoptischen Gleichnissen*, Beiträge zur Wissenschaft vom Alten und Neuen Testament 126 (Stuttgart: 1988); E. Rau, *Reden in Vollmacht, Hintergrund, Form und Anliegen der Gleichnisse Jesu*, FRLANT 149 (Göttingen: 1990).

66. Cf. P. Hoffmann, " 'Er weiss, was ihr braucht . . .' (Mt 6,7): Jesu einfache und konkrete Rede von Gott," in N. Lohfink et al., *"Ich will euer Gott werden,"* SBS 100 (Stuttgart: 1981), 151-76.

67. Cf. K. Schäfer, "Jesus on God," in J. B. Metz, ed., *New Questions on God*, Concilium 76 (New York: Herder and Herder, 1972), 58-66.

68. Cf. D. O. Via, *Parables: Their Literary and Existential Dimension* (Philadelphia: Fortress Press, 1967); W. Harnisch, *Die Gleichniserzählungen Jesu* (Göttingen: 1985).

69. P. Ricoeur, "Philosophische und theologische Hermeneutik," trans. K. Stock, in P. Ricoeur and E. Jüngel, *Metapher: Zur Hermeneutik religiöser Sprache* (Munich: 1974), 24-44, 32.

70. Cf. P. Ricoeur, "Stellung und Funktion der Metapher in der biblischen Rede," trans. B. Link-Ewert, in Ricoeur and Jüngel, *Metapher*, 45-70; H. Weder, *Die Gleichnisse Jesu als Metaphern*, 3rd ed., FRLANT 120 (Göttingen: 1984).

71. J. D. Crossan, *Raid on the Articulate* (New York: Harper and Row, 1976).

72. Ricoeur, "Stellung und Funktion der Metapher," 55.

73. Cf. E. Arens, "Ein Tischgespräch über Essen und (Ex)Kommunikation: Das Gleichnis vom Festmahl (Lk 14,16-24)," *Katechetische Blätter* 111 (1986): 449-52. P. Dschulnigg objects that Pharisees "would hardly see [themselves] in people who reject God's invitation because of worldly affairs" (P. Dschulnigg, "Positionen des Gleichnisverständnisses im 20. Jahrhundert," *Theologische Zeitschrift* [Basel] 45 [1989]: 336-52, 344, n. 30). In my opinion this objection neglects the moment of distancing in fictional-metaphoric texts.

74. Concerning this concept, cf. P. Berger and T. Luckmann, *The Social Construction of Reality: A Treatise in the Sociology of Knowledge* (Garden City, N.Y.: Doubleday, 1966); H. Peukert, *Science, Action and Fundamental Theology: Toward a Theology of Communicative Action*, trans. J. Bohman (Cambridge, Mass.: MIT Press, 1984), 224.

75. Neusner, *Rabbinic Traditions*, vol. 3, 300.

0

76. Peukert, *Science, Action and Fundamental Theology*, 224.

77. This moment has been nicely elaborated in E. Linnemann, *Parables of Jesus: Introduction and Exposition*, trans. J. Sturdy (London: SPCK, 1966).

78. Schäfer, "Jesus on God," 64.

79. "Debt" and "guilt" are equally plausible translations of the German *Schuld—Trans.*

80. Schäfer, "Jesus on God," 59.

81. Cf. Weder, *Gleichnisse*, 68.

82. W. Magass, "Bemerkungen zur Gleichnisauslegung," *Kairos* 20 (1978): 40-52, 40.

83. Cf. E. Arens, "Towards a Theological Theory of Communicative Action," *Media Development* 28, no. 4 (1981): 12-16; also, comprehensively, Rau, *Reden*, 182-407.

84. Peukert, *Science, Action and Fundamental Theology*, 224.

85. Gnilka, *Jesus von Nazaret*, 201.

86. F. Mussner, "Gab es eine 'galiläische Krise'?" in P. Hoffmann, ed., *Orientierung an Jesus: Zur Theologie der Synoptiker: Für Josef Schmid* (Freiburg: Herder, 1973), 238-52; cf. A. Polag, *Die Christologie der Logienquelle*, Wissenschaftliche Monographien zum Alten und Neuen Testament 45 (Neukirchen-Vluyn: 1977); J. Sobrino, *Christology at the Crossroads: A Latin American Approach*, 4th ed. (London: 1984), 95ff.; for a critical perspective, see L. Oberlinner, *Todeserwartung und Todesgewissheit Jesu*, SBB 10 (Stuttgart: 1980), 79-109.

87. Mussner, "Krise," 247.

88. Cf. R. Schwager, *Jesus im Heilsdrama: Entwurf einer biblischen Erlösungslehre*, Innsbrucker Theologische Studien 29 (Innsbruck: 1990), 79-109.

89. Ibid., 80.

90. Concerning Schwager's conception, cf. E. Arens, "Dramatische Erlösungslehre aus der Perspektive einer theologischen Handlungstheorie," in J. Niewiadomski and W. Palaver, eds., *Dramatische Erlösungslehre: Ein Symposium* (Innsbruck: 1992), 165-77; cf. P. Fiedler, "Beim Herrn ist die Huld, bei ihm die Erlösung in Fülle," in M. Marcus et al., eds., *Israel und Kirche heute: Beiträge zum christlich-jüdischen Dialog: Für Ernst Ludwig Ehrlich* (Freiburg: 1991), 184-200.

91. Cf. M. Reiser, *Die Gerichtspredigt Jesu*, NTA 23 (Münster: 1990).

92. Ibid., 291-92.

93. R. Pesch, Review of E. Arens, *Kommunikative Handlungen*, ThRv 79 (1983): 371-73, 373.

94. J. G. du Plessis, "Clarity and Obscurity: A Study in Textual Communication of the Relation between Sender, Parable and Receiver in the Synoptic Gospels" (doct. diss., Stellenbosch, 1985), 254.

95. R. J. Siebert, *The Critical Theory of Religion* (New York: Mouton, 1985), 422.

96. Thus Reiser, *Gerichtspredigt*, 214; cf. Mussner, "Krise," 244; for an opposing point of view, see Oberlinner, *Todeserwartung*, 86-93.

97. Thus M. Hengel, "Das Gleichnis von den Weingärtnern Mc 12,1-12 im Lichte der Zenonpapyri und der rabbinischen Gleichnisse," *ZNW* 59 (1968): 1-39.

98. Trautmann, *Zeichenhafte Handlungen Jesu*, 119.

99. Gnilka, *Jesus von Nazaret*, 280; cf. Trautmann, *Zeichenhafte Handlungen Jesu*, 122ff.; G. Theissen, *Social Reality and the Early Christians: Theology, Ethics, and the World of the New Testament*, trans. M. Kohl (Minneapolis: Fortress Press, 1992), 94-114; Oberlinner, *Todeserwartung*, 125ff. Oberlinner takes the critical prophecy against the Temple as a basis for charges being brought against Jesus, but disputes the historicity of the cleansing of the Temple.

100. H. Schürmann, *Jesu ureigener Tod* (Freiburg: 1975), 93; cf. H. Schürmann, "Die Symbolhandlungen Jesu als eschatologische Erfüllungszeichen," *Bibel und Leben* 11 (1970): 29-41, 73-78; R. Pesch, *Wie Jesus das Abendmahl hielt* (Freiburg: 1977). On the controversy concerning the eucharistic supper, cf. P. Fiedler, "Probleme der Abendmahlsforschung," *Archiv für Liturgiewissenschaft* 24 (1982): 190-223.

101. Gnilka, *Jesus von Nazaret*, 284. P. Fiedler rightly insists that the only conceivable understanding of death on Jesus' part is one that is compatible with the message of the *basileia*. Fiedler, however, slackens the dramatic tension of Jesus' situation in Jerusalem: cf. P. Fiedler, "Probleme der Abendmahlsforschung," 204-5, 214-15.

102. Thus A. Vögtle, "Jesus von Nazareth: Die Urgemeinde," in R. Kottje and B. Moeller, eds., *Ökumenische Kirchengeschichte*, vol. 1 (Munich: 1970), 3-36, 23-24.

103. On Jesus' trial, cf. K. Kertelge, ed., *Der Prozess gegen Jesus*, 2nd ed., QD 112 (Freiburg: 1989), esp. the articles by J. Gnilka and K. Müller.

104. K. Müller, "Möglichkeit und Vollzug jüdischer Kapitalgerichtsbarkeit im Prozess gegen Jesus von Nazaret," in Kertelge, ed., *Der Prozess gegen Jesus*, 41-83, 75.

105. Ibid., 81-82; cf. Gnilka, *Jesus von Nazaret*, 307-8.

106. Cf. Oberlinner, *Todeserwartung*, 158.

107. Cf. Gnilka, *Jesus von Nazaret*, 312. Gnilka cites Cicero, who calls crucifixion "the most horrible and terrible capital punishment" (Cicero, *Pro Rabirio*, 5, 16); Josephus, according to whom crucifixion is the "most pitiful of deaths" (Josephus, *De bello judaico*, 7, 203); and Tacitus, who charactizes it as *"servile supplicium"* (Tacitus, *Historiarum*, 4, 11).

108. Peukert, *Science, Action and Fundamental Theology*, 225.

109. Ibid., 330.

110. With regard to the following discussion, cf. the detailed investigations in Arens, *Bezeugen und Bekennen*, and the references there to relevant literature. Cf. also E. Arens, "Elementare Handlungen des Glaubens," in O. Fuchs, ed., *Theologie und Handeln* (Düsseldorf: 1984), 80–101.

111. The English translation only partially indicates the interrelatedness of the key terms here: *Zeuge* ("witness"), *Zeugnis* ("testimony"), *bezeugen* ("to bear witness")—*Trans.*

112. H. P. Siller, "Die Schar der Zeugen in unseren Unterricht!" in G. Biemer and A. Biesinger, eds., *Christ werden braucht Vorbilder* (Mainz: 1983), 124–35, 128.

113. For the background of this concept, cf. F. Herzog, *God-Walk: Liberation Shaping Dogmatics* (Maryknoll, N.Y.: Orbis, 1988); M. K. Taylor, *Remembering Esperanza: A Cultural-Political Theology for North American Praxis* (Maryknoll, N.Y.: Orbis, 1990).

114. K. Kienzler, *Logik der Auferstehung* (Freiburg: 1976), 155; cf. K. Rahner, *Foundations of Christian Faith: An Introduction to the Idea of Christianity*, trans. W. V. Dych (New York: Crossroad, 1984), 276–78.

115. H. Kessler, *Sucht den Lebenden nicht bei den Toten: Die Auferstehung Jesu Christi*, 2nd ed. (Düsseldorf: 1987), 255.

116. Thus is nicely put in H. P. Siller, *Handbuch der Religionsdidaktik* (Freiburg: 1991), 172–75.

117. Cf. Kienzler, *Logik der Auferstehung*, 154.

118. Rahner, *Foundations of Christian Faith*, 241.

119. Ibid.

120. K. Löning, *Die Saulustradition in der Apostelgeschichte*, NTA (Münster: 1973), 139.

121. E. Nellessen, *Zeugnis für Jesus und das Wort: Exegetische Untersuchungen zum lukanischen Zeugnisbegriff*, BBB (Cologne: 1976), 19.

122. G. Ebeling, *The Nature of Faith*, trans. R. G. Smith (London: Collins, 1961), 70.

123. Cf. W. Kramer, *Christos Kyrios Gottessohn* (Zurich: 1963), 61ff.; K. Wengst, *Christologische Formeln und Lieder im Urchristentum* (Gütersloh: 1972), 131ff.

124. F. Hahn, *The Worship of the Early Church*, trans. D. E. Green, ed. J. Reumann (Philadelphia: Fortress Press, 1973), 85.

125. Cf. G. Bornkamm, "Das Bekenntnis im Hebräerbrief," in *Gesammelte Aufsätze*, vol. 2, *Studien zu Antike und Urchristentum* (Munich: C. Kaiser, 1959); H.-J. Klauck, "Bekenntnis zu Jesus und Zeugnis Gottes: Die christologische Linienführung im Ersten Johannesbrief," in C. Breytenbach and H. Paulsen, eds., *Anfänge der Christologie: Festschrift für Ferdinand Hahn zum 65. Geburtstag* (Göttingen: 1991), 293-306.

126. Cf. P. Vielhauer, "Gottesreich und Menschensohn in der Verkündigung Jesu," in *Aufsätze zum Neuen Testament* (Munich: 1965), 55-91, 76ff.; P. Hoffmann, *Studien zur Theologie der Logienquelle*, 3rd ed., NTA 8 (Münster: 1982), 328.

127. K. Wengst, *Der 1., 2. und 3. Brief des Johannes*, Ökumenischer Taschenbuchkommentar 16 (Gütersloh: 1978), 59.

128. K. Hemmerle, "Wahrheit und Zeugnis," in K. Hemmerle et al., *Theologie als Wissenschaft* (Freiburg: 1970), 54-72, 67.

129. Ibid., 63.

130. *CD*, vol. 4/3, trans. G. W. Bromiley, 44.

131. C. Geffré, *Le Christianisme au risque de l'interprétation* (Paris: 1983), 298.

132. O. Cullmann, *The Earliest Christian Confessions*, trans. J. K. S. Reid (London: Lutterworth, 1949); V. H. Nuefeld, *The Earliest Christian Confessions* (Grand Rapids, Mich.: Eerdmans, 1963); H. Schlier, "Die Anfänge des christlichen Credo," in B. Welte, ed., *Zur Frühgeschichte der Christologie*, QD 51 (Freiburg: Herder, 1970), 13-58.

133. Where English uses "Lord" in biblical and theological contexts, German uses *Herr*. In such contexts it is thus sometimes fitting to translate *Herrschaft* as "lordship," although it is generally rendered in the present work as "rule." See n. 49 above—*Trans.*

134. Geffré, *Le Christianisme*, 296.

135. Kessler, *Sucht den Lebenden*, 110-35.

136. *CD*, vol. 3/4, trans. A. T. Mackay et al., 75.

137. Cf. Kramer, *Christos*, 61ff.; Wengst, *Christologische Formeln*, 131ff.

138. G. Bornkamm, "Jesu Wort vom Bekennen," in *Gesammelte Aufsätze*, vol. 3, *Geschichte und Glaube* 1, BevTh 48 (Munich: C. Kaiser, 1968), 25-36, 32.

139. English sometimes uses "belief" and sometimes uses "faith" where German uses the one word *Glaube—Trans.*

140. Cf. Wengst, *Johannes*, 112ff.; Klauck, "Bekenntnis zu Jesus."

141. C. Geffré, "Le témoignage comme expérience et comme langage," in E. Castelli, ed., *Le témoignage* (Paris: 1972), 291–307, 298.

142. Cf. F. Mussner, *Der Jakobusbrief*, 4th ed., HThK (Freiburg: 1981), 225–26.

143. F. Krüger, "Strukturen konfessorischer Rede," in H. Feld et al., eds., *Grund und Grenzen des Dogmas* (Freiburg: 1972), 27–46, 46.

144. E. Jüngel, "Bekennen und Bekenntnis," in S. Herrmann and O. Sohngen, eds., *Theologie in Geschichte und Kunst: Walter Elliger zum 65. Geburtstag* (Witten: Luther-Verlag, 1968), 94–105, 105.

145. Cf. *CD*, vol. 1/2, trans. G. T. Thomson and H. Knight, 440–41; J.-P. Jossua, "Zeugnis," trans. M.-T. Wacker, in *NHThG*, vol. 4, 332–42, 340.

146. The text plays on the interrelatedness of the German words *Zeuge* ("witness"), *bezeugen* ("to [bear] witness"), and *überzeugen* ("to convince or persuade")—*Trans.*

147. K. Rahner, *Theological Investigations*, vol. 10, trans. D. Bourke (London: Darton, Longman and Todd, 1973), 125–49; cf. "Lumen Gentium," in *DocVatII*, 14–101, §11.

Chapter 3.   Systematic-Practical Perspectives

1. W. Kasper, "Das Wahrheitsverständnis der Theologie," in E. Coreth, ed., *Wahrheit in Einheit und Vielfalt* (Düsseldorf: 1987), 170–93, 173.

2. Ibid., 183.

3. H. von Soden, "Was ist Wahrheit? Vom geschichtlichen Begriff der Wahrheit," in *Urchristentum und Geschichte*, vol. 1 (Tübingen: Mohr [Siebeck], 1959), 1–24, 6. With regard to the following discussion, cf. E. Arens, "Zur Struktur theologischer Wahrheit," in *ZKT* 112 (1990): 1–17; cf. also the literature referenced there.

4. Von Soden, "Was ist Wahrheit?" 8.

5. Ibid., 10.

6. Cf. R. Bultmann, "Untersuchungen zum Johannesevangelium," *ZNW* 27 (1928): 113–63; W. Pannenberg, "What Is Truth?" in *Basic Questions in Theology: Collected Essays*, trans. G. H. Kehm, vol. 2 (Philadelphia: Fortress Press, 1971), 1–27; W. Kasper, *Dogma unter dem Wort Gottes* (Mainz: 1965).

7. K. Koch, "Der hebräische Wahrheitsbegriff im griechischen Sprachraum," in H. R. Müller-Schwefe, ed., *Was ist Wahrheit?* (Göttingen: 1965), 47–65.

8. Ibid., 51; cf. Jer 28:9.

9. Koch, "Der hebräische Wahrheitsbegriff," 53.

10. J. Barr, *The Semantics of Biblical Language* (Oxford: Oxford Univ. Press, 1961), 198.

11. D. Michel, " 'Ämät': Untersuchung über 'Wahrheit' im Hebräischen," in *Archiv für Begriffsgeschichte* 12 (1968): 30–57.

12. Ibid., 55.

13. Ibid., 56.

14. H. Wildberger, " '*mn*, fest, sicher," in *Theologisches Handwörterbuch zum Alten Testament*, vol. 1, 177–209, 201; cf. the use of *chesed we'emeth* with regard to human beings in Gen 24:49, 47:29, Josh 2:14, and Prov 3:3, and with regard to God in Gen 24:47 and passim.

15. Cf. above all his major two-volume work *La vérité dans Saint Jean* (Rome: 1977).

16. R. Bultmann, *The Gospel of John: A Commentary*, trans. G. R. Beasley-Murray, R. W. N. Hoare, and J. K. Riches (Philadelphia: Westminster, 1971), 434.

17. R. Bultmann, *Theology of the New Testament*, vol. 2, trans. K. Grobel (New York: Charles Scribner's Sons, 1955), 19.

18. De la Potterie, *La vérité*, vol. 2, 1009.

19. I. de la Potterie, "History and Truth," in R. Latourelle and G. O'Collins, eds., *Problems and Perspectives of Fundamental Theology*, trans. M. J. O'Connell (New York: Paulist, 1982), 87–104, 99; cf. de la Potterie, *La vérité*, vol. 1, 158–69.

20. De la Potterie, *La vérité*, vol. 2, 1011.

21. Cf. H. Schlier, "Meditationen über den johanneischen Begriff der Wahrheit," in *Besinnung auf das Neue Testament* (Freiburg: 1964), 272–78; R. Schnackenburg, *The Gospel according to St. John*, vol. 1, trans. K. Smyth (New York: Herder and Herder, 1968); vol. 2, trans. C. Hastings, F. McDonagh, D. Smith, and R. Foley (New York: Seabury, 1980); vol. 3, trans. D. Smith and G. A. Kon (New York: Crossroad, 1982); J. Blank, "Der johanneische Wahrheitsbegriff," in *Biblische Zeitschrift* 7 (1963): 163–73; J. Blank, *Krisis: Untersuchungen zur johanneischen Christologie und Eschatologie* (Freiburg: 1964); J. Beutler, *Martyria: Traditionsgeschichtliche Untersuchungen zum Zeugnisthema bei Johannes* (Frankfurt am Main: 1972); Y. Ibuki, *Die Wahrheit im Johannesevangelium*, BBB 39 (Bonn: 1972).

22. Schlier, "Meditationen über den johanneischen Begriff," 277; cf. Ibuki, *Wahrheit im Johannesevangelium*, 355.

23. Schlier, "Meditationen über den johanneischen Begriff," 277ff.; cf. Ibuki, *Wahrheit im Johannesevangelium*, 349–52.

24. C. Geffré, *The Risk of Interpretation: On Being Faithful to the Christian Tradition in a Non-Christian Age*, trans. D. Smith (Mahwah, N.J.: Paulist, 1987), 212-13; cf. Geffré, "Postface: La question de la vérité dans la théologie contemporaine," in M. Michael, ed., *La théologie à l'épreuve de la vérité* (Paris: 1984), 281-91.

25. With Geffré, *Risk of Interpretation*, 212-13, and against I. de la Potterie, "Faire la vérité: dévise de l'orthodoxie ou invitation à la foi?" in *Le Supplément* 118 (1978): 283-93.

26. Kasper, "Wahrheitsverständnis," 171; cf. H. Peukert, *Science, Action and Fundamental Theology: Toward a Theology of Communicative Action*, trans. J. Bohman (Cambridge, Mass.: MIT Press, 1984).

27. D. Ritschl, *The Logic of Theology: A Brief Account of the Relationship between Basic Concepts in Theology* (Philadelphia: Fortress Press, 1987), 32; cf. ibid., 220-23. Cf. E. Arens, "Implizite Axiome aus der Sicht einer theologischen Handlungstheorie," in W. Huber, E. Petzold, and T. Sundermeier, eds., *Implizite Axiome—Tiefenstrukturen des Denkens und Handelns*, Festschrift für D. Ritschl (Munich: 1990), 184-96.

28. Cf. Geffré, *Risk of Interpretation*, 62-64; Geffré, "Postface."

29. Cf. F. Schüssler Fiorenza, *Foundational Theology: Jesus and the Church* (New York: Crossroad, 1984); cf. F. Schüssler Fiorenza, "The Church as a Community of Interpretation: Political Theology between Discourse Ethics and Hermeneutical Reconstruction," in D. S. Browning and F. Schüssler Fiorenza, eds., *Habermas, Modernity, and Public Theology* (New York: Crossroad: 1992), 66-91.

30. Cf. de la Potterie, "History and Truth," 97-103.

31. Ibid., 99.

32. According to de la Potterie, the Hegelian system, which is well known as the epitome of a coherence model of truth, "shows the closest analogy to biblical teaching on the eschatological dimension of truth" (ibid., 101).

33. On "asserting," cf. n. 18 added to the German Suhrkamp Taschenbuch Wissenschaft edition of Peukert, *Science, Action and Fundamental Theology* (H. Peukert, *Wissenschaftstheorie—Handlungstheorie—Fundamentaltheologie*, 2nd ed. [Frankfurt am Main: Suhrkamp, 1988], 326-27).

34. Cf. R. Zerfass, ed., *Erzählter Glaube—erzählende Kirche*, QD 116 (Freiburg: 1988).

35. Thus Theodor W. Adorno's well-known dictum in *Minima Moralia: Reflections from Damaged Life*, trans. E. F. N. Jephcott (London: Verso, 1978), 50. Cf. M. Knapp, *"Wahr ist nur, was nicht in diese Welt passt": Die*

Erbsündenlehre als Ansatzpunkt eines Dialoges mit Th. W. Adorno (Würzburg: 1983), 63ff., 85ff.; also J. B. Metz's critique of systematizing thought in Metz, *Faith in History and Society: Toward a Practical Fundamental Theology*, trans. D. Smith (New York: Seabury, 1980).

36. Cf. J. Wohlmuth, "Wahrheit als Konsens?" in *ZKT* 103 (1981): 309–23; H. Vorgrimler, "From *Sensus Fidei* to *Consensus Fidelium*," in J. B. Metz and E. Schillebeeckx, eds., *The Teaching Authority of Believers*, Concilium 180 (Edinburgh: T. and T. Clark, 1985), 3–11; K. Rahner, "A Small Fragment 'On the Collective Finding of Truth,' " in *Theological Investigations*, vol. 6, trans. K.-H. Kruger and B. Kruger (Baltimore: Helicon, 1969), 82–88; Geffré, *Risk of Interpretation*, 62ff.; Geffré, "Postface," 288ff.

37. Thus Origen in his commentary on the Gospel of John, 6, 6, 38, cited in de la Potterie, 88–89.

38. A. Auer, *Autonome Moral und christlicher Glaube* (Düsseldorf: 1971). In 1984 a second edition appeared with an epilogue on the reception of the notion of autonomy in Catholic theological ethics.

39. Cf. A. Auer, "Die Bedeutung des Christlichen bei der Normfindung," in J. Sauer, ed., *Normen im Konflikt* (Freiburg: 1977), 29–54.

40. Cf. B. Stoeckle, *Grenzen der autonomen Moral* (Munich: 1974); B. Stoeckle, *Handeln aus dem Glauben* (Freiburg: 1977); J. Ratzinger, ed., *Prinzipien christlicher Moral* (Einsiedeln: 1975).

41. This also holds for F. Böckle, "Glaube und Handeln," in J. Feiner and M. Löhrer, eds., *Mysterium Salutis: Grundriss heilsgeschichtlicher Dogmatik*, vol. 5, *Zwischenzeit und Vollendung der Heilsgeschichte* (Einsiedeln: Benziger, 1976), 23–115.

42. The subtitle of G. Höver, *Sittlich handeln im Medium der Zeit* (Würzburg: 1988).

43. Cf. ibid., 117–34.

44. Ibid., 132.

45. K. Demmer, *Moraltheologische Methodenlehre* (Fribourg: 1989).

46. Ibid., 90.

47. K. Demmer, *Die Wahrheit leben: Theorie des Handelns* (Freiburg: 1991).

48. Ibid., 14.

49. Cf. the reflections on social ethics in M. Möhring-Hesse, "Politik aus dem Glauben und ethische Auslegung: Zur theologischen Begründung christlicher Gesellschaftsethik als normative Reflexion politischer Glaubenspraxis," in *Jahrbuch für christliche Sozialwissenschaften* 32 (1991): 65–89.

50. N. Mette, *Theorie der Praxis* (Düsseldorf: 1978), 345.

51. Ibid., 346.

52. J. van der Ven, *Entwurf einer empirischen Theologie* (Kampen: 1990), 138.

53. Concerning the five phases and the fifteen subphases, cf. ibid., 138-256.

54. O. Fuchs, ed., *Theologie und Handeln: Beiträge zur Fundierung der Praktischen Theologie als Handlungstheorie* (Düsseldorf: 1984).

55. Cf., e.g., H.-U. von Brachel and N. Mette, eds., *Kommunikation und Solidarität* (Fribourg: 1985); N. Mette, *Voraussetzungen christlicher Elementarerziehung* (Düsseldorf: 1983); H. P. Siller, *Handbuch der Religionsdidaktik* (Freiburg: 1991).

56. Cf. R. Zerfass, "Herrschaftsfreie Kommunikation—eine Forderung an die kirchliche Verkündigung?" in W. Weber, ed., *Macht—Dienst—Herrschaft in Kirche und Gesellschaft* (Freiburg: 1974), 81-106.

57. R. Zerfass and H. Poensgen, "Predigt/Verkündigung," in C. Bäumler and N. Mette, eds., *Gemeindepraxis in Grundbegriffen* (Munich: 1987), 354-68, 356.

58. R. Zerfass, "Gottesdienst als Handlungsfeld der Kirche," in *Liturgisches Jahrbuch* 38 (1988): 30-58, 49.

59. Cf. H. Seibert, *Diakonie—Hilfehandeln Jesu und soziale Arbeit des Diakonischen Werkes*, 2nd ed. (Gütersloh: 1985); H. Steinkamp, *Diakonie—Kennzeichen der Gemeinde* (Freiburg: 1985); O. Fuchs, *Heilen und Befreien: Der Dienst am Nächsten als Ernstfall von Kirche und Pastoral* (Düsseldorf: 1990).

60. Zerfass and Poensgen, "Predigt," 363.

61. P. C. Bloth et al., eds., *Handbuch der Praktischen Theologie*, 4 vols. (Gütersloh: 1981-92). By contrast, Bäumler and Mette, eds., *Gemeindepraxis* is a volume oriented toward a conception of communicative community praxis. Cf. C. Bäumler, *Kommunikative Gemeindepraxis* (Munich: 1984).

62. J. Kleeman, "Zum Verständnis und Gebrauch des HPTh," in Bloth et al., eds., *Handbuch der Praktischen Theologie*, vol. 2 (1981), 7-9, 7.

63. Ibid., 9.

64. Metz, *Faith in History and Society*, 73.

65. H. Peukert, "Sprache und Freiheit: Zur Pragmatik ethischer Rede," in F. Kamphaus and R. Zerfass, eds., *Ethische Predigt und Alltagsverhalten* (Munich: 1977), 44-75, 66.

66. Cf. also the study of Barth by H. Anzinger, *Glaube und kommunikative Praxis*, BevTh 110 (Munich: 1991), esp. 260-77.

67. K. Barth, *Der Christ als Zeuge*, Theologische Existenz heute 12 (Munich: 1934), 35.

68. Cf. J.-P. Jossua, *La condition du témoin* (Paris: 1984); G. Collet, *Das Missionsverständnis der Kirche in der gegenwärtigen Diskussion* (Mainz: 1984).

69. N. Brox, *Der Glaube als Zeugnis* (Mainz: 1966), 53.

70. H. P. Siller, "Kommunikation/Öffentlichkeitsarbeit," in Bäumler and Mette, eds., *Gemeindepraxis*, 239-57, 251.

71. K. Rahner, "Theological Observations on the Concept of 'Witness,' " in *Theological Investigations*, vol. 13, trans. D. Bourke (New York: Seabury, 1975), 152-68, 164.

72. *CD*, vol. 1/2, trans. G. T. Thomson and H. Knight, 444.

73. Cf. H. Steinkamp, *Diakonie—Kennzeichen der Gemeinde* (Freiburg: 1985), 24-25, 35-36, 103ff.

74. Cf. Jossua, *La condition du témoin*, 108.

75. Cf. J.-P. Jossua, "Zeugnis," in *NHThG* 4, 332-42, 335.

76. R. Weth, "Diakonie," in Bäumler and Mette, eds., *Gemeindepraxis*, 116-28, 122.

77. Concerning the biblical grounding, cf. E. Günther, *"artys": Die Geschichte eines Wortes* (Gütersloh: 1941); N. Brox, *Zeuge und Märtyrer*, Studien zum Alten und Neuen Testament 5 (Munich: 1961); K. Elliger, *Deuterojesaja (40,1-45,7)*, Biblischer Kommentar 11/1 (Neukirchen-Vluyn: 1978); Arens, *Bezeugen und Bekennen: Elementare Handlungen des Glaubens* (Düsseldorf: 1989), 34-41.

78. J. Comblin, *Retrieving the Human: A Christian Anthropology*, trans. R. R. Barr (Maryknoll, N.Y.: Orbis, 1990), 28.

79. Ibid.

80. R. K. Fenn, *Liturgies and Trials* (Oxford: Basil Blackwell, 1982), 49.

81. J. B. Metz, "Vorwort," in Instituto Histórico Centroamericano, ed., *Sie leben im Herzen des Volkes: Lateinamerikanisches Martyrologium* (Düsseldorf: 1984), 7-12, 8; cf. L. Boff, "Martyrdom: An Attempt at a Systematic Reflection," trans. P. Burns, in J. B. Metz, E. Schillebeeckx, and M. Lefébure, eds., *Martyrdom Today*, Concilium 163 (New York: Seabury, 1983), 12-17.

82. Cf. J. Sobrino, *The True Church and the Poor*, trans. M. J. O'Connell (Maryknoll, N.Y.: Orbis Books, 1984), 171-83, 228-52.

83. Thus B. Pascal, *Pensées*, ed. L. Lafuma, trans. J. Warrington (London: Dent, 1973), no. 553.

84. P. Brunner, "Zur Lehre vom Gottesdienst der im Namen Jesu versammelten Gemeinde," in K. F. Müller and W. Blankenburg, eds., *Leiturgia:*

Handbuch des evangelischen Gottesdienstes, vol. 1, *Geschichte und Lehre des evangelischen Gottesdienstes* (Kassel: Johannes Stauda, 1954), 83-361, 260; cf. H. Fries and K. Rahner, *Einigung der Kirchen—reale Möglichkeit*, 3rd ed., QD 100 (Freiburg: 1987), 26.

85. The German is *Apostolische Glaubensbekenntnis*: literally, the Apostolic Confession of Faith—*Trans.*

86. Cf. R. Lendi, *Die Wandelbarkeit der Busse* (Bern: 1983), 347ff.

87. On ritual action, cf. V. Turner, *The Ritual Process: Structure and Anti-Structure* (Chicago: Aldine, 1969); T. F. Driver, *The Magic of Ritual: Our Need for Liberating Rites that Transfrom Our Lives and Our Communities* (San Francisco: Harper & Row, 1991); S. Wiedenhofer, "Die Tradition in den Traditionen: Kirchliche Glaubensüberlieferung im Spannungsfeld kirchlicher Strukturen," in D. Wiederkehr, ed., *Wie geschieht Tradition?* QD 133 (Freiburg: 1991), 127-72, 146-58.

88. Cf. P. Meinhold, ed., *Studien zur Bekenntnisbildung* (Wiesbaden: 1980).

89. H. de Lubac, *The Christian Faith: An Essay on the Structure of the Apostles' Creed*, trans. R. Arnandez (San Francisco: Ignatius Press, 1986), 352.

90. Cf. W.-D. Hauschild, "Das trinitarische Dogma von 381 als Ergebnis verbindlicher Konsensbildung," in K. Lehmann and W. Pannenberg, eds., *Glaubensbekenntnis und Kirchengemeinschaft* (Freiburg: 1982), 13-48.

91. K. Lehmann, "Bedarf das Glaubensbekenntnis einer Neufassung?" in P. Brunner, ed., *Veraltetes Glaubensbekenntnis?* (Regensburg: 1968), 125-86, 160.

92. Cf. J. Rohls, *Theologie reformierter Bekenntnisschriften* (Göttingen: 1987), 198-207.

93. Cf. J. N. D. Kelly, *Early Christian Creeds*, 3rd ed. (London: Longman, 1972).

94. Cf. H. Meyer and H. Schütte, eds., *Confessio Augustana: Bekenntnis des einen Glaubens* (Paderborn: 1980).

95. Cf. L. Vischer, ed., *Reformed Witness Today: A Collection of Confessions and Statements of Faith Issued by Reformed Churches* (Berne: Evangelische Arbeitsstelle Ökumene Schweiz, 1982).

96. Concerning these three texts, cf. Arens, *Bezeugen und Bekennen*, 287-314.

97. Cf. the initiatives and steps toward, as well as the resolutions of, the 1990 world convocation on "Justice, Peace and the Integrity of Creation" in Seoul. Cf. also C. F. v. Weiszäcker, *Die Zeit drängt* (Munich: 1986); U. Duchrow, *Global Economy: A Confessional Issue for the Churches*, trans. D.

Lewis (Geneva: World Council of Churches, 1987); H.-R. Reuter, ed., *Konzil des Friedens* (Heidelberg: 1987).

98. Cf. R. Hinz and F. Kürschner-Pelkmann, eds., *Christen im Widerstand: Die Diskussion um das südafrikanische KAIROS-Dokument* (Stuttgart: 1987).

99. G. Kretschmar and W.-D. Hauschild, "Die lutherischen Kirchen und die Bekenntnissynode von Barmen," in G. Kretschmar, W.-D. Hauschild, and C. Nicolaisen, eds., *Die lutherischen Kirchen und die Bekenntnissynode von Barmen* (Göttingen: 1984), 461–67, 462.

100. T. Schneider, "Unsere Hoffnung: Ein Bekenntnis zum Glauben in dieser Zeit: Einleitung," in *Gemeinsame Synode der Bistümer in der Bundesrepublik Deutschland*, vol. 1, *Beschlüsse der Vollversammlung*, 5th ed. (Freiburg: 1982), 71–84, 73.

101. Concerning such an understanding, cf. the articles by C. S. Song, D. S. Amalorvapadass, J. Hortal, and M. Dreher in G. Békés and H. Meyer, eds., *Den einen Glauben bekennen* (Frankfurt am Main: Otto Lembeck, 1982).

102. Cf. R. J. Schreiter, *Constructing Local Theologies* (Maryknoll, N.Y.: Orbis, 1985).

103. Cf. " 'Theologie impliziert Handeln . . .': Das Institut für Kontextuelle Theologie (Republik Südafrika)," in *Orientierung* 52 (1988): 219-23.

104. D. Schellong, "Zur Bedeutung von Bekenntnissen in der Gegenwart," in *Theologie im Widerspruch von Vernunft und Unvernunft*, Theologische Studien 106 (Zurich: 1971), 58-87, 81.

105. Cf. W. Kistner, *Hoffnung in der Krise: Dokumente einer christlichen Existenz in Südafrika*, ed. L. Engel et al. (Wuppertal: 1988), 16, 180-81.

106. "Gemeinsame Erklärung des ökumenischen Arbeitskreises evangelischer und katholischer Theologen," in K. Lehmann and E. Schlink, eds., *Evangelium—Sakramente—Amt und die Einheit der Kirche: Die ökumenische Tragweite der Confessio Augustana* (Freiburg: 1982), 190-92, 190.

107. Cf. R. Wischnath, ed., *Frieden als Bekenntnisfrage* (Gütersloh: 1984); U. Duchrow, *Global Economy*; H.-R. Reuter, ed., *Konzil des Friedens*.

108. D. Bonhoeffer, "Das Wesen der Kirche," in *Gesammelte Schriften*, ed. E. Bethge, vol. 5 (Munich: 1972), 227-75, 259.

109. Cf. H. Rossi, *Die Kirche als personale Gemeinschaft: Der kommunitäre Charakter der Kirche nach den Dokumenten und Akten des Zweiten Vatikanischen Konzils* (Cologne: 1978).

110. "Final Report," in *The Extraordinary Synod—1985: Message to the People of God* (Boston: St. Paul Editions, n.d.), 37-68, 53; cf. W. Kasper,

"Kirche als Communio: Überlegungen zur ekklesiologischen Leitidee des II. Vatikanischen Konzils," in *Theologie und Kirche* (Mainz: 1987), 272-89.

111. "Lumen Gentium," in *DocVatII*, 14-101, §8.

112. Ibid.

113. Ibid., §11.

114. Ibid., §13.

115. Ibid., §25.

116. "Unitatis Redintegratio," in *DocVatII*, 341-66, §2.

117. Ibid., §3.

118. Ibid., §22.

119. "Ad Gentes," in *DocVatII*, 584-630, §19, cf. §20.

120. Cf. John XXIII's opening address to the Council and the evaluation of that address in L. Kaufmann and N. Klein, *Johannes XXIII.—Prophetie im Vermächtnis*, 2nd ed. (Fribourg: 1990).

121. "Communio et Progressio," in A. Flannery, ed., *Vatican Council II: The Conciliar and Post Conciliar Documents*, rev. ed. (Boston: St. Paul Editions, 1988), 293-349, §11.

122. Cf. A. Dulles, *The Church Is Communication* (Rome: 1972); K. Kienzler, " 'Kommunikative Theologie' nach dem Vatikanum II," in *CS* 17 (1984): 277-87; J. Meyer zu Schlochtern, "Das Kirchenbild von 'Communio et Progressio' im Kontext der nachkonziliaren Ekklesiologie," in *CS* 24 (1991): 303-19.

123. Cf. H. Zirker, *Ekklesiologie* (Düsseldorf: 1984), 126-210.

124. Ibid., 133.

125. Ibid., 148.

126. Ibid., 186.

127. M. M. Garijo-Guembe, *Gemeinschaft der Heiligen: Grund, Wesen und Struktur der Kirche* (Düsseldorf: 1988), 104-7.

128. Ibid., 109.

129. Ibid., 234-36; cf. 236-50.

130. Cf. P. Lakeland, *Theology and Critical Theory: The Discourse of the Church* (Nashville: Abingdon, 1990).

131. Ibid., 103.

132. Ibid., 104.

133. "Lumen Gentium," §1.

134. Lakeland, *Theology and Critical Theory*, 119.

135. Cf. ibid., 122-37, with reference to L. Boff, *Ecclesiogenesis: The Base Communities Reinvent the Church*, trans. R. R. Barr (Maryknoll, N.Y.: Orbis, 1986); J. B. Metz, *The Emergent Church: The Future of Christianity*

in a Post-Bourgeois World, trans. P. Mann (New York: Crossroad, 1981); R. Radford Ruether, *Women-Church: Theology and Practice of Feminist Liturgical Communities* (San Francisco: Harper & Row, 1985).

136. B. Kappenberg, *Kommunikationstheorie und Kirche* (Frankfurt am Main: 1981), 205-44.

137. H.-J. Höhn, *Kirche und kommunikatives Handeln* (Frankfurt am Main: 1985), 156; cf. my review in *ThRv* 82 (1986): 214-16.

138. P. Hofmann, *Glaubensbegründung* (Frankfurt am Main: 1988), 225; cf. 215-32.

139. Cf. E. Arens, "Christus in unsere heutigen Kontexte kommunizieren: Christologische Zugänge zu einer Theologie der Kommunikation," *CS* 25 (1992): 45-62.

140. Wiedenhofer, "Tradition," 128.

141. Ibid., 161.

142. W. Huber, *Kirche*, 2nd ed. (Munich: 1988), 46; cf. 44-58; cf. J. Moltmann, *The Church in the Power of the Spirit: A Contribution to Messianic Ecclesiology* (San Francisco: Harper & Row, 1975), 314-36.

143. Huber, *Kirche*, 46. Concerning the innovative-critical potential of religious orders, cf. J. B. Metz, *Followers of Christ: The Religious Life and the Church*, trans. T. Linton (New York: Paulist, 1978); J. B. Metz and T. R. Peters, *Gottespassion: Ordensexistenz heute* (Freiburg: 1991).

144. Metz, *Followers of Christ*, 25; Duchrow, *Global Economy*, 231-41.

145. Wiedenhofer, "Tradition," 158.

146. Metz, *Faith in History and Society*, 57.

147. Cf. Schreiter, *Constructing Local Theologies*; A. Shorter, *Toward a Theology of Inculturation* (London: 1988).

148. Cf. J. Schreiner and K. Wittstadt, eds., *Communio sanctorum*, Festschrift für P.-W. Scheele (Würzburg: 1988); D. Bonhoeffer, *Werke*, vol. 1, *Sanctorum Communio*, ed. J. von Soosten (Munich: 1986).

149. Huber, *Kirche*, 90.

150. Cf. J. Hainz, *Koinonia: "Kirche" als Gemeinschaft bei Paulus*, Biblische Untersuchungen (Regensburg: 1982); K. Kertelge, "Koinonia und Einheit der Kirche im Neuen Testament," in Schreiner and Wittstadt, eds., *Communio sanctorum*, 53-67.

151. Hainz, *Koinonia*, 110.

152. Ibid., 151.

153. Kertelge, "Koinonia und Einheit," 55.

154. Cf. Garijo-Guembe, *Gemeinschaft der Heiligen*; J. D. Zizioulas, *Being as Communion* (London: 1985).

155. Cf. Fries and Rahner, *Einigung der Kirchen*; H. Döring, "Die Communio-Ekklesiologie als Grundmodell und Chance der ökumenischen Theologie," in Schreiner and Wittstadt, eds. *Communio sanctorum*, 349-69.

156. Cf. J.-M. Tillard, *Église d'églises: L'ecclésiologie de communion* (Paris: 1987), 113-215.

157. H. J. Legrand, "Die Entwicklung der Kirchen als verantwortliche Subjekte: Eine Anfrage an das II. Vatikanum," in G. Alberigo, Y. Congar, and H. J. Pottmeyer, eds., *Kirche im Wandel* (Düsseldorf: 1982), 141-74, 159.

158. Ibid., 159-60.

159. Cf. the evaluation of the Synod in G. Alberigo and J. Provost, eds., *Synod 1985—An Evaluation*, Concilium 188 (Edinburgh: T. and T. Clark, 1986), esp. the articles by J. Komonchak, J.-M. Tillard, A. Lorscheider, H. J. Pottmeyer, and G. Alberigo.

160. Meyer zu Schlochtern, "Das Kirchenbild von 'Communio et Progressio,' " 313.

161. Thus H. J. Pottmeyer, "Die zwiespältige Ekklesiologie des Zweiten Vatikanums—Ursache nachkonziliarer Konflikte," in *Trierer theologische Zeitschrift* 104 (1982): 272-88.

162. "Lumen Gentium," §§21, 22; "Presbyterorum Ordinis," in *DocVatII*, 532-76, §§7, 15; "Christus Dominus," in *DocVatII*, 396-429, §4.

163. Prefatory Note of Explanation to "Lumen Gentium," in *DocVatII*, 99; cf. Legrand, "Entwicklung der Kirchen," 150.

164. Cf. F. Ochmann, "Kirchliches Recht in und aus dem Leben der Communio—Zur Rezeption aus kanonischer Sicht," in W. Beinert, ed., *Glaube als Zustimmung: Zur Interpretation kirchlicher Rezeptionsvorgänge*, QD 131 (Freiburg: Herder, 1991), 123-63.

165. J. Habermas, *The Theory of Communicative Action*, trans. T. McCarthy, vol. 2, *Lifeword and System: A Critique of Functionalist Reason* (Boston: Beacon Press, 1989), 137ff.; J. Habermas, *Erläuterungen zur Diskursethik* (Frankfurt am Main: Suhrkamp, 1991), 16ff., 69ff.

166. K.-O. Apel, "Diskursethik als Verantwortungsethik—eine postmetaphysische Transformation der Ethik Kants," in R. Fornet-Betancourt, ed., *Ethik und Befreiung* (Aachen: 1990), 10-40, 11; cf. K.-O. Apel, *Diskurs und Verantwortung* (Frankfurt am Main: 1990).

167. See J. Habermas, *The New Conservatism: Cultural Criticism and the Historians' Debate*, ed. and trans. S. W. Nicholsen, Studies in Contemporary German Social Thought (Cambridge, Mass.: MIT Press, 1990).

168. J. Habermas, *The Philosophical Discourse of Modernity*, trans. F. Lawrence (Cambridge, Mass.: MIT Press, 1987), 15.

169. Cf. T. Balasuriya, *Planetary Theology* (Maryknoll, N.Y.: Orbis, 1984).

170. For political theology, cf. Metz, *Faith in History and Society*; Peukert, *Science, Action and Fundamental Theology*; M. L. Lamb, *Solidarity with Victims* (New York: 1982); R. J. Siebert, *From Critical Theory to Communicative Political Theology: Universal Solidarity* (New York: 1989); G. Baum, *Compassion and Solidarity: The Church for Others* (New York: 1990). For the theology of liberation, cf. G. Gutiérrez, *A Theology of Liberation: History, Politics and Salvation*, trans. C. Inda and J. Eagleson (Maryknoll, N.Y.: Orbis, 1973); J. Sobrino and J. Hernández Pico, *Theology of Christian Solidarity* (Maryknoll, N.Y.: Orbis, 1985); A. Nolan, *God in South Africa: The Challenge of the Gospel* (Grand Rapids, Mich.: Eerdmans, 1988).

171. Cf. E. Arens, "Internationale, ekklesiale und universale Solidarität," in *Orientierung* 53 (1989): 216-20.

172. Cited in W. Schieder, "Brüderlichkeit etc.," in *Geschichtliche Grundbegriffe*, vol. 1, 552-81, 574.

173. In this paragraph two different German words are translated as *brotherhood*. The word used here is *Verbrüderung*, denoting a brotherhood in the sense of a group or grouping. The word generally used in this section, denoting brotherhood as a quality of relation, is *Brüderlichkeit*— *Trans.*

174. Cited in Schieder, "Brüderlichkeit," 575.

175. "Engels to the Communist Correspondence Committee in Brussels, 23 Oct. 1846," in *MECW*, vol. 38, 85.

176. K. Marx, "The June Revolution," in *MECW*, vol. 7, 147.

177. K. Marx, "The Class Struggles in France, 1848 to 1850," in *MECW*, vol. 10, 57-58.

178. With regard to the following discussion, cf. U. Essbach-Kreuzer and W. Essbach, *Solidarität und soziale Revolution* (Frankfurt am Main: 1974), 12ff.; W. Weigand, *Solidarität durch Konflikt* (Münster: 1979), 193ff.

179. K. Marx and F. Engels, "Manifesto of the Communist Party," in *MECW*, vol. 6, 506.

180. K. Marx and F. Engels, "The German Ideology," in *MECW*, vol. 5, 214.

181. Marx and Engels, "Manifesto," 503.

182. "Universal Society of Revolutionary Communists," in *MECW*, vol. 10, 614.

183. K. Marx, "Provisional Rules of the Working Men's International Association," in *MECW*, vol. 20, 14.

184. Cited in Schieder, "Brüderlichkeit," 579.

185. "Third Annual Report of the International Working Men's Association," in *MECW*, vol. 20, 437.

186. Concerning this movement's self-reflection and self-criticism, cf. W. Balsen and K. Rössel, *Hoch die internationale Solidarität: Zur Geschichte der Dritte-Welt-Bewegung in der Bundesrepublik* (Cologne: 1986).

187. Cf. S. Welch's feminist theological presentation, arising out of the women's movement, in *Communities of Resistance and Solidarity: A Feminist Theology of Liberation* (Maryknoll, N.Y.: Orbis, 1985). Cf. also the reflections in F. Hengsbach, "Katholische Soziallehre als Ethik sozialer Bewegungen," *Religionsunterricht an höheren Schulen* 32 (1989): 153–61.

188. Cf. "Quadragesimo Anno," trans. F. J. Hans and M. R. P. McGuire, in C. Carlen, ed., *The Papal Encyclicals, 1740–1981*, vol. 3 (Wilmington, N.C.: McGrath, 1981), 415–43, §73.

189. "Apostolicam Actuositatem," in *DocVatII*, 489–521, §14.

190. "Gaudium et Spes," in *DocVatII*, 199–308, §32.

191. Ibid., §57.

192. Ibid., §90.

193. Ibid.

194. "Ad Gentes," in *DocVatII*, 584–630, §21.

195. "Mater et Magistra," in Carlen, ed., *Papal Encyclicals*, vol. 5, 59–90, §§23, 75, and 155.

196. "Pacem in Terris," in Carlen, ed., *Papal Encyclicals*, vol. 5, 107–29, §§98 and 114.

197. I do not enter here into a discussion of the problem of an ecclesial social teaching. For such discussion, cf. M.-D. Chenu, *Kirchliche Soziallehre im Wandel* (Fribourg: 1991); W. Palaver, ed., *Centesimo Anno: 100 Jahre kirchliche Soziallehre* (Thaur: 1991).

198. "Laborem Exercens," in Carlen, ed., *Papal Encyclicals*, vol. 5, 299–326, §33.

199. Cf. the edition with commentary by W. Korff and A. Baumgartner (Freiburg: 1988).

200. "Sollicitudo Rei Socialis," in G. Baum and R. Ellsberg, eds., *The Logic of Solidarity: Commentaries on Pope John Paul II's Encyclical "On Social Concern"* (Maryknoll, N.Y.: Orbis, 1989), 1–62, §9.

201. Ibid., §22.

202. Ibid., §24.

203. Ibid., §26.

204. Ibid., §36.

205. Ibid., §38.

206. Ibid., §39.

207. Ibid., §45.

208. Most recent when the present work appeared in German in 1992— *Trans.*

209. This would be the point at which to discuss the documents of the Conferences of Latin American Bishops at Medellín and Puebla. Cf. R. Antoncich and J. M. Munárriz, *La doctrina social de la iglesia,* Colección Cristianismo y sociedad (Buenos Aires: Ediciones Paulinas, 1986), 90ff.

210. Pontifical Commission "Iustitia et Pax," *The Church and Racism: Towards a More Fraternal Society* (Vatican City: 1988).

211. Ibid., §23.

212. Cf. J. B. Metz, "Im Aufbruch zu einer kulturell polyzentrischen Weltkirche," in F. X. Kaufmann and J. B. Metz, *Zukunftsfähigkeit* (Freiburg: 1987); W. Bühlmann, *Weltkirche,* 2nd ed. (Graz: 1985).

213. Cf. J. B. Metz, "Unterwegs zu einer nachidealistischen Theologie," in J. B. Bauer, ed., *Entwürfe der Theologie* (Graz: 1985), 209-33.

214. See Habermas, *The New Conservatism.*

215. Cf. European Assembly "Peace with Justice," Basel, May 15-21, 1989, *Das Dokument* (Bonn: 1989), no. 45. Not the least significant element of this document is the fact that it was ratified within the framework of the conciliar process "Justice, Peace and the Integrity of Creation" by the first church gathering for all of Europe—a gathering to which, for the first time since the Reformation, the Conference of European Churches and the Council of European Bishops' Conferences issued a joint invitation.

216. Ibid., no. 27.

217. Ibid., no. 45.

INDEX